Rituals and Traditional Events in the Modern World

Many events have evolved over centuries, drawing on local customs and conditions. However, as the world becomes increasingly globalised, traditional events and the identities they support are increasingly being challenged and rituals may be lost. Reacting against this trend towards homogeneity, communities strive to preserve and even recreate their traditional events, which may require rituals to be resurrected or reinvented for a new audience.

The aim of this book is to explore the role of traditional events and rituals in the modern world. The 16 chapters cover a range of case studies of the performance of ritual through events, including their historical antecedents and development over time, as well as their role in society, link with identities both seemingly fixed and fluid and their continued relevance. The cases examined are not museum pieces, but rather vibrant festivals and events that continue to persist. Drawing on the power of history and cultural tradition, they are manifestations of heritage, existing in three temporalities: celebrating the past, occurring in the present and aiming to continue into and influence the future. Iconic events including Chinese New Year, Hogmanay and the New Orleans Mardi Gras are examined and examples are drawn from a diverse range of countries such as South Korea, China, the United States, Scotland, Italy, India and Haiti.

This volume provides a deep understanding of the role of tradition and ritual within events from a global perspective and will be valuable reading for students, researchers and academics interested in events, heritage and culture.

Jennifer Laing is a Senior Lecturer in Tourism and Events at La Trobe University, Australia. Her research interests include travel narratives, the role of events in society and heritage tourism. She has co-written books with Warwick Frost on the influence of books on travel, commemorative events and explorer travellers and adventure tourism.

Warwick Frost is an Associate Professor in Tourism and Events at La Trobe University, Australia. His research interests include heritage, events, nature-based attractions and the interaction between media, popular culture and tourism. He has co-written books with Jennifer Laing on the influence of books on travel, commemorative events and explorer travellers and adventure tourism.

Routledge advances in event research series
Edited by Warwick Frost and Jennifer Laing
Department of Marketing, Tourism and Hospitality, La Trobe University, Australia

Rituals and Traditional Events in the Modern World

Edited by Jennifer Laing and Warwick Frost

Routledge
Taylor & Francis Group

LONDON AND NEW YORK

First published 2015
by Routledge
2 Park Square, Milton Park, Abingdon, Oxon OX14 4RN

and by Routledge
711 Third Avenue, New York, NY 10017

Routledge is an imprint of the Taylor & Francis Group, an informa business

British Library Cataloguing in Publication Data
A catalogue record for this book is available from the British Library

Library of Congress Cataloging in Publication Data
Rituals and traditional events in the modern world / edited by Jennifer Laing and Warwick Frost.
  pages cm. – (Routledge advances in event research series)
  Includes bibliographical references and index.
  1. Rites and ceremonies–Cross-cultural studies. 2. Ritual–Cross-cultural studies. I. Laing, Jennifer, editor of compilation. II. Frost, Warwick, editor of compilation.
  GN473.R5945 2014
  203'.8–dc23   2014019111

ISBN: 978-0-415-70736-7 (hbk)
ISBN: 978-1-315-88687-9 (ebk)

Typeset in Times New Roman
by Wearset Ltd, Boldon, Tyne and Wear

Contents

Illustrations

Figures

Tables

Contributors

Sue Beeton, Associate Professor in the Department of Marketing, Tourism and Hospitality, La Trobe University, Melbourne, Australia. Email: s.beeton@latrobe.edu.au.

Ubaldino Couto, Lecturer in Event Management at the Institute for Tourism Studies (IFT), Macau SAR, China. Email: dino@ift.edu.mo.

Elspeth Frew, Associate Professor and Head of the Department of Marketing, Tourism and Hospitality, La Trobe University, Melbourne, Australia. Email: e.frew@latrobe.edu.au.

Warwick Frost, Associate Professor in the Department of Marketing, Tourism and Hospitality, La Trobe University, Melbourne, Australia. Email: w.frost@latrobe.edu.au.

Mary Rachel Gould, Assistant Professor of Communication and Co-Director, SLU Prison Arts and Education Program, Saint Louis University, St Louis, USA. Email: mgould9@slu.edu.

Yu Hua, Lecturer, School of Linguistics, Shanghai International Studies University, Shanghai, China. Email: yuhuafish@gmail.com.

Monica Iorio, Dipartimento di Scienze Sociali e delle Istituzioni, Università degli Studi di Cagliari, Cagliari, Italy. Email: iorio@unica.it.

Aise Kim, Senior Lecturer and Program Director – Bachelor of Tourism and Event Management, School of Management, University of South Australia, Adelaide, Australia. Email: Aise.Kim@unisa.edu.au.

Jennifer Laing, Senior Lecturer in the Department of Marketing, Tourism and Hospitality, La Trobe University, Melbourne, Australia. Email: jennifer.laing@latrobe.edu.au.

Sunny Lee, Lecturer in Event and Tourism Management, School of Management, University of South Australia, Adelaide, Australia. Email: sunny.lee@unisa.edu.au.

Daniel Leung, Researcher and Lecturer, Department of Tourism and Service Management, MODUL University, Vienna, Austria. Email: daniel.leung@modul.ac.at.

Judith Mair, Senior Lecturer, School of Business, University of Queensland, Australia. Email: j.mair@business.uq.edu.au.

Catherine Matheson, Senior Lecturer and Associate of the International Centre for the Study of Planned Events, School of Arts, Social Sciences and Management, Queen Margaret University, Edinburgh, UK. Email: CMatheson@qmu.ac.uk.

Emma Nolan, Lecturer in Event Management and Programme Leader – BA (Hons) Event Management, University of Winchester, UK. Email: Emma.Nolan@winchester.ac.uk.

Haywantee Ramkissoon, Research Fellow, Monash Sustainability Institute, Monash University, Australia. Email: haywantee.ramkissoon@monash.edu.

Hugues Séraphin, Lecturer in Event Management, University of Winchester, UK. Email: Hugues.Seraphin@winchester.ac.uk.

Kiran Shinde, Principal, College of Architecture, Bharati Vidyapeeth Deemed University, Pune, India. Email: kiran.shinde@bharatividyapeeth.edu.

Ross Tinsley, Head of Research, International Hospitality and Tourism Research Centre, Hotel and Tourism Management Institute, Soerenberg, Switzerland. Email: rtinsley@htmi.ch.

Geoffrey Wall, Professor of Geography and Environmental Management, University of Waterloo, Canada. Email: gwall@uwaterloo.ca.

Leanne White, Senior Lecturer in Marketing, College of Business, Victoria University, Melbourne, Australia. Email: Leannek.White@vu.edu.au.

Zhu Yujie, Postdoctoral Fellow, The Australian Center on China in the World, Australian National University, Canberra, Australia. Email: yujie.zhu@anu.edu.au.

1 From pre-modern rituals to modern events

Warwick Frost and Jennifer Laing

> People nowadays often bemoan the disappearance of festivals. It was the same in
> the eighteenth century ... we should hesitate before speaking, in the singular, of
> 'the traditional festival'. If it is at all possible to do so, it is only because all fest-
> ivals were the object of general disapproval. The traditional festival conjured up
> a repellent image.
>
> (Ozouf 1976: 1)

Introduction

In pre-modern times, rituals and events were major elements of everyday life.
Whether agricultural or hunter-gatherer, communities needed traditional ceremonies to mark the important dates in the seasonal calendar, pay homage to their
deities, formalise rites of passage and reinforce local identities. In more complex
societies where there were small urban and military elites, ritualised events both
cemented hierarchies and reassured community members of the social exchange
of surplus production for protection. Survival in uncertain times required people
to band together, forming tight-knit parochial groups based on trust and personal
connectedness. Events and their rituals held a dual role in creating identities.
They brought people together, reinforcing their connections and obligations; but
they also distinguished other groups as different and potentially hostile. All
around the globe, the social roles of events followed similar patterns, even if
there were marked variations in form.

With the advent of industrialisation and urbanisation, communal societies
rapidly evolved into much larger and more complex nation states. As Benedict
Anderson (1983) has argued, modern times saw the rise of *imagined communities*. Instead of knowing everybody in the group, people were now connected to thousands, if not millions, of others whom they could never personally
interact with. For such national societies to work, new institutions, symbols and
ceremonies needed to develop to convince people that they now shared in this
much larger national identity.

Accordingly, as nation states developed, new events, rituals and traditions
were created. These had the purpose of affirming national identities and the
authority of rulers and governments. Often these were organised and promoted

by governments with the quite deliberate intention of encouraging loyalty and disseminating a national story that everybody could feel part of. For example, in our recent work *Commemorative Events: Memory, identities, conflict* (Frost and Laing 2013), we examined how state-sponsored events had proliferated in modern times, utilising commemorations of important historical events and national days to keep large and sometimes diverse societies glued together. Similarly, mega-events, despite their international format, are typically used by the governments of host nations as a means to stimulate national pride and solidarity.

However, despite the changing roles of events related to the rise of nation states, traditional rituals and events remain with us in the modern world. This is quite a puzzle. If they originally developed in response to the needs of traditional societies that were insular and geographically limited, why should they persist? The local customs and conditions that drove their evolution have now been replaced by globalisation, urbanisation and mass media. The features and constraints of the modern world have created new types of events – such as mega-events like the Olympics, World Cups and World Fairs – but they have not blotted out the traditional. Indeed, far from disappearing, there are many traditional rituals and events that remain popular and continue to be enthusiastically staged. And this phenomenon is global.

The aim of this book is to explore the role of traditional events and rituals in the modern world. The 16 chapters cover a range of case studies of the performance of ritual through events, including their historical antecedents and development over time, as well as their role in society, link with identities both seemingly fixed and fluid and their continued relevance. The cases examined are not museum pieces, but rather vibrant festivals and events that continue to persist. Drawing on the power of history and cultural tradition, they are manifestations of heritage, existing in three temporalities: celebrating the past, occurring in the present and aiming to continue into and influence the future.

Many events have evolved over centuries, drawing on local customs and conditions. However, as the world becomes increasingly globalised, traditional events and the identities they support are increasingly being challenged and rituals may be lost. Reacting against this trend towards homogeneity, some communities strive to preserve and even recreate their traditional events. Globalisation and modernity thus occupy important spaces in the staging and development of events. On the one hand, they may be viewed as *challenges*, encouraging homogeneity and threatening the continuation of tradition. However, on the other hand, they may also be viewed as *drivers*, stimulating a reaction whereby people and societies place greater value on maintaining their heritage. The latter concept is widely acknowledged within heritage studies (see, for examples, Laing and Frost 2012; Lowenthal 1998), but is more commonly applied to tangible buildings rather than the intangibility of events.

The processes are complex and varied, but four major patterns of the continuance of traditional rituals and events may be identified:

- *Preservation*. Rituals and traditional events are staged continually, with organisers and participants placing great value on maintaining the format and components as closely as possible to how they were in the past. The resultant event is promoted as preserving traditions against modernity and globalisation and claims high levels of *authenticity* and *provenance*.
- *Adaption*. The event evolves over time, incorporating new elements, but still maintaining some customary rituals. The authenticity of these remnants is highly valued and may be juxtaposed with modern components to promote an appealing mix.
- *Appropriation*. Events take rituals and customs from elsewhere and incorporate them into their staging. These may be from other events, or from other parts of customary life. The Maori Haka, for example, is performed by teams from New Zealand and other Pacific Ocean nations at sporting events, whereas it originated as a warrior's challenge. Furthermore, it is performed by team-mates from both Maori and European heritage. In 2006, players in an indigenous Australian junior football team were so impressed by a Haka performed by their Papua New Guinean opponents that they developed their own ritual. Since then, this has been performed by other indigenous teams (for example, versus Ireland in 2013), though it is presented as a 'Challenge', with no reference to the Haka.
- *Invention*. This concept, made famous by historian Eric Hobsbawm, refers to the process of the creation of rituals and symbols that quickly take on the appearance and reputation of being traditional (see the next section for a more detailed exploration). An example of this is the closing ceremony of the Olympic Games, where athletes of all countries parade together – in contrast to the opening where they march as national teams. This was suggested in 1956 by a Melbourne schoolboy and taken up by organisers who wished to defuse tensions arising from the deterioration of the Cold War.

Some key theories

Two particular theories are often invoked to explain the significance and resilience of traditional rituals and events. These are Falassi's *Ritual Structure* and Hobsbawm's *Invention of Tradition*. Interestingly, both of these were published in the 1980s, well before the rise of events studies. Accordingly, their application to events studies has been somewhat uneven; mainly being utilised by those taking a social sciences or humanities perspective and often noticeably lacking from those following a business paradigm. In the case studies that constitute this book, most authors refer to one or both, reflecting their importance to the general study of traditional events.

Falassi (1987) introduced an anthology of writings on events by arguing that most follow a *ritual structure*, that is a series of common rites or components. He argued that this structure was rarely deliberately planned by organisers, but rather grew organically or subconsciously as a response to our basic human needs and beliefs. In essence, these represented a series of underlying meanings that underpinned most events and their significance to societies. Particularly apparent in traditional events that had evolved over centuries, Falassi argued that they were still apparent in recently constructed events. Other researchers, for example Seal (2004), have found Falassi's ritual structure a valuable framework for explaining modern events and their meanings.

According to Falassi, the chief rites commonly found in events are:

- *Valorisation.* Time and space are claimed for the event through an opening ceremony. The event is now marked as symbolically different from normal time and space.
- *Purification.* There are ceremonies to cleanse and safeguard the festival and its participants.
- *Passage.* Rituals that mark transition from one stage of life to another, particularly for young people.
- *Reversal.* Normal behaviours and roles are reversed. The illicit may be respectable. A common form is the coronation of a 'fool' as the king of the festival.
- *Conspicuous display.* The most valued objects are displayed, for example, religious relics are paraded.
- *Conspicuous consumption.* Abundant, even wasteful, consumption, particularly of food and drink.
- *Dramas.* Treasured stories are told through dramatic or musical performances.
- *Exchange.* Symbolic exchanges of money, valuables or tokens. The wealthy might distribute gifts and money to the poor.
- *Competition.* Typically games and sporting contests, often between rival groups. Such games may be a substitute for armed conflict.
- *Devalorisation.* A closing ceremony marks the return to normal time and space, perhaps with a promise of a future repeat of the festival.

As with Falassi, Hobsbawm (1983) set out his theory in an introductory essay to an edited collection. His thesis was that 'traditions which appear or claim to be old are often quite recent in origin and sometimes invented' (1983: 1). A specialist in modern history, he observed that this tendency towards invention was a characteristic of modern society, being particularly apparent in Western Europe during the late nineteenth and twentieth centuries. Here was a major paradox in modernity. In a period of increasing change, many old traditions, rituals and festivals were disappearing at a rapid rate. However, at the same time, societies were creating new traditions. This propensity to invent, Hobsbawm reasoned, was a product of the stresses of modernity and accelerating change. These new traditions were purposefully functioning to maintain social cohesion and support changing institutions. Published in the same year as Hobsbawm's work, Anderson (1983) had argued that the development of nation states demanded that there be symbolic events reinforcing loyalty and inclusiveness. Hobsbawm took this a step further in arguing that these would have to be specifically created. Most importantly, Hobsbawm demonstrated that it only takes a short space of time for new rituals to be widely accepted as traditional and venerable.

A historical overview of traditional events and rituals

To better understand the role of traditional events in the modern world, it is valuable to consider how they originally functioned and developed in pre-modern societies. Due to constraints of space, we can only do this in a limited way. Rather than a comprehensive examination of traditional events and rituals, the following sections serve only as an introduction. Furthermore, our choices are highly subjective, reflecting our interests and knowledge – in many ways Anglocentric. Instead of attempting to cover a wide range of societies and cultures, our focus is on a small group of case studies. These are merely intended as examples and their purpose is to provide a general historical foundation to the events and rituals covered in the later chapters. Nonetheless, it is important to understand that historical cases and description have a key role in examining and analysing the evolution of events. As historian David Cannadine argued:

> Like all cultural forms which may be treated as texts, or all texts which may be treated as cultural forms, 'thick' rather than 'thin' description is required … in order to rediscover the 'meaning' of … ritual during the modern period, it is necessary to relate it to the specific social, political, economic and cultural milieu within which it was actually performed. With ceremonial, as with political theory, the very act of locating the occasion or the text in its appropriate context is not merely to provide the historical background, but actually to begin the process of interpretation.
>
> (1983: 105)

Prehistoric events

In a general sense, prehistoric signifies before recorded history – before societies developed writing. This immediately raises problems of evidence. How do we know what events and rituals were like in such traditional communities? How do we interpret their meanings and significance? What we have is only fragmentary. In some instances, archaeology has unearthed artefacts, though these are skewed towards certain materials. Stones, for example, may survive; whereas iron may rust and wood, skins and other organic materials will decay. Occasionally, material finds will be complemented by folklore, though this raises further problems of veracity. Stonehenge in England illustrates this well. Built around 4,000 years ago, its structure and fabric are still well intact. Archaeological research has identified the source of the stones, how they were raised and even how they have been periodically rearranged. There is a consensus that Stonehenge was constructed as an important ceremonial site. However, there is substantial disagreement as to what those rituals were and most importantly what their purpose was. Furthermore, recent years have seen the highly controversial invention of

Druidic rituals, particularly around the midsummer solstice. It is a fascinating and provocative example of the difficulties of interpreting a heritage site that still has significance and appeal, but where the original meanings are lost or disputed.

Archaeology has pushed back the beginning of human rituals well beyond Stonehenge. Cave paintings around the world are linked to hunting, religious, possibly even astrological ceremonies. For example, the famous cave paintings of prehistoric wildlife at Lascaux in France (approximately 17,000 years old) are often seen as being created for rituals before a hunt. Like Stonehenge, there are also alternative theories, the only agreement being that they are for ritual purposes. In Outback Australia, Mungo Woman, excavated in the Willandra Lakes, is dated to between 20,000 to 25,000 years ago. She is evidence of

> The world's oldest known cremation ... Her body was burnt and the bones collected, broken and buried in a small pit. This shows that complex rites could accompany death, including the death of a woman, and is a very similar ritual to that accorded to the dead in traditional Tasmanian Aboriginal society, which may have retained an extremely ancient custom which was originally more widespread.
>
> (Flood 1990: 250)

In recent years, archaeologists and anthropologists have become more speculative about prehistoric rituals and ceremonies. Applying a comparative approach, underpinned by a premise of the universality of human experience, they have complemented material finds with more recent ethnography of prehistoric peoples. Further underpinning this is the concept that our ancestors were essentially rational and that their rituals evolved primarily to help their societies survive and flourish.

An intriguing example of this paradigm is the propensity of some prehistoric societies to engage in building massive monumental works. Examples include Stonehenge and Avebury in England, New Grange in Ireland, Inca, Mayan and Aztec temples, the moundbuilders of the Mississippi Valley and the *Moai* (statue) of Easter Island. In the past, these ceremonial sites have tended to be seen as wasteful, illustrative of traditional priest-dominated societies expending nearly all of their surplus resources on religious practices. However, a new interpretation sees such *cultural elaboration* as monument building as a rational rather than wasteful strategy. As archaeologists Terry Hunt and Carl Lipo explained: 'any form of cultural elaboration requires an investment of time and energy in activities that do not have a clear or direct role in enhancing survival or enabling reproduction'. Building monuments and burying grave goods use resources that could, in the short term, support higher populations. Expending resources on rituals rather than children is a form of *bet-hedging* (i.e. balancing risks over the longer term), so that, 'where we find unpredictability in resources, those who have fewer offspring in any one generation tend to have more descendants overall' (Hunt and Lipo 2011: 136).

Such decision making was probably not conscious, as prehistoric peoples 'often engage in customs that happen to have evolutionary benefits, but without ever thinking about them in that way' and 'those reaping the benefits of any given practice need not understand why it contributes to their survival'. Indeed, all that is needed is that society flourishes, demonstrating that ceremonial expenditure was justified in propitiating the gods. Focusing specifically on Easter Island (Rapanui), Hunt and Lipo argued:

> we are not saying the islanders consciously decided to spend more time making and moving statues in efforts to take time and resources away from reproduction ... [but doing this] didn't threaten Rapanui survival, and indeed probably help to sustain it.
>
> (Hunt and Lipo 2011: 136)

Following this new interpretation, Easter Island is seen not as an example of feckless wastage of limited resources, but rather of the importance of ceremonies in ensuring a stable society.

For prehistoric hunter-gatherers, ceremonial feasting developed as a reaction to inconsistent food supplies. Periodically there would be massive surpluses of food, far more than small groups could consume and with little prospect of preserving for future years. Sometimes seasonal, but unpredictable in their scale and reliability, such bounty was the cause of joyous celebration. In prehistoric Australia, the two most notable were summer swarms of Bogong moths in the high country around modern Canberra and the harvesting of bunya nuts (*araucaria bidwilli*) in south-eastern Queensland. While the latter fruited each year, it was generally at three-year intervals that there were massive harvests. Both instances provided fat-rich feasting. While these events brought communities together, they also had the highly important effect of facilitating contact with other tribes and clans, often from hundreds of kilometres away. Sharing the bounty with others allowed for trade, settling disputes and encouraging cross-tribal marriages (Flood 1990; Lourandos 1997). Just as important as feasting, many societies developed rituals of fasting and consumption taboos; again this may be rationalised as a response to inconsistency in food supply.

Inter-tribal contact and exchange required the development of standardised rituals signifying peaceful intentions and friendship. First contact was particularly problematic and open to misunderstandings. Here, the evidence of rituals has often come from Western explorers and accordingly may be misinterpreted.

In concluding this brief overview of prehistoric rituals, it is worth noting how these changed in intent with the incursion of European colonial powers. One by-product of the Age of Enlightenment was a major Western fascination with *the Other*, often manifested through anthropological interest in studying and recording these ceremonies (Bell *et al.* 2013; Catlin 1841; Griffiths 1996). This paralleled European antiquarianism and folklore studies at home and was closely linked to a growth in ethnographic museums and displays. As they did with rare fauna and flora, European colonials were keen to record, classify and dissect cultures and traditions before they died out in the face of modernity.

Such interest generated a commodification of traditional rituals. In Australia, Aboriginals quickly realised there was a market for performing modified versions of their rituals, particularly the *corroboree*. Even as missionaries and officials sought to forbid indigenous religious ceremonies, there was a trend towards performance for payment, often with the reassurance that these were secular dances and stories. William Thomas, Assistant Protector of Aborigines in the Melbourne area in the 1840s, attended many ceremonies and recorded them in his diary. While he thought some had no religious elements, at other times he was puzzled, recording of an initiation ritual: 'I think there may be more in the meaning of this than I am acquainted with' (quoted in Ellender and Christiansen 2001: 52). At almost exactly the same time, the painter George Catlin was recording ceremonies and costumes among Native American tribes along the Missouri River. Acutely aware that these traditions could be soon lost, he noted:

> The Mandans, like all other tribes, lead lives of idleness and leisure: and of course, devote a great deal of time to their sports and amusements, of which they have a great variety ... to the eye of the traveller who knows not their meaning or importance, they are an uncouth and frightful display of starts, and jumps, and yelps ... but when one ... has been lucky enough to be initiated into their mysterious meaning, they become a subject of the most intense and exciting interest.
>
> (Catlin 1841: 128)

As European contact increased, some indigenous people gained a certain measure of status in the new transitional society through performing and mediating their traditional rituals. The most prominent of these in Melbourne was Barak, who through to the 1890s drew pictures of traditional corroborees for visitors. His works are now seen as of the highest significance and held in art collections around the world (Sayers 1994). Similarly, in Vanuatu the ritual of land-diving was discouraged by missionaries and colonial authorities. However, late in the twentieth century, it became very popular with tourists, especially after it was performed during a royal tour. In a society in transition from traditional to modern, the revenue from land-diving was important for the local economy (Cheer *et al.* 2013).

The classical world

The development of new political, social and economic institutions created new types of events. In the popular imagination, the two events most associated with the classical world were the Olympics and the arena contests of Rome. In both scale and style, these established strong ideas of what major events should be like and the impact they could have on society and leisure. It is particularly notable that many modern events and venues have looked backwards to the classical period for inspiration.

The ancient Olympics are usually dated as beginning in 776 BCE. This is also the date that is often used as marking the beginning of history for the Greeks. Before then we have myths and archaeological evidence, but no firm history. Homer probably composed the *Iliad* in the eighth century BCE. Placing the birth of the Olympics at approximately the same time is based on the calculations of Hippias, who wrote in around 400 BCE. There were probably earlier games and contests, but the 776 date gives the Olympics a special resonance of marking the *birth* of Greek culture and history (Lane Fox 2008).

Similarly, the foundation of Rome by Romulus and Remus was later specifically dated to provide a festival. Like the Olympics, the auspicious date was situated by scholars around the middle of the eighth century BCE, a convenient bridge between the semi-mythical past and recorded history. As the Romans developed a calendar that had the same dates re-occurring each year, the opportunity presented itself for a specific foundation day. This was decided as 21 April and became the basis for the Parilla, a commemorative and celebratory festival (Feeney 2008). In 1925, Mussolini revived this anniversary as the Natale di Roma (Birth of Rome) and it continues as a carnivalesque celebration of ancient Rome (Frost and Laing 2013).

What evolved among the ancient Greeks was the idea of combining festivals, rituals and religious significance. This is probably what occurred at many prehistoric events, but with the Olympics and other festivals, the details were now recorded and preserved. The Olympics were held to honour Zeus, with the appropriate religious ceremonies matched by athletic games. As classicist Lionel Casson argued, it provided

> In one unique package the spectrum of attractions that have drawn tourists in all times and places: the feeling of being part of a great event and of enjoying a special experience; a gay festive mood punctuated by exalted religious moments; elaborate pageantry; the excitement of contests between performers of the highest calibre – and, on top of this, a chance to wander among famous buildings and works of art. Imagine the modern Olympics taking place at Easter in Rome, with the religious services held at St Peter's.
>
> (1974: 76–77)

While the Olympics highlighted athletics, other events had different ways of honouring the gods. The Pythian Games, dedicated to Apollo, featured song and dance. In Athens, an annual festival for Dionysus focused on music and drama and is credited as the birthplace of theatre. All of these functioned as early versions of hallmark events, branding particular towns and cities with their distinctive festival, attracting large numbers of visitors and stimulating the local economy. As had occurred with many prehistoric events, there was a strong tradition of keeping the peace and being tolerant of strangers through the course of these festivals (Casson 1974).

Highly urbanised Rome is strongly associated with the spectacle of arena events – including gladiatorial contests and chariot races. In the modern imagination, this has been strongly reinforced through film, including *Quo Vadis*

(1951), *Ben-Hur* (1959), *Gladiator* (2000) and the Italian *Peplum* (or *sword and sandal*) movies of the 1950s and 1960s. In many Roman cities and towns, arenas were constructed on a massive scale and many survive today. The best known is the Colosseum in Rome. Constructed between 70 and 80 CE, it was commissioned by the Emperor Vespasian as a means of rebuilding faith in imperial rule following the disastrous reign of Nero. With free entry and daily events, it provided one-half of the *bread and circuses* recipe for stable rule. In providing this focus on events, the Romans combined the reinforcement of the authority of their imperial state, allowed for the inclusion of subject peoples within their culture and distracted potential dissenters (Korstanje 2009).

With the collapse of the Western Empire, what remained to influence European societies were the relics of rituals and ceremonies. The festival of Saturnalia – held towards the close of the year and featuring the gifting of presents – evolved gradually into Christmas. The resilience of the Eastern Empire provided a continuing exemplar of imperial excellence, continuing to diffuse westwards through trade, Varangian mercenaries, Orthodox missionaries and ultimately the Crusades (Herrin 2007). However, for most medieval societies, the glories of Rome remained only as a shadowy and legendary influence, perhaps best exemplified by the persistence and eventual revival of Arthurian romance.

Romanticising the medieval

The Dark Ages were characterised by a decline in centralised power, cities and trade. The chief exception was Byzantium, where magnificent pageantry and rituals still captured the imagination of visitors from the periphery. Elsewhere across Europe, there was a return to agriculture and insularity. Social life became centred on villages, autarky and variants of feudalism. Inward-looking communities developed rituals and customs that heavily emphasised agricultural production, promoting fertility and attempting to ward off natural disasters. As Christianity spread across Europe, there was a tendency for missionaries to incorporate old folkways and mythology – particularly those connected with seasonal cycles – into the Christian canon. Such hybridised rituals would remain well into the modern era.

It is the rituals of the medieval period that are most popularly associated with traditional festivals and events. Even more than that, these are the ceremonies and customs that are lauded and romanticised (and form a significant part of this book). The fascination with the medieval is a paradoxical, yet common, feature of modernity. For over 200 years, the urbanised societies of the West have looked backwards at the medieval and imagined a romanticised Golden Age of chivalry and legend that runs to the core of modern identities (Laing and Frost 2012; Wood 1999). This hyper-real heritage draws on fact and fiction, combining *The Canterbury Tales*, the Crusades, *The Court Jester*, Robin Hood, *Indiana Jones*, *Lord of the Rings* and *El Cid*. Central to this imaginary world are carnivalesque images of traditional rituals, albeit mediated by Hollywood. In popular consciousness, the medieval is characterised by feasting, maypoles, jousting, tournaments, masked balls, festivals and processions. Furthermore, modern trends – such as slow food and foraging – draw on their medieval heritage for authenticity.

Medieval European agricultural communities and their rituals

In a predominantly agricultural world, societies were organised around villages with strongly communal structures for support, defence and production. Rituals and festivals brought people together, reinforcing these bonds through the celebration of the local community and marking of seasonal milestones. Not surprisingly, given the emphasis on agriculture, most ceremonies were centred on tasks such as planting and harvesting. These were highly symbolic and ritualised, and even after the spread of Christianity, contained echoes of earlier animism and paganism. According to archaeologist Yosef Garfinkel (2003), the shift from hunting and collecting to agriculture required people to group together in sedentary societies. Collective ceremonies were necessary to encourage bonding and Garfinkel nominated ritualised dancing as paramount for defining identities. To this we would add a wider range of experiences that were staged as a group, including singing, music, initiations, decision making, worship, feasting and brewing.

Many rituals were designed to capture or encourage natural powers of fertility and closely followed a seasonal calendar. At the beginning of spring, the birch was the first tree to sprout leaves and so was viewed as a harbinger of new life. Young trees were uprooted or cut and carried in a procession through the village. They then became the centrepiece for dancing and festivities, before being torn up and scattered to return energy to the soil. Young unmarried girls, viewed as filled with potential fertility, were involved in this dancing and rituals (Barber 2013).

According to linguist and archaeologist Elizabeth Barber, in such traditional communities rituals were constructed on the basis of analogy. Girls and birch trees were symbolic of fecundity and they were central to rituals to ensure sufficient rainfall and ward off droughts and storms. While festive, at their core such rituals were about survival: 'one must invite – indeed coax – the spring to arrive. If one simply waited, Spring (being wilful) might not *choose* to come, and then, with last year's food bins already almost empty, one could not survive' (Barber 2013: 41).

Here we see differences in the interpretation of medieval agrarian rituals. The mythologist Joseph Campbell was adamant that it was wrong to see these as attempts to control or influence nature. Rather, 'the wonderful cycle of the year, with its hardships and periods of joy, is celebrated' and these 'rites all prepare the community to endure' (Campbell 1949: 384). While such a rational interpretation seems convincing to twenty-first century researchers, it is also clear that medieval peoples sought to literally change nature through the appropriate use of rituals.

As the year progressed, there was a burst of feasting and merrymaking just prior to Lent:

> For days people gorged themselves – the 'Christian' reason being to eat up the remaining stores that the church would not allow during Lenten fasting, but the pre-Christian reason being that much food on the table at the end of winter would by analogical magic produce copious food in the next agricultural cycle.
>
> (Barber 2013: 43)

The analogical slaying and defeat of Winter occurred across Europe. In Russia, there were mock funerals and burnings of an effigy and

> In parts of Germany, two men arrayed as Summer and Winter would fight, with Summer invariably trouncing Winter. In other areas in Germany, Poland, France, and the Basque country, people burned, stoned, clubbed, shredded, or drowned a straw doll representing Winter or Death, while the Swiss of Zurich incinerated a huge cotton 'snowman.' As in Russia, the residual magical energies were often buried or strewn about the fields where the seeds of the new crops awaited the returning warmth to rise again.
>
> (Barber 2013: 44)

Midsummer was a time of great festivity, as it remains in much of Europe today (Figures 1.1 and 1.2). The longest day of the year was marked with bonfires, singing and dancing. Many cultures constructed symbolic effigies made out of straw. These were burnt with laughter and mock mourning, again a way of returning the life force to the soil to ensure future fertility. There was also a practical element in the burning off of potentially hazardous vegetation. The autumn harvest was a celebration of success and the end of the year's farmwork (American relics include Thanksgiving and the Hoe-Down – literally a dance to celebrate putting farm implements away). By harvest, symbolism was less important, the key rituals had been performed earlier and would soon be commenced again.

Medieval towns

As towns redeveloped after the Dark Ages, they too evolved their own rituals and events. In contrast to the natural cycles of the surrounding countryside, these developments were often more about identity, trade and independence; though worries about dangerous magic were just below the surface. Another interesting contrast was that urban traditions were more likely to be recorded by contemporary chroniclers and officials.

For many towns, events and rituals grew up around their semi-mythical origins. Such traditions were important in demonstrating how historically the town had been created as a special place with rights and privileges worthy of preservation. Three examples are worth noting. The first is Reims in France. In 496, its Bishop

Figure 1.1 Midsummer festival in the Marais district, Paris (source: W. Frost).

Figure 1.2 Hungarian folk dancers taking part in the Szentendre Summer Festival, Hungary (source: J. Laing).

Remy had baptised Clovis, King of the Franks. From then to the nineteenth century, its cathedral was where French kings were traditionally crowned and its economy was centred on associated royal production and events. The second is Coventry, whose origins were traced to the establishment of a monastery and market town by the eleventh-century Lord Leofric and Lady Godiva. By the thirteenth century, an elaborate myth had developed about Godiva and her special role as protector of the welfare of the townspeople and this gradually evolved into an annual festival. The third is the Palio in Siena (Italy), a horse race marking the end of the festival to celebrate Mary as the patron saint of the town. In medieval times, many Italian cities and towns staged such events, though Siena's is now the only one to have run continuously. Symbolically, it is staged in the very centre of the city (the Campo), bringing together all the districts or factions to compete, but also stress their identity and unity in terms of their special relationship with the town's patron saint (Dundes and Falassi 1975).

Many medieval urban festivals combined religion and rites of reversal, often leading to carnivalesque excesses. For example, in fourteenth-century France,

> In the annual Feast of Fools at Christmastime, every rite and article of the Church no matter how sacred was celebrated in mockery. A *dominus festi*, or lord of the revels, was elected from the inferior clergy ... whose day it was to turn everything topsy-turvy. They installed their lord as Pope or Bishop or Abbot of Fools in a ceremony of head-shaving accompanied by bawdy talk and lewd acts; dressed him in vestments turned inside out; played dice on the altar and ate black puddings and sausages while mass was celebrated in nonsensical gibberish ... wearing beast masks and dressed as women or minstrels ... [then] all rush violently from the church to parade through the town, drawing the *dominus* in a cart from which he issues mock indulgences while his followers hiss, cackle, jeer, and gesticulate ... Naked men haul carts of manure which they throw at the populace. Drinking bouts and dances accompany the procession.
>
> (Tuchman 1978: 32–33)

In analysing the works of Rabelais, literary researcher Mikhail Bakhtin recognised the profound importance of ritual spectacles in towns. These 'took on a comic aspect as clowns and fools, constant participants in these festivals, mimicked serious rituals such as the tribute rendered to the victors at tournaments, the transfer of feudal rights, or the initiation of a knight' (1965: 5). Immersion in such parody, mimicry and general tomfoolery 'offered a completely different, nonofficial, extraecclesiastical and extrapolitical aspect of the world, of man, and of human relations; [and] ... built a second world in which all medieval people participated' (1965: 6). Furthermore, these festivals were all-encompassing for the towns and their people, with essentially no barriers between performers and audience, nor between a stage and public space.

In medieval Paris, Midsummer was converted to St John's Day. As in the surrounding countryside, the highpoint was an enormous bonfire symbolising purification. Customarily it was lit by a person of high office who on this day came down and mingled with the masses. In 1648, it was King Louis XIV himself, lighting the fire and dancing while crowned with a wreath of roses. The concept of purification by fire was taken to the extreme with the burning of a barrel or sack of live cats, a ritual that persisted in Paris until well into the eighteenth century (Goudsblom 1992).

Town festivals often developed elaborate sporting competitions. Symbolic of warfare, they involved different districts within towns, but also served to unite those within its boundaries. Many were linked to religious holidays, forging that uneasy relationship between authority and chaos that characterised many urban traditional festivals. The Palio of Siena is a prime example. Another persists at Ashbourne in Derbyshire (UK), where an annual football match was played in the streets on Shrove Tuesday (McCabe 2006). With few rules and hundreds of players, it was anarchic and dangerous, though sanctified by its connection to a holy day. Like the Palio, such folk football competitions were once widespread, but now only continue in a few places.

While much of the research into medieval festivals has emphasised their role in bringing communities together, there is a counter-argument. Some historians have argued that there were also patterns of divisiveness, that many of these festivals privileged certain groups – typically the elites – and excluded or marginalised others. Accordingly, they argue, festivals were distinguished by ongoing tensions, as various groups battled for control and prominence (Hanawalt and Reyerson 1994).

The decline of traditional rituals

For Hobsbawm (1983), nineteenth-century modernity, characterised by increased connectivity through steam trains, telegraph and newspapers, sounded the death-knell for insular traditions. While these also encouraged new traditions, what was invented – according to Hobsbawm – was still far less than what disappeared. Compelling as this explanation seems, it is important to understand that the processes of decline and replacement were occurring far earlier in the modern era.

In Western Europe, the economic and social development of the early modern period (early 1500s to late 1700s) was the catalyst for the decline of many traditional rituals. Religious turmoil, the growth of commerce and nascent beginnings of industrialisation, the collapse of feudalism and acceleration of the drift to the cities all combined to create a new world where past customary practices were anachronistic.

In England, state support for the Reformation (and abject fear of the Counter-Reformation) created the need for new festivals and commemorations to promote unity and loyalty. Most prominent of these was Guy Fawkes or Bonfire Night, commemorating the defeat of an attempt to blow up parliament. In creating a new tradition to reinforce their legitimacy, the authorities intended that this

Unequivocally Protestant celebration on 5 November therefore provided a handy replacement for what was now regarded as a redundant Catholic holy day, and also filled All Saints' Day's role as a festival marking the onset of winter, with celebratory bonfires defying the November darkness ... Bonfire Night had replaced Hallowe'en.

(Sharpe 2005: 85; see also Cressy 1994; Frost and Laing 2013)

As religious fundamentalism took a stronger and stronger grip on sixteenth-century England, the Puritans focused their wrath on age-old rituals:

Most Catholic rites were regarded as thinly concealed mutations of earlier pagan ceremonies ... much energy was spent in demonstrating that holy water was the Roman *aqua lustralis*, that wakes were the *Bacchanalia*, [and] Shrove Tuesday celebrations *Saturnalia* ... ecclesiastical injunctions prohibited the entry into the church or churchyard of Rush-bearing processions, Lords of Misrule and Summer Lords and Ladies ... the Puritans wanted the abolition of all remaining holy days, a ban on maypoles ... the bagpipes and fiddlers who accompanied the bridal couple to the church and to the throwing of corn (the sixteenth-century equivalent of confetti) ... [and] the custom of giving New Year's gifts ... the custom of drinking healths was also seen as a heathen survival.

(Thomas 1971: 74–76)

However, civic authorities in the growing towns were concerned about these new developments. Replacing medieval carnivalesque with sectarian violence threatened social stability and the new economic order. Events needed to be carefully staged – allowing people to blow off steam, but with no lasting damage. With Guy Fawkes Night, 'the trick was to maintain a solemn Protestant commemoration without inspiring too much anti-Catholic enthusiasm' (Cressy 1994: 70). Even then, it remained (and remains today) on the edge of disorder. At Lewes in south-east England, late-nineteenth-century Guy Fawkes Night was characterised by riots and property damage directed at merchants; provocative clashes between tradition and the new civic order of municipal corporations and town police forces (Sharpe 2005). It is not surprising that Guy Fawkes – reversed now into a hero – has emerged as the symbolic face of protest groups like Anonymous (Frost and Laing 2013).

The reining in of traditional events was not confined to the Protestant world. In France, the eighteenth-century Age of Enlightenment encouraged a view that the *Ancien Régime* was distinguished by too many festivals and religious holidays. These were seen as entrenching insularity, conservatism and ignorance and restricting economic production. While there was resistance, French aspirations to be the major European power required embracing modernity (Ozouf 1976).

Conclusion

In this introductory chapter, our aim has been to set the scene for the later case studies through a general discussion of the changing nature of traditional events and rituals. While we have only been able to touch lightly on various periods of history, patterns are apparent. Two are worth highlighting.

First, interest in the role of events in society is spread across a broad academic spectrum. Rather than being a narrow domain, events – as seen in this chapter – are central to research in archaeology, history, classics, literature, sociology, folklore and cultural studies. With such a breadth of perspectives, a wide range of theories are being proposed, tested, contested and debated. For those of us in events studies, it is important that we engage with and understand these relevant disciplines.

Second, the persistence of traditional rituals and events into the modern world is complex. As events serve to satisfy contemporary needs in society, a rapidly changing world – it might be thought – demands that events and rituals also be constantly changing. Following this logic, much of what was staged in the past is now anachronistic and should wither away. However, what we see occurring – and which requires explanation and understanding – is quite different. Even in the face of modernity and globalisation, there are traditional events that are retained and treasured. Some are even growing in popularity. Furthermore, there are trends towards invention based on romanticised views of the past and appropriation and adaptation of other culture's rituals and customs. Traditions, and how we use them, lie at the very foundation of many of our contemporary events. To understand events better, we need to examine and analyse this relationship.

References

Anderson, B. (1983) *Imagined Communities: Reflections on the origins and spread of nationalism*, London and New York: Verso, 2006 edn.

Bakhtin, M. (1965) *Rabelais and His World*, Cambridge MA: MIT Press, 1968 English translation.

Barber, E.W. (2013) *Dancing Goddesses: Folklore, archaeology, and the origins of European dance*, London and New York: Norton.

Bell, J.A., Brown, A.K. and Gordon, R.J. (eds) (2013) *Recreating First Contact: Expeditions, anthropology and popular culture*, Washington, DC: Smithsonian Institution.

Campbell, J. (1949) *The Hero with a Thousand Faces*, New York: Princeton University Press, 1968 edn.

Cannadine, D. (1983) 'The context, performance and meaning of ritual: The British Monarchy and the 'invention of tradition', c. 1820–1977', in E. Hobsbawm and T. Ranger (eds), *The Invention of Tradition* (pp. 101–164), Cambridge: Cambridge University Press.

Casson, L. (1974) *Travel in the Ancient World*, Baltimore and London: Johns Hopkins University Press, 1994 edn.

Catlin, G. (1841) *North American Indians*, New York: Viking, 1989 edn.

Cheer, J., Reeves, K. and Laing, J. (2013) 'Tourism and traditional culture: Land diving in Vanuatu', *Annals of Tourism Research*, 43, 435–455.

Cressy, D. (1994) 'National memory in early modern England', in J.R. Gillis (ed.), *Commemorations: The politics of national identity* (pp. 61–73), Princeton: Princeton University Press.

Dundes, A. and Falassi, A. (1975) *La Terra in Piazza: An interpretation of the Palio of Siena*, Berkeley: University of California Press.

Ellender, I. and Christiansen, P. (2001) *People of the Merri Merri: The Wurundjeri in colonial days*, Melbourne: Merri Creek Management Committee.

Falassi, A. (1987) 'Festival: Definition and morphology', in A. Falassi (ed.), *Time Out of Time: Essays on the festival* (pp. 1–10), Albuquerque, NM: University of New Mexico Press.

Feeney, D. (2008) *Caesar's Calendar: Ancient time and the beginnings of history*, Berkeley: University of California Press.

Flood, J. (1990) *The Riches of Ancient Australia* (3rd edn), Brisbane: University of Queensland Press, 1999.

Frost, W. and Laing, J. (2011) *Strategic Management of Festivals and Events*, Melbourne: Cengage.

Frost, W. and Laing, J. (2013) *Commemorative Events: Memory, identities, conflicts*, London and New York: Routledge.

Garfinkel, Y. (2003) *Dancing at the Dawn of Agriculture*, Austin: University of Texas Press.

Goudsblom, J. (1992) *Fire and Civilization*, London: Allen Lane.

Griffiths, T. (1996) *Hunters and Collectors: The antiquarian imagination in Australia*, Cambridge: Cambridge University Press.

Hanawalt, B.A. and Reyerson, K.L. (eds) (1994) *City and Spectacle in Medieval Europe*, Minneapolis: University of Minnesota Press.

Herrin, J. (2007) *Byzantium: The surprising life of a medieval empire*, London: Penguin.

Hobsbawm, E. (1983) 'Introduction: Inventing traditions', in E. Hobsbawm and T. Ranger (eds), *The Invention of Tradition* (pp. 1–14), Cambridge: Cambridge University Press.

Hunt, T. and Lipo, C. (2011) *The Statues That Walked: Unraveling the mystery of Easter Island*, New York: Free Press.

Korstanje, M.E. (2009) 'Reconsidering the roots of event management: Leisure in Ancient Rome', *Event Management*, 13(3), 197–203.

Laing, J. and Frost, W. (2012) *Books and Travel: Inspiration, quests and transformation*, Bristol: Channel View.

Lane Fox, R. (2008) *Travelling Heroes: Greeks and their myths in the epic age of Homer*, London: Penguin.

Lourandos, H. (1997) *Continent of Hunter-Gatherers: New perspectives in Australian prehistory*, Cambridge: Cambridge University Press.

Lowenthal, D. (1998) *The Heritage Crusade and the Spoils of History*, Cambridge: Cambridge University Press.

McCabe, S. (2006) 'The making of community identity through historic festive practice: The case of Ashbourne Royal Shrovetide Football', in D. Picard and M. Robinson (eds), *Festivals, Tourism and Social Change: Remaking worlds* (pp. 99–118), Clevedon: Channel View.

Ozouf, M. (1976) *Festivals and the French Revolution*, Cambridge, MA: Harvard University Press, 1991 edn.

Sayers, A. (1994) *Aboriginal Artists of the Nineteenth Century*, Melbourne: Oxford University Press.

Seal, G. (2004) *Inventing ANZAC: The Digger and national mythology*, Brisbane: University of Queensland Press.

Sharpe, J.A. (2005) *Remember, Remember: A cultural history of Guy Fawkes Day*, Cambridge, MA: Harvard University Press.

Spivey, N. (2004) *The Ancient Olympics: A history*, Oxford: Oxford University Press.

Thomas, K. (1971) *Religion and the Decline of Magic: Studies in popular belief in sixteenth and seventeenth century England*, London: Penguin, 1988 edn.

Tuchman, B. (1978) *A Distant Mirror: The calamitous 14th century*, London: Papermac, 1989 edn.

Wallace, T. (2007) 'Went the day well: Glamour and performance in war-weekends', *International Journal of Heritage Studies*, 13(3), 200–223.

Wood, M. (1999) *In Search of England: Journeys into the English past*, London: Viking.

Part I
Asia

2 Ganesh festival

A ten-day extravaganza; a life full of meanings

Kiran Shinde

Introduction

Parades, processions and festivals have long been studied in the Western world to understand their complex relationships with social identities and cultural change, and often highlight issues of authenticity, staging and their exploitation for tourism (Chambers 1997; Kraft 2007; Picard and Robinson 2006). In the case of Hindu festivals and processions, a majority of the extant studies explore their mysticism and examine aspects related to mythology, cosmology and the socio-cultural milieu while occasionally underlining the political context and content (Lutgendorf 1994; Raj and Morpeth 2007; Shapiro 1987). Scholars from different disciplines such as religious studies, anthropology, ethnography and geography have offered their insights on topics ranging from studies of the colossal gatherings at the pan-Indian *Kumbha mela* to ethnographic accounts of village-level festivals (Maclean 2003; Shackley 2001). However, many provide snapshots and often tend to reinforce the romanticism associated with Hindu culture (Rinehart 2004). Some emphasise the value of festivals for cultural tourism (Ichaporia 1983; Jaitly 2001) while others raise concerns over increasing visitor flows during festivals and their socio-economic and environmental impacts on the place and the community (Shinde 2010). In this expanding field, however, a systematic analysis of Hindu festivals and processions is wanting. This paucity is felt even more acutely given that festivals are celebrated because they constitute and function as 'ritual' for transmitting and maintaining continuity of religious and cultural traditions and have a significant social role.

This chapter aims to offer some insights into the complex relationship between religion, culture, economy and social significance of Hindu festivals and processions by focusing on Ganesh, the elephant-headed deity (also popularly known as Ganpati) widely worshipped by Hindus as the supreme god of wisdom, prosperity and good fortune, and the Ganesh-*utsav* (*utsav* meaning festival) dedicated to him. This festival, generally celebrated every year around the month of September, follows a basic structure where people bring an idol of Ganesh, worship it in private homes or public spaces for around ten days and then take out the idol in a procession and finally immerse it in flowing waters; every aspect of the festival being a ritual in itself. In addition, cultural performances and social events are added that enhance the festive fervour and simultaneously contribute to a surge in economic activities associated with the festival.

The Ganesh festival is a pan-Indian festival that is celebrated by most Hindus globally but its fullest expression is found in the state of Maharashtra among the predominantly Marathi-speaking Hindus. Outside Maharashtra, states like Punjab, West Bengal, Bihar and Tamilnadu, also actively promote public celeb-rations of the Ganesh festival (*Pudhari Reporter* 2013b). In recent years, the Indian diaspora has actively promoted public celebrations of Ganesh festivals as a distinct marker of their culture and identity in cities including London, Sydney, New York and Singapore (A. Joshi 2013; Naidoo 2007).

The purpose of this chapter is to explore different layers of the Ganesh festi-val in all its variations from a private ritual to its public celebrations and the meaning it imparts in creating and reinforcing a Hindu identity. The focus is on the public nature of the festival, which has received little scholarly attention in the literature around religion, festivals and tourism. I examine social, cultural, economic and environmental dimensions of the festival with the findings from the study of its celebrations as reported in Pune in 2013.

Ganesh and the Ganesh festival

According to Hindu mythology, Ganesh is the putative son of Shiva (one of the trinity of Hindu gods) and his consort Parvati. The legend states that in a fit of anger Lord Shiva severed Ganesh's head; repenting his actions, he thereafter transplanted an elephant's head on Ganesh. Furthermore, a privilege was bestowed upon Ganesh in that he will be the first of the gods to be invoked whenever a *puja* is performed for whatever reason or purpose (Barnouw 1954).

The Ganesh festival is celebrated in the dark half of the Hindu month of *bhaadrapada* for ten days, starting on the fourth day (the *Vinayak Chaturthi*) and culminating with the *Visarjan* (immersion in flowing waters) ceremony on the fourteenth day (the *Chaturdashi*). Symbolically, Lord Ganesha visits the home on Ganesh *Chaturthi* day but there are no strict rules for the duration of the festival and performance of rituals as they usually depend on family tradi-tions. The idol can be immersed the very next day, or on the third, fifth, sixth, seventh and tenth day. Hindus believe that the history of immersion of Ganesh idols is as old as Ganesh himself (Crowley 2010).

The physical appearance of Ganesh is such that, instantly, it invokes its uniqueness and a bemused appeal. Barnouw brings to life the image of Ganesh idols that are brought home during the Ganesh festival:

> In all the variety of poses Ganpati retains the same identifiable features. He has a large elephant head with a long trunk, small eyes, and big ears. His body is short, his stomach bulging, traditionally he has only one tusk... His trunk almost always turns to the left, although there are some exceptions. He has four hands, with one of which (the lower right) he is often shown giving a blessing. Usually he is in a seated posture... [and] wears a golden

crown on his head.... The top part of his body is usually bare, although he may wear the sacred thread. His *dhoti* is generally red or saffron in color.

(1954: 78)

This kind of imagery and the features discussed above continue to inspire the composition of devotional poetry that is used in His prayers (*aarti*) generally and particularly during the festival. The day of the arrival of Ganpati is marked with an elaborate *puja* (ritualised worship of the deity performed as per religious scriptures). The elaborateness of rituals is accurately described by Barnouw in his narrative of a *puja* in which he participated in 1952:

> [In front of the Ganesh idol] is a dish full of food and other items prepared by the women of the household, including two kinds of sandalwood paste, some yellow powder called *haldi* (turmeric), and red powder called *Kunku* (turmeric which has been soaked in lime water and dried). There are also betel nuts, a coconut, and assorted flowers and leaves. One of these, santa-mum leaf, is offered to Ganesha on this day only and must not be offered on any other day. Another specialty is a clump of *dhurva* grass *(cynodon dactylon)*, of which Ganesha is said to be fond. There must be exactly twenty-one shoots of this grass, each containing three leaves, twenty-one being a number especially associated with him. There are also containers for the *panchamrita* or five nectars: milk, ghee, curds, honey, and sugar, with which the statue is anointed.... One by one the other things are taken from the tray and offered to the statue. Strips of cotton and silk are draped around Ganesha's shoulders, and at length his elephant trunk is barely to be seen in the heap of flowers. To complete the *puja*, the family represent-ative makes a final prostration to the deity ... Special sweet-balls called *modak*, associated with Ganapati, are eaten at this time, twenty-one in number.

(Barnouw 1954: 77)

This detailed account of the puja for the installation of the Ganesh idol holds true in present times also. Once the idol is installed in the designated place, an abridged version of this *puja* is performed with almost the same sequence every day including the day of immersion. After the final *puja* in the home, the head of the family, typically a male, lifts the idol and carries it walking bare-foot out of the door. He is not allowed to look back and the family, friends and neighbours participate in this journey to the river or flowing water chanting '*Ganpati Bappa Morya, phud chya varshi lavkar ya* [praise Ganesh, please come back soon next year]'. This procession, after reaching the river bank, once again performs the last departure *puja* and then the idol is carried into the river and immersed.

A vivid description of how the immersion ritual turns into a cultural proces-sion is found in the notes of Count Gubernatis, who witnessed the Ganpati celeb-rations in Bombay city in 1885:

I followed with the greatest curiosity crowds who carried in procession an infinite number of idols of the god Ganesh ... A crowd, more or less numerous, accompanies the idol, clapping hands and raising cries of joy, while a little orchestra generally precedes the idol.

(cited in Cashman 1970: 351)

This basic structure of the festival is also followed in public celebrations as well but there is a marked difference. A public Ganpati statue is not connected with any one family but with a larger group or community that is essentially place-based and location-specific. A group of people, who usually represent a locality, a neighbourhood as defined by a collection of streets or housing societies, or even professional workplaces like factories, workshops, government institutions, etc., take charge of their public Ganpati statues and the annual festival celebrations. Since the public celebrations are essentially a social phenomenon, it is necessary to understand their organisation in greater depth and therefore some reference to their history is important here.

Historical context

Tracing the history of public celebrations of the Ganesh festival, Barnouw notes that the eighteenth-century Maratha governors, known as Peshwas, practised elaborate festivities in honour of Ganesh. He mentions records wherein detailed accounts of expenses of the festival in 1795 were presented in the Peshwa court. Similar kinds of records are referred to by Kadam (2013), finding that 'the festival organised by Peshwas were imitated and followed by several smaller landlords and leaders'. He refers to rituals pertaining to social hierarchy (*'maan-pan'*) and hereditary rights accorded by the royal court to the owners (*'haqq'*) and alludes to the public celebration of the Ganesh festival in Aundh. Barnouw's conclusion that 'worship of Ganesha, therefore, is an old and sanctified tradition in Poona and was associated with the ruling court, whose elaborate Ganesha festivities bore many of the characteristics of a public festival' (1954: 80) is of utmost relevance as it highlights the public nature of the festival as its inherent characteristic in spite of the popular belief that the modern type of public celebrations evolved in 1893.

It is in the nineteenth century, in the socio-political context of colonialism, unrest and the freedom struggle, that the public nature of the festival became pronounced. The popularising of the Ganesh festival as a public celebration is largely credited to the leadership of Lokmanya Tilak, a radical freedom fighter who called for outdoor installations of large idols and large-scale public immersion of idols on the last day of the festival. In general, Tilak had two aims: first, to use the festival as a platform for organising lectures about social reforms and anti-British propaganda; and second, to bring the Hindu community together vis-à-vis the Muslims and provide a sense of Hindu solidarity (Barnouw 1954). Much has been said about the intertwining of political ambitions of Tilak and appropriation of the Ganesh festival in the cause of the nationalist movement (for this debate refer to Cashman 1970; Kaur 2004), but for the purpose of this chapter it is best to sidestep this debate and focus on the shaping of the public nature of the festival under the prevalent socio-political context and its cultural underpinnings.

In principle and spirit, the rituals of worship performed at public celebrations (*sarvajanik*) remained similar to the private home-based celebrations. The publicness evolved in aspects primarily related to scale, size and organisation of social and cultural events as a part of the festival. Neighbourhoods or localities were to erect temporary *mandaps* (decorated pavilions and platforms) to house Ganesh idols and its collective worship. They were also to provide a venue for offering musical programmes and dramatic skits. Informal groups and athletic clubs (*mandals*) that represented their neighbourhoods collected subscriptions for organising the festival. However, they were required by the government to form local committees and register them as charitable trusts under the legislation related to such charities and donations. While doing so, the group aspects of the festival were consolidated. All public idols were to converge together on the final day for their immersion in a united ceremony. Alongside this was introduced the '*mela* movement' of singing parties, which were attached to the public Ganpatis. Cashman observes that 'in many streets, *wadas* (compounds) or *peths*, a *mela*, composed of from twenty to several hundred singers, mostly boys and students, rehearsed verses in honour of the god and marched for weeks before the annual procession' (1970: 352). The festival, used for propagating nationalist ideas, began to attract the attention of the British administration. The administrators introduced censorship and strict control on registration of festival programmes to monitor the manoeuvres of the organisers. Each public Ganpati was to be registered with the police and required to obtain an official permit so that the organisers could carry the Ganpati statue in the final procession.

The procession became an integral part of the festival. It simultaneously signified social solidarity and translated into a cultural parade. Cashman offers a vivid description of the public procession of 1894 in Pune:

> The procession itself was a colorful occasion. It included one hundred sarvajanik ganapatis, conveyed in palanquins carts and horse-carriages, preceded by seventy-five bands of musicians, some seventy *melas*, twenty groups of *lejimavalas* (acrobats who dance to the music of the instrument named *lejim*) and a concourse of 25,000 people. They were in turn showered with sweets, parched rice and *gulal* by an estimated crowd of 50,000 which watched from the streets and balconies.
>
> (1970: 354)

In the procession, it became a practice to take out the large idols but immerse a second, smaller idol, and therefore several of the original larger Ganpati idols and *mandals* acquired a hegemonic position in the procession and continue to do so to this day (Kaur 2004).

The erection of large statues in public spaces and the cultural processions gave the festival its distinct public nature where the 'nationalist feeling provided the necessary social cement' (Barnouw 1954: 83). These ideas of politicising the festival were aptly transmitted by the local Marathi newspaper, *Kesari*, which was started by Tilak. Two dominant characteristics were central to the public nature: one, the festival was considered as a powerful vehicle for disseminating ideas, and two, its inclusive approach involved a loose structure for its organisation that enabled individuals to develop their own particular projects within the larger festival framework (Cashman 1970: 366). In the socially inclusive approach of public celebrations, caste and class hierarchies had no significant place, which helped in making Ganesh a genuinely pan-Hindu god (Crowley 2010). These characteristics shaped the template of the public celebrations that was followed in most cities in Maharashtra and elsewhere.

Post-independence, considerable emphasis has been placed on the cultural component of the festival that made it popular as a cultural marker for its organisers, participants and spectators. In his 1952 study, Barnouw observed 'a certain amount of competition among the different groups of the city in erecting elaborate and unusual Ganpati statues' (1954: 77) and found that

> People go from one Ganpati to another to see the sights. In front of some statues there are long queues waiting, while crowds sit on the streets to watch the entertainments, so that many thoroughfares are closed to traffic. The entertainments seem to consist largely of comic or dramatic dialogues interspersed with music.
>
> (Barnouw 1954: 78)

Commensurate with the socio-economic and political contexts, the nature and organisation of public celebrations also experienced qualitative changes. Barnouw alludes to some of these changes in his translation of a report in the Marathi newspaper *Sakal*:

> [The] editorial ... complained about the poor quality of the public entertainments. Rising prices have made it difficult for people to contribute generously to the local committees. The entertainments, therefore, have become cheap and mechanical ... Older men, who remember the early days of the festival, say that its whole character has changed in the past few years. Lecturing and speech-making have given way to commercialized entertainment. The high moral purpose of the festival has become lost in the course of its expansion.
>
> (Barnouw 1954: 83)

In this historical journey it is clear that the public celebration of the festival, although initially a religious event, was appropriated and moulded with political goals to reach out to people and then over time was broadened to include social and cultural agendas. In line with these changes there was 'inventiveness in devising new Ganpatis, the competition among the local committees, the crowds attending the entertainments, and the enthusiasm of the young men [which] testify to continuing good health' of the festival (Barnouw 1954: 84). Over time, the focus might have shifted, yet the rituals of public celebrations did not change (Crowley 2010); rather they now followed new goals and themes with the idea of enhancing the celebrations and impressing people. The ability of the Ganesh festival to mould itself to include new societal functions has kept it evolving into a major marker of identity, as is discussed in the next section.

The 2013 Ganesh festival in Pune

With the growth of the city and the increase in population, the number of idols has also increased and enthusiasm has grown manifold (Crowley 2010). In 2013, Pune is a bustling metropolis of more than 4.5 million people and for the Ganesh festival this means thousands of *mandals* participating in public celebrations. A newspaper reported approximately 3,955 *mandals* in the city (TNN 2013a).

In presenting the contemporary version of the public Ganesh festival, I follow the methodology of newspaper reporting of the festival that was adopted by Barnouw and Cashman. According to records maintained by police, 1,370 large and small public Ganpati *mandals* participated in the immersion procession around the core city in 2013 (*Loksatta Reporter* 2013b). To accommodate this scale of immersions, the local municipal body constructed 17 immersion spots along the river (Dutta 2013b).

The individual subscriptions and donations remain the main source of income for most *mandals* organising the festival, yet increasingly public Ganpatis seek sponsorship to put on ostentatious entertainment programmes and cultural events. While the influence of socio-economic and political changes often is tacit, the most significant in the present context is the increasing recognition of the impacts of the festival on the physical environment and health of the city. Several studies have established negative environmental impacts associated with the festival, particularly due to its scale. These include water pollution due to immersion of idols, noise pollution during the procession and overcrowding and traffic problems throughout the festival duration. Detailed investigations in different contexts of idol immersions, such as Chhatri Lake in Amravati (Shirbhate *et al.* 2012), Shivaji Park in Mumbai and Masunda Lake in Thane (Kaur 2012) and in lakes in Bhopal (Vyas *et al.* 2006), all conclude that since idols are generally prepared using plaster of Paris, mud and other materials that contain different chemicals, heavy metals, etc., the addition of these substances to the water changes its physiochemical characteristics and causes pollution. The blaring of loudspeakers and continuous playing of musical instruments such as *dhol-tasha* (percussion instruments with high decibel levels used during processions) cause severe health hazards (Saler and Vibhute 2011). The beats are heavy and are likely to cause disturbance to the central nervous system that leads to fatigue, insomnia, headache and shakiness (Dutta 2013a).

Against this backdrop, a myriad of spectacle and displays marks the festival. A cursory analysis of newspaper reports on public celebrations show that a sizeable proportion of *mandals* follow the convention of displaying mythological legends and historical tableaux in their pavilions (Rashid 2013a), while there is increasing numbers of Ganesh *mandals* that stand up for bringing to the fore several relevant social issues and critiquing them (Lipare 2013). By and large the themes include problems associated with rapid urbanisation, ineffective political governance, corruption, traffic concerns, rising incidences of rape, gender inequalities, female foeticide and so on (Puri 2013b). Contemporary issues are always the favourite subject for displays. For instance, in the wake of the outbreak of swine flu in the city, many *mandals* used it as a theme for their decoration and organised several social events and camps to raise awareness about health issues (Kadu 2013). One can also find positive themes where the focus is on achievements such as the success of launching an indigenous satellite, winning international sports championships, etc., and honouring citizens for exemplary services to society. In recent times, the greening of the Ganesh festival has drawn a great deal of interest because of the environmental aspects that are associated with the festival.

The festival continues to attract the involvement of a range of stakeholders and agencies. The local government organises its own version of the festival, known as the 'Pune Festival', during the same period. The Pune Festival was started in 1989 with the joint involvement of the Pune Festival Committee, Department of Tourism (Government of India) and Maharashtra Tourism Development Corporation (MTDC). The Pune Festival, spread over two weeks, offers an array of 'free for all' cultural events including performances in all formats of music and dance by nationally and internationally renowned artists, literature meets, folk performances, theatre, poetry, drama and traditional and modern sports.

In addition, several community-based organisations and NGOs are active in public celebrations. For instance, the Pune police have trained over 10,000 NSS students of the University of Pune as volunteers, to assist them in managing crowd movement. A more recent innovation is that of an informal group of 20 bikers riding with medical practitioners as pillion passengers, who in case of emergencies provide immediate assistance to patients and help them get to an ambulance or reach a nearby hospital (Dastane 2013). An NGO named MANS (Maharashtra Andhshraddha Nirmoolan Samiti), which has been working towards eradicating superstitions, is also actively involved in collecting idols and immersing them in quarries: in 2012, the NGO collected almost 190,000 idols from the entire state (Dutta 2013b). Another environmental NGO helps with waste disposal: it placed a total of 90 waste collectors and 450 volunteers on the 13 river-*ghats* in Pune from where they collect, reuse and recycle much of the decorative items that are brought along for immersion (*Loksatta Reporter* 2013c).

Even corporate institutions use their corporate social responsibility agenda to promote social causes in the festival. Most notable examples are the initiatives by newspapers such as the *Times of India* and *Sakal*. The *Sakal-Adarsh Ganesh-utsav* is a four-day event that seeks to enhance people's participation and includes several programmes for all age groups, mainly children and elderly. (*Sakal Reporter* 2013a). A joint initiative of the *Times of India*, State Ministry of Environment and Maharashtra Pollution Control Board is the annual Times Green Ganesha (TGG) campaign. As part of this campaign, volunteers conduct Ganpati idol-making workshops in schools and colleges and educate students about the impacts of plaster of Paris idols and non-biodegradable products on the environment; TGG awards are given to eco-friendly *mandals* and housing societies (TNN, 2013b).

Communal harmony continues to be the hallmark of the Ganesh festival (Barnouw 1954; Cashman 1970). One of the oldest *mandals* (which also ranks as the third most prestigious Ganpati), namely the Guruji Talim *Mandal*, was started by Muslim and Hindu families 127 years ago and continues to enjoy active participation by many Muslim families (Biswas 2013b). Dutta (2013c) adequately captures the sentiments through one of her Muslim interviewees, who reiterates that 'For us Ganesh-utsav is not a Hindu festival, but a community event that we all participate in'. Dutta further mentions how proudly the organisers talk about the spirit of inclusiveness, which is reinforced by holding a *qawwali* (primarily an Islamic cultural performance) contest on the same stage on which spiritual discourses, Marathi theatre and music and dance competitions are held (Dutta 2013c). Similar harmony is reported in many places outside Pune. For instance, in Kurundwad town seven mosques have continued the 100-year-long tradition of celebrating the Ganesh festival on their premises. In the Dhepanpur mosque, the *mandal* is named Shivaji Tarun *Mandal* (it should be noted that the organisation is named after the Maratha King Shivaji who fought against Islamic rule) and it takes the lead in organising events including social discourses, de-addiction and live plays on historical events (Lipare 2013). Here, the festival acquires a predominant social rather than religious role.

The social role of the festival helps to build social capital. According to Rao (2001), festival celebrations at the community level enhance social cohesion in building social capital, while at the level of the family, they provide households with an opportunity to access social networks and generate returns from investments in social capital. A family, by participating in the highly associational activity of public celebration of the festival, signals its commitment to being an active member of the community; a 'good citizen' who forms mutually beneficial reciprocal relationships (Rao 2001: 77). This is amply demonstrated in the case of Ganpati celebrations in Shivtej Nagar in the fringe areas of Pune:

> With over 3000 houses and a population of more than two hundred thousand, till 2006 this area commonly saw several small *mandal*s sprout up all during Ganesh-utsav. But this changed after 2006 with the idea of consolidating all these into a one large *mandal* named *Shivtej cha Raja Mandal*. According to the Founder-President of the *mandal*, this target was achieved in 2013 and it changed festivities in many ways; rather than spending money on ostentatious decorations, they are investing the subscriptions in the development of the area. Various cultural and sport competitions for

children, women and elderly are conducted over 10 days ... Besides bringing people together, the residents feel that 'the working together has been a
boon for volunteers as the spirit of cooperation helps them [overcome any]
obstacle they face due to lack of education ... Even the women in the area
get the opportunity to help as volunteers during Ganesh-utsav now.'

(quoted in Bengrut 2013b)

Nevertheless, it is important to note that the size, structure and practices of a festival all affect the logic of participation and investment and therefore may have
different implications for social capital formation (Rao 2001: 78). In the Ganesh
festival, donations made to the festival are generally not anonymous and the
largest donors are publicly honoured by being invited to perform the *aarti* on a
particular day or being offered a prominent place in the procession. The building
of social capital can further be seen in the ways that the festival provides a participatory role for women.

The role of women has considerably increased in public celebrations in recent
years, and their presence is widely felt: in 2013, on the second day of Ganesh-
utsav, 10,000 women of all age groups from the city gathered before sunrise to
recite the *Atharvashirsha shlokas* and chant the 1,000 names of Ganesha and
other *bhajans* as a ritual of Ganesha worship (Bengrut 2013a). There has been an
increase in all-girl groups, with one group boasting more than 120 members
(Chatterjee 2013); teams called *Mahila Gansevaks* (female servants of Ganesh)
have been formed in Mumbai for the security of women within the *mandals*
(Ashar and Mhaske 2013); and 1,800 women participated in a competition for
preparing the customary *modaks* (*Loksatta Reporter* 2013a).

Riding the technology wave, Ganpati celebrations have also gone the electronic way. A newspaper report highlights how social networking has made the
Ganesh festival 'huge':

Ganesh's presence in new media is overwhelming: Wallpapers, ringtones,
songs all mediums are promoting Ganesh. His songs are most watched on
YouTube. There are several apps where people search for information and
updates about Ganesh and his festival. In the last two days there has been
enormous increase in net traffic related to [the] Ganesh festival.

(*Pudhari Reporter* 2013a)

The highlight of the festival continues to be the immersion-procession (*visarjan-
miravanuk*) on the final day. Crowley (2010) has likened this procession to a
'cross between the Macy's parade and an ambulatory prayer service ... featuring
stunning performances of densely percussive religious songs played with traditional instruments'. The musical performances are orchestrated by *dhol-tasha*
groups (or *pathaks*) that use different kinds of percussion instruments including
drums. More than 200 such groups exist in the city and prepare months in
advance for their performance in the procession. These performers are hired by
Ganpati *mandals* to add the cultural entertainment quotient to their floats and

parade during the procession (Chatterjee 2013). Performing in the procession also means creating and reinforcing an identity for the participants. This is amply demonstrated by the line-up at the head of the traditional procession – the cart carrying *nagaara* (huge drums), the *pathak* of Raman Baug school (the school that started the tradition), *zanz-pathak* of Kamayani School for Blind, the *pathak* of the *Art of Living* of Sri Sri Ravishankar, and the *pathak* comprising foreign students organised by Rotary (*Loksatta Reporter* 2013b). According to Puri's report,

> An estimated 25,000 people between six and 60 years of age participated [in the procession], including 5000 women, school and college students, retired and serving army officers and even well-placed professionals like doctors, engineers, and IT professionals, who come together for their love for the drums, and for Lord Ganesha.
>
> (Puri 2013a)

The Ganesh festival continues to be a socio-cultural identifier. The public displays range from using the public platform to voice concerns and critiques about society to the banal, simple, plain, joyous celebrations like any other occasion to party, and the procession acts as a major ritual for the cultural life of the city.

Discussion and conclusion

This study of the Ganesh festival in Pune has focused on what has continued as a ritual rather than tracing and documenting what has changed from the late nineteenth century to contemporary times (2013 at time of writing). The study is also about how public rituals are shaped in relation to the broader socio-economic and political contexts. It has aimed to illustrate that in spirit the festival remains unaltered but its manifestation adapts to prevalent conditions. In this section, I summarise salient features and draw attention to emerging concerns of the Ganesh festival.

In the twenty-first-century globalised world, the Ganesh festival has travelled far across the globe with the Indian diaspora. The loose structure of the ten-day festival and the emphasis on solidarity, inclusiveness and worship of a god with universal appeal has all added to the popularity of the festival and its acceptance by non-Maharashtrians as well. It has come to symbolise Hinduism globally and has emerged as a significant cultural and religious marker for a Hindu identity. Joshi, in her overview of Ganpati celebrations all across the world, reports that

> In the USA more than 50 marathi *mandal*s affiliated with the Brihan Maharashtra *Mandal* are celebrating the Ganesh festival this year ... often the festival is celebrated on weekends rather than the actual dates for the convenience of all involved. For the last 23 years this festival has been continuously celebrated in London ... The local government has allowed the organisers to immerse the clay idols in the Thames river. This year eight

more towns in UK will have public celebrations. For the last 19 years, the Maharashtra *mandal* in Singapore is also celebrating the festival.

(A. Joshi 2013)

While the diaspora is adding to the globalisation of the Ganesh festival, significant changes are also observed on the home turf. According to a newspaper report, one of the older Ganesh *mandals* that achieved 50 years of existence has decided to close down the *mandal* and its Ganesh-*utsav* in light of the increasing numbers of public Ganesh-*utsav mandals* and their economic impacts on citizens (*Sakal Reporter* 2013b). A similar cause for concern is the gradual decline in the number of volunteers in the *mandals* (Biswas 2013a). A few social problems associated with group formations are also evident from the remarks made by the Chairman of Shrimant Dagdusheth Halwai Ganpati Temple, one of the most prestigious *mandals*:

> The festival has changed with each generation. Several bad practices have come into festivals. During the 10 sacred days instead of indulging in prayers and good work, people engage in drunken obscene dances and gambling right inside the pandals. However, it would be wrong to colour all the *mandal*s with the same brush. I would say that as many as 70 percent of *mandal*s are good with their workers staying away from bad things.
>
> (quoted in Rashid 2013b)

A better organisation of the festival is routinely plagued by the uneasy relationship between government control and public celebrations by *mandals*. *Mandals* and several political parties or groups backing them argue that the duty of the police is to maintain law and order during Ganesh-*utsav* but they should not enforce their restrictions on *mandals*, and not go overboard with their demands for security measures (*Sakal Reporter* 2013c). On the need for installing security scanners and equipment, the Chairman of a prestigious Ganpati Temple reiterates the sentimental feelings against the security needs: 'we don't want to desanctify a devotee's offerings that he or she brings with so much devotion and love due to the security procedure' (Rashid 2013b). Similar use of religious garb is evident when a trustee of a school finds the government directives on use of *dhol-tasha* as 'irrational and as something that will kill the spirit of the festival', which he further justifies by stating that

> we play the *dhol-tasha* for hours every year, yet there has been no health complaint [about] us, we only feel the spiritual vibe that the drums generate, and not the kind of sound pollution that is seen on congested roads of the city.
>
> (quoted in Dutta 2013a)

Thus, the real threats towards security and safety of people and health issues are overlooked (P. Joshi 2013) in the zeal to celebrate the festival.

The environmental impacts are the other major concerns that the festival has somehow to address. Of course, there are early moves in that direction such as promoting eco-friendly idols made of clay and changes to the rituals of the immersion process, but much more needs to be done. Once again, one can refer to the instance of noise pollution. In the case of Kolhapur, Saler and Vibhute (2011) reported that noise levels were exceeding the permissible limit during the Ganesh festival in spite of legal standards in place and the efforts of regulatory agencies such as official declaration of eight areas as *silent zones*. They conclude that 'this indicates lack of support of people in making Ganesh festival free from noise pollution' (Saler and Vibhute 2011: 6882). Initiatives like TGG and NGO activity in collecting idols and other religious waste is laudable but water pollution due to immersion remains a challenge given its ritual necessity in the festival celebration.

A similar difficulty occurs with the procession, which takes days to complete. For instance, in 2012, the immersion procession took 29 hours and almost the entire city came to a standstill to watch the spectacle. But this comes with its problems of law and order, risk of drowning, stampedes and so on. However, these are relegated to a secondary concern; the primary issue being the imaging of the route, the procession and the mandap as a sacred territory (Ley 2005: 30). The festival, in bringing about this rupture, moves beyond being a purely religious practice into the domain of a social and cultural engagement. More than 60 years ago Barnouw noted that

> For the mass of the people, the Ganpati festival, like many other Indian festivals, is a time of let-down and release, bright lights, and excitement ... The Ganpati festival serves to break down boundaries to some extent, if only momentarily.
>
> (1954: 85)

The *publicness* of the festival remains its high point.

In highlighting the public nature of the Ganesh festival, I have glossed over several nuances of personalised worship and the changes taking place in that domain. Similar to Barnouw's seminal study and Cashman's work, further ethnographic research may be able to offer insights on the contemporary individualised ritual worship and festival of Ganesha. Even more rigorous research from a geographical perspective, particularly in examining the public domain of processions (following on from Ley's speculative work on their territorial claims), can provide better understanding about the spatiality of processions and festivals. The spectacle of a public festival comes at a cost; and therefore the economics of a festival like the Ganesh festival requires more research than has been possible here. Patronage, sponsorship, market surveys and consumer data analyses are some aspects that can help in bringing out the economic dimension of the festival. When emotions and religious beliefs are discussed, the governance and involvement of government agencies generally takes a back seat but some thought as to the institutional structure for public celebrations can help in better management of the festival. Some attention to these newer directions for research in festivals and rituals will lead to a comprehensive repertoire that is not only emotionally evocative of what has been done in the past but may also provide better understanding of the impacts and influences that they can have on society at large.

References

Ashar, S. and Mhaske, P. (2013) 'Dus ka dum, formula for Mumbai Mandals', *Pune Mirror*, 12 September.

Barnouw, V. (1954) 'The changing character of a Hindu festival', *American Anthropologist*, 56, 74–86.

Bengrut, D. (2013a) '10,000 hues of devotion', *Pune Mirror*, 11 September.

Bengrut, D. (2013b) 'Getting it together for Ganpati', *Pune Mirror*, 11 September.

Biswas, P.S. (2013a) 'Our social work doesn't end with festival, it goes on for the year – says a Ganpati mandal', *The Indian Express*, 12 September.

Biswas, P.S. (2013b) 'Religious amity cornerstone of this Ganesh mandal', *Times of India*, 11 September.

Cashman, R. (1970) 'The political recruitment of God Ganapati', *Indian Economic Social History Review*, 7, 347–373.

Chambers, E. (ed.) (1997) *Tourism and Culture: An applied perspective*, Albany, NY: State University of New York Press.

Chatterjee, S. (2013) 'Pune's favourite dhol-tasha groups this year', *Times of India*, 13 September.

Crowley, T. (2010) 'Ganesh Chaturthi: Recovering the ecological roots of an ancient festival', *Reality Sandwich*. Online: http://realitysandwich.com/61399/ganesh_eco_festival.

Dastane, S. (2013) 'RTO, bikers to offer medical services', *The Indian Express*, 12 September.

Dutta, A. (2013a) 'Dhol-tasha equally deafening: Study', *Times of India*, 11 September.

Dutta, A. (2013b) 'Festival must connect to nature: MANS calls for eco-friendly immersion', *Times of India*, 11 September.

Dutta, A. (2013c) 'Harmony comes first for Hadapsar mandal', *Times of India*, 11 September.

Ichaporia, N. (1983) 'Tourism at Khajuraho: An Indian enigma', *Annals of Tourism Research*, 10(1), 75–92.

Jaitly, J. (2001) 'Canned culture: Temples, fairs and festivals – Cultural impact of tourism in India', *The Eye*, II.

Joshi, A. (2013) 'Pardeshat hi morya cha gajar ghumla' [Ganesh festival celebrated with pomp even abroad], *Loksatta*, 14 September.

Joshi, P. (2013) 'Curbs on dhol-tasha may bring down immersion duration', *The Indian Express*, 18 September.

Kadam, K. (2013) 'Aundh cha ganesh-utsav pavne-teenshe varshanpurvi chaa' [The ganesh-utsav of Aundh dates from last 275 years], *Sakal-Pratibimb*, 12 September.

Kadu, S. (2013) 'Ganesh utsava barobarch aarogya jan-jagruti che upakram' [Health awareness programs along with Ganesh utsav], *Pudhari*, 13 September.

Kaur, R. (2004) 'At the ragged edges of time: The legend of Tilak and the normalization of historical narratives', *South Asia Research*, 24(2), 185–202.

Kaur, R. (2012) 'Effect of idol immersion on marine and fresh water-bodies', *Advances in Applied Science Research*, 3(4), 1905–1909.

Kraft, S.E. (2007) 'Religion and spirituality in Lonely Planet's *India*', *Religion*, 37, 230–242.

Ley, P. (2005) *Everybody Loves a Parade: Indian religious processions*. Chattanooga: The University of Tennessee.

Lipare, D. (2013) 'Kurundwad madhe hindu-muslim ekatmate cha shatki sohla' [The centennial celebration of Hindu-Muslim unity in Kurundwad], *Loksatta*, 15 September.

Loksatta Reporter. (2013a) ' "Modak banwa" spardhet Meena Mehta pratham' [Meena Mehta stood first in the competition on preparing modak], *Loksatta*, 18 September.

Loksatta Reporter. (2013b) 'Sangvi teel ganpatin che satvya divashi visarjan' [Ganpatis in Sangvi suburb immersed on seventh day], *Loksatta*, 16 September.

Loksatta Reporter. (2013c) 'Swatcha sansthe tarfe nadi-ghatan war nirmalya gola karnyachi mohim' [A campaign by an NGO called Swatcha to execute the campaign of collecting flowers, garlands and other ritual material offered to Ganpati at riverbanks], *Loksatta*, 15 September.

Lutgendorf, P. (1994) 'My hanuman is bigger than yours', *History of Religions*, 33(3), 211–245.

Maclean, K.K. (2003) *Power and Pilgrimage: The Kumbha Mela in Allahabad, 1765–1954*, unpublished PhD thesis, La Trobe University, Melbourne.

Naidoo, L. (2007) 'Re-negotiating identity and reconciling cultural ambiguity in the Indian immigrant community in Sydney, Australia', *Anthropologist Special Issue: Indian Diaspora – The 21st Century – Migration, Change and Adaptation*, 2, 53–66.

Picard, D. and Robinson, M. (eds) (2006) *Festivals, Tourism and Social Change: Remaking worlds*, Clevedon: Channel View Publications.

Pudhari Reporter. (2013a) 'Ganesh utsava aata netmanya "sanganesha": Social media madhye bappancha bolbala; mandale zali net-connected' [Ganesh utsav becomes net-approved 'e-ganesha': bappa rules social media; mandals connected to internet], *Pudhari*, 13 September.

Pudhari Reporter. (2013b) 'Punjab, hariyana teel ganesh-utsava cha rangach nyara' [The unique colour of Ganesh-utsav in Punjab and Hariyana], *Pudhari*, 15 September.

Puri, T. (2013a) 'Dhol-tasha troupes make big bucks', *Times of India*, 13 September.

Puri, T. (2013b) 'Ganpati mandal focus on concern for women, girl child: Slide and puppet shows, music videos used to convey message', *Times of India*, 15 September.

Raj, R. and Morpeth, N.D. (eds) (2007) *Religious Tourism and Pilgrimage Festivals Management: An international perspective*, Wallingford: CABI.

Rao, V. (2001) 'Celebrations as social investments: Festival expenditures, unit price variation and social status in rural India', *Journal of Development Studies*, 38(1), 71–97.

Rashid, A. (2013a) 'The Lord is here', *The Indian Express*, 9 September.

Rashid, A. (2013b) 'Security is paramount but so is the sanctity of the temple', *The Indian Express*, 8 September.

Rinehart, R. (2004) *Contemporary Hinduism: Ritual, culture, and practice*. Santa Barbara, CA: ABC-CLIO.

Sakal Reporter. (2013a) 'Abaal vridhana chya kala-gunan na spardhet milnar vyaspeeth' [Children and old, both will get a forum to show their talents], *Sakal*, 12 September.

Sakal Reporter. (2013b) 'Mandal band karnyacha "jai-bharat" cha nirnaya' [Jai-Bharat mandal decides to close down its mandal], *Sakal*, 15 September.

Sakal Reporter. (2013c) 'Police ni madnalan war nirbandh ladu nayet' [Police should not force restrictions on mandals], *Sakal*, 12 September.

Saler, P. and Vibhute, S. (2011) 'Monitoring of noise during Ganeshotsav', *International Journal of Engineering Science and Technology*, 3(9), 6876–6882.

Shackley, M. (2001) *Managing Sacred Sites: Service provision and visitor experience*, London: Continuum.

Shapiro, A. (1987) 'Sanjhi: A festival of Vraja', in A. McDowall and A. Sharma (eds), *Vignettes of Vrindavan* (pp. 80–103), New Delhi: Books and Books.

Shinde, K.A. (2010) 'Managing Hindu festivals in pilgrimage sites: Emerging trends, opportunities and challenges', *Event Management*, 14(1), 53–69.

Shirbhate, N.S., Malode, S.N., Wadankar, G.D. and Shelke, P.B. (2012) 'Impacts of idol immersion in Chhatri lake of Amravati, Dist Amravati', *International Journal of Innovations in Bio-Sciences*, 2(1), 51–54.

TNN. (2013a) 'Pol says security for immersion a task: Urges Mandals to wind up procession early', *Times of India*, 17 September.

TNN. (2013b) 'Times Green Ganesha flags off eco-friendly celebrations', *Times of India*, 9 September.

Vyas, A., Mishra, D.D., Bajapai, A., Dixit, S. and Verma, N. (2006) 'Environment impact of idol immersion activity lakes of Bhopal, India', *Asian Journal of Experimental Science*, 20(2), 289–296.

3 Divali festival in Mauritius

The development of a conceptual framework for understanding attitudes towards and intentions to celebrate traditional cultural festivals

Haywantee Ramkissoon

Introduction

The promotion of local festivals as an instrument to bring social and community cohesion is an emerging and important area of research. This is often reflected in the increasing number and diversity of local events (Felsenstein and Fleischer 2003; Gursoy *et al.* 2004). With a rich history in both the ancient and modern eras, festivals are known to exist in virtually all human cultures (Falassi 1987). These symbolic products, with their social and cultural significance, create a sense of identity for those in quest of cultural pursuits (Lee and Beeler 2007; Prentice and Andersen 2003). In festival celebrations, the history, context and culture play a significant role to ensure their continued relevance. Festivals also serve the needs of residents (Derrett 2003), offering a range of participatory opportunities. Ranging in size from small to large community functions, festivals provide the opportunity for the community to participate in collective experiences distinct from everyday life as well as demonstrate community solidarity (Jeong and Santos 2004). People not only identify themselves and associate meanings with the places they live in, but also are interpreted by others according to where they live. Festivals contribute to a sense of belongingness with the community as well as strengthen an individual's sense of place identity, as in the cases of Mardi Gras, the Jacaranda Festival in Australia and the Kangnung Dano Festival in Korea (Derrett 2003; Jeong and Santos 2004). Static spaces become animated with cultural celebrations that allow a better understanding of sense of community and place.

As the importance and significant benefits of festivals on local communities are being recognised (Tkacczynski and Rundle-Thiele 2011; Yolal *et al.* 2012), place identity is receiving increasing attention from scholars interested in studying the association between local festivals and the community (De Bres and Davis 2001). It is also an important element for festival stakeholders. They need to understand not only the factors underlying festival participation, but also how to promote the community's place identity to encourage future participation. Residents' satisfaction with local festivals is also important to measure its success and continued relevance. Empirical studies of diverse festivals have emphasised the importance of festival satisfaction and future intentions (e.g. Lee and Beeler 2009; Lee and

Hsu 2013). These studies show that individuals with satisfying experiences have higher repeat intentions. Being attitudinal in nature, one's sense of identity with a place is considered as an antecedent of satisfaction and behaviour (e.g. Ramkissoon *et al*. 2013a). Additionally, festival satisfaction is critical in providing shared positive experiences across the community leading to future intentions. While it has been recognised that residents' festival satisfaction is important for its continued relevance, its effects on one's sense of place has been largely undocumented, calling for more research in the field (Lee *et al*. 2012).

This chapter draws on existing theories from social and environmental psychology and builds a conceptual model to explore the salient factors that drive residents' festival satisfaction, place identity and future intentions. It is underpinned by an attitudinal approach to the study of residents' festival intentions based on attitude-behaviour models. Future studies could draw from the propositions that emanate from the proposed framework and contribute further to this important research area. This will help increase the popularity of traditional festivals, promoting cultural tourism at the local level. It uses a case study of the traditional Hindu festival *Divali* to discuss its importance for residents of the island of Mauritius in communicating its historical significance and cultural practices and promoting the community's place identity.

The case study: *Divali* festival in Mauritius

Mauritius, an island with a land area of around $1,860 \text{km}^2$, is situated in the Western Indian Ocean, off the south-east coast of Africa, with a mixed population originating from India, Africa, Europe and China. During the past decades, the island has witnessed a growing interest in celebrating festivals to revive local traditions and culture. *Divali* is an important part of the diaspora Indian community, celebrated around the new moon night in the month of *Kartik* (October–November) every year. Originating from the term *Deepavali*, which signifies rows of lamps (Macmillan 2008), *Divali* symbolises the triumph of good over evil, darkness over light and victory over defeat. The festival of lights, previously celebrated only as a religious festival among Hindus in the island, has over the years become a national event (Hitillambeau-Mirthil 2013) celebrated by Mauritians of all origins and generations. Its multicultural significance has promoted a bonded community leading to communal identity in the island. The self is expressed through celebrations and performances appropriate to the social settings of the place (Duffy 2010). *Divali* on the island symbolises a cohesive community, lessening the cultural and social differences within the community and proving to be an effective tool for social integration (Crespi-Vallbona and Richards 2007).

With the numerous legends and tales associated with *Divali*, the festival has gained a powerful symbolic meaning among the Mauritian community. In times past, it was believed that the citizens of Ayodhya in India had lit up the whole city with tiny oil lamps made of clay to celebrate Rama and his wife Sita's return to the town of Ayodhya (Hitillambeau-Mirthil 2013; Jha 1976). This symbolic tradition is still followed by hundreds of families in Mauritius. Traditional earthen lamps, *diyas*, are sold in almost every retail store in the island during the several weeks preceding the festival of lights. Balconies and verandas are beautifully decorated with rows of *diyas* often with a flickering but reassuring light, as perceived by the Mauritians. Fine silky paper is used to convert the *diyas* into colourful lanterns to light up home gardens. However, in certain homes, the traditional earthen lamps have been replaced by electric fairy lights attracting several people to admire the brightly lit houses.

Divali is recognised as a national holiday. The importance of the festival attracts local government sponsorship. District and village councils decorate their respective areas, host concerts allowing locals to showcase their talents and display fireworks with the aim to gather Mauritians of all origins in a spirit of unity and national brotherhood. *Divali* hence occupies a special position in such settings (Johnson 2007) leading to identity construction between the Mauritian community and the place. Expressive celebrations such as music, dance, lighting of lamps and fireworks and sharing of sweets through its sets of meanings tap into people's emotional and intuitive selves and translate into place identity. Emotions promote social ties and interactions, constructing individual and group identities (Duffy 2010) and a strong sense of place (Ramkissoon *et al.* 2013a, 2013b). Hence, *Divali* is seen as a performative spectacle displaying constructions of identity in several forms.

Divali in the island is also celebrated to worship the deity *Laxmi*, the goddess of wealth. *Laxmi* is considered to bring wealth, happiness and prosperity and has immense relevance for Mauritians. The festival of lights has several rituals that begin with extensive preparations to welcome the goddess. Several days prior to the festival, homes are thoroughly cleaned and decorated with electric lights, non-vegetarians abstain from meat and people shop for new clothing, new kitchen utensils and other things they might need. Two days prior to the festival, clay lamps are lit and *Laxmi puja* (traditional worship of the goddess with chanting of hymns) is performed (Figure 3.1). The worshippers believe that the *diyas* will drive evil spirits away (Johnson 2007). The next phase of activities is the preparation of delicious treats that will be distributed to neighbours, families and friends at the workplace. Family members unite in the kitchen sharing recipes that have been passed on for generations. Some of the traditional sweets are colourful *barfi*, coconut *laddoos*, *naan khatai*, syrupy *gulab jamun*, but the most anticipated every year remains the Mauritian delicacy *gateau patate* made of a flour and sweet potato mix with sugar, vanilla and grated coconut filling (Hitillambeau-Mirthil 2013).

Literature review

Festival satisfaction and behavioural intentions

Satisfaction is a psychological construct, viewed as an emotional response to experiences (Ramkissoon, Smith and Kneebone 2014). It is considered the con-

Figure 3.1 Traditional lighting of *Diya* and *Puja* (source: H. Ramkissoon).

sumer's judgement about goods and services (Oliver 1997) and has an assumed impact on their behaviour depending on the strength with which they are satisfied with the product (or, in this case, festival) (Tudoran *et al.* 2012). Satisfaction in the present context is conceptualised as the collective evaluation of individual experiences with the *Divali* festival. Behavioural intention defined as residents' future intentions to celebrate *Divali* is another important dependent variable in this study. Residents' future festival intentions depend on achieving festival satisfaction as evidenced in literature (e.g. Oliver and Burke 1999; Yuan and Jang 2008).

Drawing on Lazarus's (1991) theoretical framework, researchers have concluded that individuals engage in activities to achieve an outcome. Their appraisals trigger an emotional response (satisfaction) that in turn generates a coping response (behavioural intentions) to maintain or increase their festival satisfaction levels (Yuan and Jang 2008). In their empirical reviews of studies, scholars argue that people with high levels of festival satisfaction have repeat intentions (Baker and Crompton 2000; Lee and Beeler 2007; Oliver 1997). Yuan and Jang (2008) noted that satisfaction with the Vintage Indiana wine and food festival had a significant influence on people's intentions to purchase wines and visit local wineries. Convention attendees with higher satisfaction levels were seen to report higher revisit intentions than those who were less satisfied (Severt *et al.*

2007). Given that satisfying experiences predict future intention (Lee *et al.* 2012), this study proposes that residents' satisfaction with the *Divali* festival will have a positive influence on their future intentions to celebrate the festival.

Festival authenticity

The concept of authenticity plays an important role in festival production and consumption (Getz 1997; Ramkissoon and Uysal 2011; Richards 2007). Different perspectives of authenticity can lead to changes in the cultural content of a festival, giving rise to new meanings (Cohen 1998). From a marketing perspective, the milieu in which festivals operate also adds value to the core product and can increase festival satisfaction (Robinson and Clifford 2012). There is some evidence in the literature (e.g. Shin *et al.* 2012; Song *et al.* 2013) showing authenticity to be an antecedent of festival satisfaction. These researchers argue in their study of the oriental medicine festival in South Korea that authenticity can be increased by the perceived theme of the festival.

Further, authenticity can be an important driver, value, motive or interest (e.g. Grayson and Martinec 2004; Ramkissoon and Uysal 2010; Ramkissoon, Uysal and Prebensen 2014) for locals to participate in cultural festivals. Some studies have shown a positive effect of authenticity on repurchase intentions (loyalty) (e.g. Kolar and Zabkar 2010; Zhou *et al.* 2013). A similar finding was reported by Ramkissoon and Uysal (2010) in their study of perceived authenticity and cultural behavioural intentions in the island of Mauritius. However, others have argued that findings on the association between these two constructs are inconclusive and warrant more research (Song *et al.* 2014). From a cultural festival perspective, this study proposes to investigate the association between residents' perceived authenticity of *Divali* and their future intentions to celebrate the festival in Mauritius. Results from this body of research will advance theoretical knowledge in the subject. Moreover, understanding perceived authenticity as an antecedent of residents' festival satisfaction and cultural behavioural intentions will allow the Mauritian government and other stakeholders to concentrate on this aspect and fully support and promote the importance of traditions in the island.

Festival motivation

Studies of festival motivation place critical emphasis on the association between festival satisfaction and future behavioural intentions (e.g. Park *et al.* 2008; Yolal *et al.* 2012), with different dimensions reflecting specific contexts of festivals. Motivational schemes are crucial in formulating effective marketing strategies (Lee and Hsu 2013). Backman *et al.* (1995) and Crompton and McKay (1997) came up with different motives, for example, excitement, external, family, socialising, cultural exploration and relaxation, for festival consumption. More recently, Yolal *et al.* (2012) identified socialisation, excitement, event novelty, escape and family togetherness as motives to attend a festival in Turkey.

Socialisation and the beliefs in helping one's community were offered as motives for some Australian festival attendees (Slaughter and Home 2004). This may imply that festivals provide individuals with expectations for place-based activities.

Several studies in the literature have concluded that motivation is an antecedent of satisfaction (e.g. Baker and Crompton 2000; Severt *et al.* 2007) and behavioural intentions (e.g. Lee and Beeler 2009; Rittichainuwat *et al.* 2003). However, there is still a research gap in understanding the association between festival motivation, satisfaction and future intentions (Lee, Lee *et al.* 2007; Yoon *et al.* 2010) in the festival and event literature. Yoon *et al.* (2010) suggest that motives need to be factored into attractive festival qualities that may positively influence satisfaction and behavioural intentions. Baker and Crompton (2000) found positive effects of festival quality on both festival satisfaction and behavioural intentions. Educational benefit, a key motivator for convention attendees, was a significant predictor of their satisfaction with the event (Severt *et al.* 2007). On the basis of the preceding discussion, it is proposed to investigate the relationships between the motivations to celebrate *Divali* and residents' satisfaction with the festival. It is also proposed to investigate the association between residents' satisfaction with the *Divali* festival and their future intentions.

Place identity

An important area of scholarship in the festivals and events literature is that of place identity. Place identity refers to the cognitive connection depicting the symbolic link between a person and a place. When people participate in local festivals, the attributes of the place may give rise to a strong sense of identity (Gu and Ryan 2008; Ramkissoon *et al.* 2012) involving not only the specific, localised festival experiences but also more specific memories about the place (Devine-Wright and Clayton 2010). While cultural festivals and events have attracted the attention of scholars for decades (e.g. Coulon 1999; Qui *et al.* 2013), few studies have investigated the relationship between festivals and residents' levels of place identity. Festivals create opportunities for community development (Getz 1997; O'Keach 2011) by forging strong and distinct identities (Derrett 2003) in specific settings to assert local cultural values. As such, festivals help in preserving the traditions and culture that are passed from generation to generation. Festivals offer an integrated approach and promote a sense of identity (Alonso and Liu 2010; O'Keach 2011), providing a vision for participants (Derrett 2003). This is very evident in the *Divali* celebrations in the island of Mauritius that range from physical manifestation of religious ceremonies to participation at social gatherings (Hitillambeau-Mirthil 2013). Lee *et al.* (2012) argued that individuals often make an effort and commitment to a festival to maximise the benefits and fulfil their needs. As such, it promotes a sense of connectedness between residents, their neighbours and their spatial environment (Ramkissoon *et al.* 2013a). Only a handful of studies have dealt with residents' festival satisfaction, place identity and satisfaction, with ambiguous findings (e.g. Lee *et al.* 2012) calling for further examination of the association between these constructs.

Some researchers argue that place identity is predicted by overall level of satisfaction (George and George 2004; Lee *et al.* 2012). In contrast, other work has demonstrated a direct effect of individuals' place identity on satisfaction (e.g. Ramkissoon *et al.* 2013a; Veasna *et al.* 2013; Yuksel *et al.* 2010). Place identity has also been proposed as an antecedent of behavioural intentions. Lee, Graefe *et al.* (2007) and Yuksel *et al.* (2010) reported the positive influence of place identity on loyalty (revisit intentions). Similarly, Ramkissoon *et al.* (2013a, 2013b) demonstrated that individuals' place identity had a positive influence on people's pro-environmental intentions. These inconclusive findings on the association between festival satisfaction, place identity and behavioural intentions suggest the need for further research. Based on theoretical frameworks (e.g. Ramkissoon *et al.* 2012) and empirical evidence (e.g. Lee *et al.* 2012), this study proposes that there is a direct and positive relationship between residents' satisfaction with the *Divali* festival and their place identity. It also proposes the direct effect of residents' place identity on their future intentions to celebrate the *Divali* festival.

The proposed model

Following the empirical and theoretical discussion, the propositions are developed. The structural model in Figure 3.2 describes a logical flow between the constructs related to festival satisfaction and residents' future intentions in festival celebrations. Given the centrality of authenticity in the consumption of culture, the model proposes that residents' perceived festival authenticity has a direct positive influence on their festival satisfaction and future intentions. As evidenced by the literature, motivation is a central concept in understanding satisfaction and behaviour. Drawing from existing motivational theories (Crompton and McKay 1997), the proposed structural model depicts a positive influence of residents' festival motivation on their festival satisfaction and their future intentions. Finally, borrowing from the human attachment theory and empirical evidence from the environmental psychology literature, the model proposes that residents' satisfaction with the festival drives their emotional attachment to the festival settings (place identity) that underlies their future intentions to celebrate the festival. The following propositions are developed.

Proposition 1 Festival authenticity positively influences satisfaction with the *Divali* festival.

Proposition 2 Festival authenticity positively influences behavioural intentions to celebrate *Divali*.

Proposition 3 Festival motivation positively influences satisfaction with the *Divali* festival.

Proposition 4 Festival motivation positively influences behavioural intentions to celebrate *Divali*.

Proposition 5 Festival satisfaction positively influences place identity.

Proposition 6 Place identity positively influences behavioural intentions to celebrate *Divali*.

Proposition 7 Festival satisfaction positively influences future intentions.

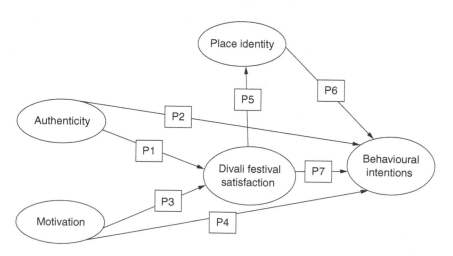

Figure 3.2 Theoretical framework.

Conclusion

Festivals evoke keen interest and are grandly celebrated by the various communities at the local and national level. With their increasing significance, the need for further research on determinants of festival satisfaction and residents' future intentions to celebrate traditional cultural festivals is reinforced. Borrowing from existing theories in social and environmental psychology, this study develops a conceptual model in an attempt to contribute to the comparative lack of studies on residents' levels of festival satisfaction, place identity and their future intentions. The conceptual framework proposes that authenticity and motivation are determinants of residents' festival satisfaction and future intentions to celebrate *Divali*. It is further proposed that residents' festival satisfaction influences their place identity and future intentions to celebrate *Divali*.

This chapter offers researchers a framework that is grounded in theory and past research and has the potential to deliver valuable theoretical and practical implications for promoting cultural festivals at the local and national level. It provides a good rationale for cultural festival marketers to enhance residents' emotional ties not only to festivals but also to the spatial settings where they are celebrated. This may reinforce their levels of identity with the festival and place settings and may result in their future intentions to celebrate local festivals. The limitation of this study is the lack of empirical evidence. Researchers are encouraged to use structural equation modelling to test the model. They can consider extending the framework to include other potential predictors of festival satisfaction and future festival intentions. Inclusion of other determinants may enhance the predictive power of the framework and provide further insights.

References

Alexandris, K., Kouthouris, C. and Meligdis, A. (2006) 'Hindu festivals of India', *Journal of Popular Culture*, 20(2), 175–182.

Alonso, A. and Liu, Y. (2010) 'Wine tourism development in emerging Western Australian destinations', *International Journal of Contemporary Hospitality Management*, 22(2), 245–262.

Backman, K., Backman, S., Uysal, M. and Sunshine, K. (1995) 'Event tourism: An examination of motivations and activities', *Festival Management and Event Tourism*, 3(1), 15–24.

Baker, D. and Crompton, J. (2000) 'Quality, satisfaction and behavioral intentions', *Annals of Tourism Research*, 27(3), 785–804.

Cohen, R. (1998) 'Authenticity and commoditization in tourism', *Annals of Tourism Research*, 15, 371–386.

Coulon, C. (1999) 'The Grand Magal in Touba: A religious festival of the Mouride brotherhood of Senegal', *African Affairs*, 98(391), 195–210.

Crespi-Vallbona, M. and Richards, G. (2007) 'The meaning of cultural festivals', *International Journal of Cultural Policy*, 13(1), 103–122.

Crompton, J. and McKay, S. (1997) 'Motives of visitors attending festival events', *Annals of Tourism Research*, 24, 425–439.

De Bres, K. and Davis, J. (2001) 'Celebrating group and place identity: A case study of a new regional festival', *Tourism Geographies: An International Journal of Tourism Space, Place and Environment*, 3(3), 326–337.

Derrett, R. (2003) 'Festivals and regional destinations', *Rural Society*, 13(1), 35–53.

Devine-Wright, P. and Clayton, S. (2010) 'Introduction to the special issue: Place, identity and environmental behavior', *Journal of Environmental Psychology*, 30, 267–270.

Duffy, M. (2010) 'Performing identity within a multicultural framework', *Social and Cultural Geography*, 6(5), 677–692.

Falassi, A. (1987) *Time out of Time: Essays out of the festival*, Albuquerque, NM: University of New Mexico Press.

Felsenstein, D. and Fleischer, A. (2003) 'Local festivals and tourism promotion: The role of public assistance and visitor expenditure', *Journal of Travel Research*, 41, 385–392.

Fodness, D. (1994) 'Measuring tourism motivation', *Annals of Tourism Research*, 21(3), 555–581.

George, B.P. and George, B.P. (2004) 'Past visit and the intention to revisit a destination: Place attachment as a mediator and novelty seeking as the moderator', *Journal of Tourism Studies*, 15(2), 51–66.

Getz, D. (1997) *Event Management and Event Tourism*, New York: Cognizant.

Grayson, K. and Martinec, R. (2004) 'Consumer perceptions of iconicity and indexicality and their influence on assessments of authentic marketing offerings', *Journal of Consumer Research*, 31(2), 296–312.

Gu, H. and Ryan, C. (2008) 'Place attachment, identity and community impacts of tourism: The case of a Beijing hutong', *Tourism Management*, 29(4), 637–647.

Gursoy, D., Kim, K. and Uysal, M. (2004) 'Perceived impacts of festivals and special events by organizers: An extension and validation', *Tourism Management*, 25(2), 171–181.

Hitillambeau-Mirthil, N. (2013) *Air Mauritius In-Flight Magazine Islander*, No. 73.

Jeong, S. and Santos, C. (2004) 'Cultural politics and contested place identity', *Annals of Tourism Research*, 31(3), 640–656.

Jha, J. (1976) 'The Hindu festival of Divali in the Caribbean: East Indians in Caribbean', *Caribbean Quarterly*, 22(1), 53–61.

Johnson, H. (2007) '"Happy Divali!" performance, multicultural soundscapes and intervention in Aotearoa/New Zealand', *Ethnomusicology Forum*, 16(1), 71–94.

Kolar, T. and Zabkar, V. (2010) 'A consumer-based model of authenticity: An oxymoron or the foundation of cultural heritage marketing?' *Tourism Management*, 31, 652–664.

Lazarus, R. (1991) *Emotion and Adaptation*, New York: Oxford University Press.

Lee, J. and Beeler, C. (2007) 'The relationships among quality, satisfaction and future intentions for first-time and repeat visitors in a festival setting', *Event Management*, 10, 197–208.

Lee, J. and Beeler, C. (2009) 'An investigation of predictors of satisfaction and future intention: Links to motivation, involvement, and service quality in a local festival', *Event Management*, 13(1), 17–29.

Lee, J., Graefe, A. and Burns, R. (2007) 'Examining the antecedents of destination loyalty in a forest setting', *Leisure Studies*, 29, 463–481.

Lee, J., Kyle, G. and Scott, D. (2012) 'The mediating effect of place attachment on the relationship between festival satisfaction and loyalty to the festival hosting destination', *Journal of Travel Research*, 51(6), 754–767.

Lee, T. and Hsu, F. (2013) 'Examining how attending motivation and satisfaction affects the loyalty for attendees at Aboriginal festivals', *International Journal of Tourism Research*, 15, 18–34.

Lee, Y.K., Lee, C.K., Lee, S.K. and Babin, B. (2007) 'Festivalscapes and patrons' emotions, satisfaction, and loyalty', *Journal of Business Research*, 61(1), 56–64.

MacMillan, D. (2008) *Diwali: Hindu festival of lights*, Berkeley Heights, NJ: Enslow.

O'Keach, R. (2011) 'Promoting sustainable festival events tourism: A case study of Lamu Kenya', *Worldwide Hospitality and Tourism Themes*, 3(3), 193–202.

Oliver, R.L. (1997) *Satisfaction: A behavioral perspective on the consumer*, New York: Irwin/McGraw-Hill.

Oliver, R. and Burke, R. (1999) 'Expectation processes in satisfaction formation: A field study', *Journal of Service Research*, 1(3), 196–214.

O'Sullivan, D. and Jackson, M. (2002) 'Festival tourism: A contributor to sustainable local economic development?' *Journal of Sustainable Tourism*, 10(4), 325–342.

Park, K., Reisinger, Y. and Kang, H. (2008) 'Visitors' motivation for attending the South Beach Wine and Food Festival, Miami Beach, Florida', *Journal of Travel and Tourism Marketing*, 25(2), 161–181.

Prayag, G., Hosanny, S., Nunkoo, R. and Alders, T. (2013) 'London residents' support for the 2012 Olympic games: The mediating effect of overall attitude', *Tourism Management*, 36, 629–640.

Prentice, R. and Andersen, V. (2003) 'Festival as a creative destination', *Annals of Tourism Research*, 30(1), 7–30.

Qui, H., Yuan, J., Ye, B. and Hung, K. (2013) 'Wine tourism phenomena in China: An emerging market', *International Journal of Contemporary Hospitality Management*, 25(7), 1115–1134.

Ramkissoon, H. and Uysal, M. (2010) 'Testing the role of authenticity in cultural tourism consumption: A case of Mauritius', *Tourism Analysis*, 15, 571–583.

Ramkissoon, H. and Uysal, M. (2011) 'The effects of perceived authenticity, information search behaviour, motivation and destination imagery on cultural behavioural intentions of tourists', *Current Issues in Tourism*, 14(6), 537–562.

Ramkissoon, H., Smith, L. and Kneebone, S. (2014) 'Visitor satisfaction and place attachment in national parks', *Tourism Analysis*, 19(3), 287–300

Ramkissoon, H., Smith, L.D.G. and Weiler, B. (2013a) 'Relationships between place attachment, place satisfaction and pro-environmental behaviour in an Australian national park', *Journal of Sustainable Tourism*, 21(3), 434–457.

Ramkissoon, H., Smith, L. and Weiler, B. (2013b) 'Testing the dimensionality of place attachment and its relationships with place satisfaction and pro-environmental behaviours: A structural equation modelling approach', *Tourism Management*, 36, 552–566.

Ramkissoon, H., Uysal, M. and Prebensen, N. (2014) 'Authenticity as a value co-creator of tourism experiences', in N. Prebensen, J. Chen and M. Uysal (eds), *Experience Value in Tourism*, Boston, MA: CABI.

Ramkissoon, H., Weiler, B. and Smith, L. (2012) 'Place attachment and pro-environmental behaviour in national parks: The development of a conceptual framework', *Journal of Sustainable Tourism*, 20(2), 257–276.

Richards, G. (2007) 'Culture and authenticity in a traditional event: The views of producers, residents, and visitors in Barcelona', *Event Management*, 11, 33–44.

Rittichainuwat, B.N., Qu, H. and Leong, J.K. (2003) 'The collective impacts of a bundle of travel determinants on repeat visitation', *Journal of Hospitality and Tourism Research*, 27(2), 217–236.

Robinson, R. and Clifford, C. (2012) 'Authenticity and food service experiences', *Annals of Tourism Research*, 39(2), 571–600.

Severt, D., Wang, Y., Chen, P. and Breiter, D. (2007) 'Examining the motivation, perceived performance, and behavioral intentions of convention attendees: Evidence from a regional conference', *Tourism Management*, 28(2), 399–408.

Shin, C.Y., Song, H.J. and Lee, C.K. (2012) 'A study on the structural relationships among festival quality, perception of festival theme, perceived value, and satisfaction: The case of 2011 Jecheon International Oriental Medicine Expo', *Korean Academic Society of Tourism Management*, 26(6), 205–255.

Slaughter, L. and Home, R. (2004) 'Motivations of long term volunteers: Human services vs. events', *Journal of Hospitality, Tourism and Leisure Science*, 2, 1–12.

Song, H.J., Moon, J.H., Choi, S.S. and Lee, C.K. (2013) 'Estimating the economic impact of Oriental medicine festival: The case of 2011 Jecheon Oriental medicine bio expo', *Korean Academic Society of Hospitality Administration*, 22(3), 221–233.

Song, H., You, G., Reisinger, Y., Lee, C. and Lee, S. (2014) 'Behavioral intentions of visitors to an oriental medicine festival: An extended model of goal directed behavior', *Tourism Management*, 42, 101–113.

Tkacczynski, A. and Rundle-Thiele, B. (2011) 'Event segmentation: A review and research agenda', *Tourism Management*, 32, 426–434.

Tudoran, A., Olsen, S. and Dopico, D. (2012) 'Satisfaction strength and intention to purchase a new product', *Journal of Consumer Behaviour*, 11(5), 391–405.

Veasna, S., Wu, W. and Huang, C. (2013) 'The impact of destination source credibility: The mediating effect of destination attachment on destination image', *Tourism Management*, 36, 511–526.

Yolal, M., Woo, E., Cetinel, F. and Uysal, M. (2012) 'Comparative research of motivations across different festival products', *International Journal of Contemporary Event and Festival Management*, 3(1), 66–80.

Yoon, Y., Lee, J. and Lee., C. (2010) 'Measuring festival quality and value affecting visitors' satisfaction and loyalty using a structural approach', *International Journal of Hospitality Management*, 29(2), 335–342.

Yuan, J. and Jang, S. (2008) 'The effects of quality and satisfaction on awareness and behavioral intentions: Exploring the role of a wine festival', *Journal of Travel Research*, 46, 279–288.

Yuksel, A., Yuksel, F. and Bilim, Y. (2010) 'Destination attachment: Effects on customer satisfaction and cognitive, affective and conative loyalty', *Tourism Management*, 31(2), 274–284.

Zhou, Q., Zhang, J. and Edelheim, J. (2013) 'Rethinking traditional Chinese culture: A consumer-based model regarding the authenticity of Chinese calligraphic landscape', *Tourism Management*, 36, 99–112.

4 Transforming tradition

Performing wedding ritual in modern China

Yu Hua and Zhu Yujie

Introduction

This research is focused on the changing roles of wedding rituals from early modern China to the contemporary modern world. Wedding ritual, especially the ritual of 'obstruction' in Gouliang Miao (Hmong) village in Fenghuang town, West Hunan Tujia and Miao Minority Autonomous Prefecture, was interpreted in different cultural contexts, forming a different relationship with the state. Travelling through different national discourses on ritual in three stages of modern China, namely the Qing dynasty (early modern), the modern state (1910s–late 1970s) and post-reform China (1978–), wedding ritual in Gouliang village takes on different practices. The meanings of ritual are fluid with transforming discourses. What is the meaning of wedding ritual when it is transformed into the nature of *other* people, feudal superstition, cultural resources, the object of tourists' gaze and the heritage product? What is the role of wedding ritual in the locals' contemporary life when ethnic tourism and heritage industry gradually penetrate into the village? What is the role of the state in transforming wedding ritual practices? Guided by these questions, this chapter explores diversified meanings of traditional wedding ritual in a transforming process of national discourses and needs.

Wedding ritual of Miao in early modern China

Ritual used to penetrate into every sphere of Chinese life in imperial China. It was said to be 'the determinate fabric of Chinese culture, and further, defines sociopolitical order. It is the language through which the culture is expressed' (Hall and Ames 1998: 269). The emperor, as the Son of Heaven, governed the society and the universe through 'inauguration ceremonies, the diffusion of the calendar, the bestowal of titles and names, the classification of the various cults and deities' and offered sacrifices to the Heaven and his ancestors (Gernet 1985: 105, cited in Rawski 2001: 214). When the Qing empire started to legitimate the expansion of its territory and sought to include different ethnic and linguistic groups in its own rule, one of the techniques of expansion that the Qing employed was the use of ethnography and cartography of customs and rituals of various peoples based on direct observation within the context of the early modern world (Hostetler 2000). One of the frequent topics recorded in the early ethnography of the Miao area is marriage and courtship practices, which was of great interest to the Confucian literati because of their own strong training in the importance of proper rites (Hostetler 2000). The ultimate goal of direct observation, ethnography and cartography is to govern non-Han peoples. As Tian Wen, who assumed governorship of Guizhou in 1688, observed, 'Consulting literary sources is not as satisfactory as observation ... If one wants to control the barbarian frontier area, one must judge the profitability of the land, and investigate the nature of its people' (Hostetler 2000). The wedding ritual depicted in the local gazetteers thus presents the Confucian scholar and official's observation and interpretation of the Miao practice partly as the object of governance and partly as the cultural Other. While describing the cultural phenomena of another culture, the author is seeing the Other in the perspective of his or her own culture and language. In this case, the official scholar is describing the wedding ceremony in traditional Confucian culture in order to know and investigate the nature of his people.

In the category of 'ethnography of populace customs' (*feng su zhi*) of the *Fenghuang Town Gazetteer* (Vol. 7) composed during the Daoguang period (1820–1850), the wedding in Fenghuang town was described and interpreted in the language of a classic Confucian ritual book, such as *Yili* (*Book of Rites*) or *Zhuxi Jiali* (*Zhuxi Family Rituals*) (Ebrey 1991). It might be the case that the official scholar described the wedding ritual in Fenghuang town according to the Confucian ritual procedures.

> **Wedding** The family of the boy invite an intermediary to ask the family of the girl for the permission (of wedding). The girl's family member writes down the girl's date of birth on a piece of red paper, which is called the phoenix note, to indicate their approval.... The boy's family then present such betrothal gifts as hairpins, clothes, pigs and spirit, which is called delivering gifts, bearing the meaning of *na cai* (presenting betrothal gifts, a phrase from *Yili*). When they are ready to get married, an auspicious date of wedding is selected by divination and presented to the girl's family together with some more gifts. It is called *shang tou* (taken as a priority), bearing the meaning of *na ji* (sending news of auspicious divination). On the wedding day, the bridal sedan chair is sent to the bride's to the sound of drums. On the day the groom goes to meet the bride in person, two geese are offered in front of the ancestors' altar, which is called offering sacrifice of goose.... At the arrival of the groom's home, the bride and the groom perform the ritual of drinking the wedlock wine, offering sacrifices to the ancestors, kowtowing to the parents and elders of the two families.

The Qing official scholar tends to integrate the procedures and meanings of each ritual step in the Confucian classic into the writing of the wedding ritual in Fenghuang town in the local gazetteer. There is a cultural integration among

Miao, Tujia and Han in this area, since 'there has been a mutual assimilation in customs and ethnic characteristics (among Miao, Han and Tujia), like the alloying of tin and lead in the making of a pot' (Kinkley 1987: 247). It is not strange to find the traditional Confucian wedding procedures embedded in the wedding ritual practice in the Miao area. Wedding ritual was a process of constructing and negotiating a relationship between the two families to be joined, from presenting the betrothal gifts, to sending news of auspicious divination of the wedding day and offering sacrifice to the ancestors of the groom. The meaning of the wedding narrated in the local gazetteer can be traced in the *Book of Rites* (51–21 BCE):

> The ceremony of marriage was intended to be a bond of love between two (families of different) surnames, with a view, in its retrospective character, to secure the services in the ancestral temple, and in its prospective character, to secure the continuance of the family line.
>
> (trans. Legge 1885)

Another form of wedding ritual can also be located in the earlier version of the gazetteer. The wedding ceremony in the Miao area was described as a process of walking and drinking without any rite of drinking wedlock wine or offering sacrifices to the ancestors. The *Qianzhou Town Gazetteer* (Vol. 7), composed during *Qianlong* period (1735–1796), recorded that:

> The bride walked to the groom's, holding the umbrella herself on the way. Her brothers carried the bamboo basket filled with wooden pillow, quilts, and dresses. The bride's kinsmen sent her to the groom's and enjoyed the drinking for three days and nights.

This entry described a simpler ritual in which the bride walked to the groom's residence by herself. It was called *zouhun* (walking wedding) later by the Miao in Gouliang village. This form of wedding enjoyed popularity during the 1970s and 1980s when post-Mao China was still in the last wave of 'anti-feudalism' and 'anti-superstition' governance, according to the local villagers.

Struggle of rituals in the modern state

In modern (1840–1919) and contemporary Chinese history (1919–present), conventional and folk ritual as a whole has declined almost to the point of extinction in Chinese culture and life. To pave the way for modernity (famously identified with 'democracy and science' by Chen Duxiu) in China, traditional Chinese culture, especially ritual, was systematically denounced as feudalistic remnants and superstitious practice in the New Culture and May Fourth movements (1916–1919). The New Culture Movement promoted the elimination of tradition, Confucianism and classical language, leading to the rupture of traditional Chinese culture. Through the movement of 'Destroying the Four Olds' – old ideas, cultures, customs and habits – and the movement of 'Criticising Confucius' during the Cultural Revolution (1966–1976), the ritual tradition has been expunged from ideology and the political domain in the process of Chinese modernisation (Hu 2011: 61).

Rituals and the temples related to ritual performances in Gouliang were inescapably suppressed and destroyed during the Cultural Revolution, but were revived with the onset of Deng Xiaoping's Opening Up and Reform policy and the rise of ethnic tourism from 1979 onwards. However, the shackles of 'anti-feudalism' and anti-ritual were still in the minds of the villagers. In the 1980s, locals in Gouliang did not restore the traditional way of staging a wedding in the Confucian wedding procedure. Instead, they revived the ritual of *zouhun* which was recognised as the typical Miao wedding. The marriage is completed by walking to the groom's home without wedding banquet or sacrifice to the ancestors. Long Hexiu, who got married in the 1980s, walked to her husband's home on her wedding day. She recalled:

> At that time we did *zou hun*, unlike today's wedding that is reverting to our traditional way. Now I admire those who had a matchmaker and got a marriage rite. We belonged to the *zou hun* [generation]. Since it was typical of that time, there was no regret for me. But those who were introduced by the matchmaker and got a wedding ceremony are the best. They enjoyed superior status. My status is lower since I walked to my husband's house. When I walked here, my mother-in-law gave me a wardrobe for my clothes. There was no banquet until I gave birth to Xiao Hui [her first daughter].
>
> (fieldwork notes 2009)

Long thought that the traditional wedding ritual could endow the bride with superior status compared with *zouhun* in which the bride walked to the groom's house. The 'superiority' of the traditional wedding was presided over by Miao song experts. The whole ritual procedure is performed in the form of antiphonal Miao songs, which involves prolonged chanting of the rhymed verses (Ling and Rui 2003: 283). It is regarded as 'superior' by the villagers to the equally traditional but simpler *zouhun*. Currently, local villagers prefer the ritual of obstructions instead of *zouhun*, which will be discussed later in this chapter.

In cultural practices, the villagers seem to have restored their traditional way. In discourses and ideology, conflicts persist. Due to the continuous control of local ritual practices by the state (Oakes and Sutton 2010), a tension exists among the state's socialistic discourses and the discourse of developing ethnic tourism. A large billboard headed 'Village Rules and Folk Covenants' hangs on the wall of an old wooden mansion which is both the tourists' site and the officials' office. One of the folk laws issues the order of keeping away from feudalism and superstition, and simplifying the wedding ceremony and funeral ritual and acting in accordance with Socialist Spiritual Civilisation. On one hand, the tourism industry has appropriated some elements in the wedding ritual and performs the artistic and amusing parts in front of the tourists. On the other hand, the state discourse insists on the simplification of wedding ritual and warns the villagers away from the 'superstitious' part of it. If the 'feudalist' and superstitious part refers to the sacrificing to the ancestors during the wedding, the traditional meaning of a wedding will be lost. If the wedding were to be simplified, then what will be reserved for the ethnic culture? If the wedding performance for the tourists can be complex, why not the wedding in the locals' everyday life? We suppose that it is under such tension that the traditional wedding ceremony is enjoying more and more popularity among the locals.

Wedding ritual in the Intangible Heritage Movement

China was one of the first countries to ratify the Convention for the Safeguarding of the Intangible Heritage (Intangible Cultural Heritage Convention, ICHC) in 2004. In the following years, intangible cultural heritage has been promoted in China through a number of policies and practices at the national, provincial and local levels. Although 'Intangible Cultural Heritage' is used to maintain and promote local cultural diversity, the government's adoption of the notion has become a tool to legitimise its cultural and social control, particularly over ethnic minorities, through defining and formulating local folklore, performing arts, rituals and social practices, and transforming them into a unified national body of knowledge.

Intangible heritage in China has thus become a new form of social-cultural 'movement' (*yundong*) (Peng 2008) by local governments and related agencies. The discourse of intangible heritage includes culture and ethnic traditions, which are packaged as consumable tourist attractions. The growth of ethnic tourism – both by domestic and international tourists – has motivated a search for and consumption of original culture and intangible heritage, especially in the minority areas.

West Hunan Tujia and Miao Autonomous Prefecture is hailed as a 'treasure house' of intangible heritage (Wang *et al.* 2013). A recent government report (Ministry of Culture of the People's Republic of China 2013) claims that West Hunan has taken possession of 3,200 items of intangible heritage cultural resources, among which 24 were listed on the national level. The increasing number of intangible heritage items demonstrates the achievements of the officials, who are working hard for the bidding. Wedding ritual is segmented into the prescribed categories with aesthetic and artistic significance rather than its ritual and moral value. The antiphonal Miao songs were taken as a form of art and listed in the category of 'folk music' in the bidding. The 'Miao ancient words', which can be chanted during the ritual of 'paying the mother's milk' in the wedding to thank the bride's parents and elders, is decontextualised and categorised as 'folk literature' (Huang 2012: 173). Officials from the Cultural Department are trained to write up application reports to apply for the next, higher level of the intangible heritage programme. The intangible heritage movement, on the one hand, has forced local officials to enter normal villagers' lives and listen to their stories. Large numbers of local legends and folklore have been collected, recorded and stored in the Cultural Department across the country. On the other hand, the writing of these collected stories is channelled by the categories of intangible heritage prescribed by UNESCO and turned into standardised expert knowledge aiming for success in bidding, compared with the Qing officials' writings which were largely shaped by the ritual meaning in the Confucian ritual classics.

Despite of being categorised as a branch of knowledge and forced to stand outside its life context, the intangible heritage movement does liberate the cultural practices that were once labelled as the remnants of 'superstition' and offers a free space for the locals to perform the rituals in their everyday life without suspicion.

Traditional Miao weddings in the contemporary world

Contemporary Miao weddings are found to follow the wedding ritual shared among Miao, Tujia and Han in Fenghuang town during the Daoguang period (1820–1850). The whole wedding involves negotiating and constructing the relationship between the two families to be conjoined through the chanting of Miao songs. This section describes in detail the ritual of the 'obstruction of song', recorded as a part of wedding rituals in 2008 in Gouliang Miao village. Note that the following section describes the ritual of 'obstruction of songs' in its original context for the comparison of the same ritual genre in the context of tourism. The ritual of 'song obstruction' is performed in the style of antiphonal Miao chanting. The bride's family attempts to obstruct the way of the groom's party by blocking its way and singing traditional songs.

In the traditional wedding, the Miao song masters who improvise the lyrics are called *Geshi* (master composer) and the singers are called *Geshou* (chanter). The *Geshi* composes the lyrics according to the repertoire and immediate context. The male *Geshi* (song composer for the groom's family) and female *Geniang* (song composer and chanter for the bride's family) learn a complex repertoire of formulaic chants from the Miao song masters in the village by oral transmission in their daily life (Zhao 2008: 86). The chanters are the apprentices of the master composer. Together, they serve as ritual instructors throughout the traditional wedding process, namely in how to receive the bride, obstruct the gate and set the feast for the groom, as well as on how the bride should depart from her natal home, enter into the groom's house, prepare the wedding banquet at the groom's house and see the guests off at the end of the celebration.

Ritual, as the texture of traditional Chinese culture, discloses its meaning in images revealed in the ritual performances rather than in propositions established within a system of signs (Wu and Hu 2010). The following attempts to describe in detail the 'obstruction' ritual in the traditional wedding form and to present the cultural fabric of the traditional ritual in a contemporary context.

In the afternoon, the groom's party arrived. As the bride's home was located at the bottom of a hill, cars cannot drive directly to the door. They unloaded all the betrothal gifts onto a spacious terrace. The bridegroom's four kinsmen carried a heavy pig, the groom took the bride's new wedding dress, a red umbrella and a silver crown in the two baskets. Also, the Assistant carried the two muttering geese and the Helper took the wine, soft drinks and the two full baskets of grain. The bride and her relatives were waiting for the groom on the terrace. The *Geniang* stood opposite the groom's group, chanting to them. Two *Geniang* chanted their welcome and compliments on the groom's betrothal gifts slowly and loudly. The surrounding mountains echoed with their song:

> We are here waiting for the guests aye~aye~aye~
> We come here to see new in-laws aye~aye~aye~
> You come to our place for the first time aye~
> We see you carry such a large pig aye~aye~aye~
> Every basket you are carrying is loaded so full aye~aye~aye~
> We are obstructing the way for your songs aye~
> Your arrival has gained much fame for us aye~aye~aye~
> You must sing us some songs to pass here aye~

The groom's *Geshi* spoke to them: 'You asked us to sing. We do not know how. We come to receive the bride. Our love for the bride can be expressed by mouth? As you asked us to sing, we will chant one or two sentences.' Instead of immediately returning a song, the groom's *Geshi* responded humbly by saying that they did not know how to chant Miao songs, signifying that they have no talent for singing. They did not chant until the *Geniang* pleaded again. A classic Chinese ritual book *Liji* (475–221 BCE) states: 'When the elder asks a question, to reply without acknowledging one's incompetency and (trying to) decline answering, is contrary to propriety (ritual)' (Legge 1885). This may also explain why the Chinese tend to decline a kind offer of food or answering immediately on some social occasions. On this occasion, *Geshi* claimed themselves to be incompetent before they began to answer the *Geniang*. This action is taken to be in accordance with ritual propriety.

As '*li* is seen in humbling oneself and giving honour to others' (Legge 1885), the lyrics improvised by the groom's *Geshi* constitute one of the rhetorical constructions of ritual performance that one can easily find in both ancient and contemporary Chinese cultural phenomena. The two families officially met for the first time during the ritual of obstruction, in which the groom presented the betrothal gifts. They praised the bride's kinsmen and belittled their own betrothal gifts by chanting:

> You all know well *li* aye~aye~aye~
> You come out to receive us with your smiling faces aye~aye~aye~
> And treat us as if we were high officials oh~aye~
> We see you aunts stood there aye~aye~aye~
> Your mouths are as sweet as candy aye~aye~aye~
> You are here with smiling faces aye~
> The things we carry here are only a few aye~aye~aye~
> We are sorry for it aye~

Immediately after they honoured the bride's kinsmen and humbled themselves, they proposed to enter the bride's home, a suggestion to go through the obstruction. The bride's *Geniang* did not easily give way to their request. The rule is that if they obviously lose the singing competition, they have to unlock the obstruction. Yet, obstructing the groom's way is a ritual performance rather than a real intention. Forced to confront the 'obstruction' directly as the groom's *Geshi* had proposed, they started to negotiate and banter with each other. We will see how the bride concedes without losing face and passes the 'obstruction' in the following dialogue:

THE GROOM'S GESHI: We know ourselves. Our gifts are so few. Come on! Let's go to your home [in a beseeching way].

THE BRIDE'S GENIANG: No, you cannot enter the door now [steadily and loudly refuse for the first time].

THE GROOM'S GESHI: We feel sorry for our bride. Others will see our shabby betrothal presents. We could compete neither with the wealthy nor the poor. We feel sorry [grinning].

THE BRIDE'S AUNT: Your presents are so many. You are good at singing and speaking. Find a stone. Let us sit down and chat along [everyone laughs. Gently refuse for the second time].

THE GROOM'S GESHI: No. No. No. Shall we go home and sit? [in a pleading tone, his face broadened out into a grin].

THE BRIDE'S AUNT: Our home is poor and shabby, very shabby. Let us have a rest on the flagstone [expressing her refusal with a smile for the third time].

THE GROOM'S GESHI: We are here to receive the bride. You are very good at receiving the guests. Let's go to your home. You know *li* [ritual] very well. Let us sit at home instead of standing on the path [in an imploring way].

THE BRIDE'S GESHI: You always said that you did not know how. We are here as if we have stirred up a nest of hornets. You have so many songs. Sing one more. Though we do not know how to sing back, we put them on credit. Others owe money on credit. We owe Miao songs on credit as we have already stirred up the hornet's nest [everyone laughed].

For the first time the groom's *Geshi* requested to go to the bride's home, which was the suggestion to go through the 'obstruction', which the bride's *Geniang* sternly refused with her apparent negative response. Then an excuse was raised by the groom's *Geshi* that their shabby betrothal gifts would be exposed to others and mocked by outsiders. They humbly expressed their apology, dropping a hint of hiding the wretched gifts at home as soon as possible. The bride's aunt reacted with the opposite observations of the betrothal gifts. They praised the betrothal gifts and Miao songs, which presented sufficient reason to ask the groom's *Geshi* to stay and sing. They insisted on deterring the groom's proceeding by saying that they would like to find a stone, sit down and chat. Thus the groom's *Geshi* were denied their request for the second time. They immediately replied with three 'nos' and proposed to go home again in a pleading tone after the second refusal. The bride's aunt found a third excuse to turn down the request by articulating that their home was 'poor and shabby'. Finally the *li* was proposed to support their appeal of entering the bride's home. The groom's *Geshi* complimented the bride's *Geniang*: 'you are very good at receiving the guests.... You know *li* very well.' Instead of directly replying the *Geshi*'s request, the bride's *Geniang* compared their opponents' chanting to 'a nest of hornets'. They negotiated in the metaphoric language: 'Others owe money on credit. We owe Miao songs on credit.' The imagery of the hornet's nest was employed to compliment the groom's *Geshi* as well as to mock themselves facing their strong opponent. When they stirred up the hornet's nest, the numerous hornets (Miao songs) flew out. They had to put the Miao songs on credit and let the 'hornets' play. The imagery of a hornet's nest acted as a funny rhetorical device to deter the groom and obstruct the gate. By saying 'putting Miao songs on credit', the bride's *Geniang* euphemistically expressed that they would not or could not respond to the songs and continue to obstruct the way. The ones who were eager to move on, and who got the hint, laughed. The groom's cousin, who was increasingly feeling the difficulty of keeping a heavy pig on his right shoulder, could not help asking for clarification.

THE GROOM'S COUSIN: Owe what? You owe the Miao songs? If you are not singing back, we will go ahead [carrying the heavy white pig on his shoulder, grinning].

EVERYONE IN THE GROOM'S GROUP ECHOED: Great! [Amused.]

THE BRIDEGROOM: Oh! Let's go ahead! Go ahead! Go ahead! [Laughed and stepped forward.]

Thus the groom finally went through the obstruction. With smiles on everyone's face, they walked forward to the bride's home. It is the initial stage to establish the relationship between the bride's and the groom's family, as well as a chance to inaugurate a relaxed and fun atmosphere for the wedding. For the bride's family, Miao songs were chanted to express their welcome of the groom and appreciation for the gifts. For the groom's family, Miao songs were chanted to express their humility and sincerity. The composition of the lyrics they were chanting to each other was improvised from their repertoire as well as from the immediate surroundings.

When they revived the tradition, they also introduced some new elements. In this case, the Miao songs chanted by the elders and the middle-aged during the young couple's wedding preserved a traditional way of thinking and acting. Local stories, legends and metaphors were inherited through composing and chanting the Miao songs (Yu 2013). So the content of the singing demonstrated established sayings, metaphors, legends and improvised sayings based on the immediate surroundings. This aspect of the ritual of 'obstruction of song' makes a space to embrace both old traditions and new invention in a specific context.

Ritual of 'obstructions' in the realm of tourism

Ethnic cultures have been exploited as cultural resources since 2000 in West Hunan. The local tourism company made Miao rituals a key selling point. The ritual features prominently in public performances created for the entertainment and edification of tourists. In Miao wedding programmes on stage, tourists are invited to act either as the bride or the groom to experience a staged Miao wedding. These performances are designed by the villager Mr Long, who had travelled to various sites of ethnic tourism in Guizhou, Yunan, Hainan and Guangxi provinces. As head of the Miao cultural performance team, he is responsible for designing the cultural performances and training the tourist guides, as well as the actors and actresses. In creating these touristic performances, however, Long has incorporated a wide variety of elements that are not historically part of Miao tradition. For instance, the bamboo pole dance was imported from the *li* ethnic group in Hainan province. Performance of Miao bullfighting and the use of the farm tools are derived from Mr Long's agricultural life. And the wedding ritual is derived from the Miao wedding ritual. He said the design of the performances was intended to entertain tourists by involving them in order to experience the local agricultural and ethnic life. In his words, the main point of these performances is to enable the tourists to have fun.

The wedding ritual of 'obstruction of song' was appropriated to welcome the tourists. When the village was opened to tourists in 2002, local villagers built a wooden frame gate at the south-west entrance of the village and designed the performance of 'obstruction of song', 'obstruction of alcohol' and 'obstruction of drums' at the gate as the Miao's first encounter with the tourists. The ritual of 'obstructions at the gate' is the first 'ritual performance' most tourists experience when they enter the village.

It is typical for a tour guide, usually a Miao girl, to introduce to tourists the ritual of obstructions as the highest form of ritual to receive the guests from afar while a tourist group is on their way to the village. Tourists will be taught to sing a simple song, either in Mandarin or Miao language, to deal with the 'obstruction of songs'. As soon as the tourists get off the bus, six or seven girls in blue embroidered Miao attire begin to sing a welcoming song in Miao (Figure 4.1). They stand in a line in front of the wooden gate, holding a long strip of red silk in their hands as the obstruction for the tourists. A big red flower hangs in the middle of the silk band, which seems to express the actual welcome to the tourists. The girls chant in Miao:

> Welcome to Gouliang Miao village!
> We have sweet wine and beautiful song to welcome you.
> Welcome to our village.

At the end of the song, the leading girl speaks in Mandarin to explain the ritual:

> The ritual of obstructions at the gate is our Miao's highest form of cere-mony to welcome the distinguished guests. We have obstruction of songs, obstruction of alcohol and obstruction of drums. According to our custom, you have to sing a song, drink a cup of sweet wine, and play the drum to gain the right to pass the gate. Now it is your turn to sing a song!

(fieldwork notes 2008)

Figure 4.1 The Miao girls during the obstruction of songs ritual in the village of Gouliang, China (source: Y. Hua).

Tourists, scattered in front of the girls, are required to sing a song back (Figure 4.2). Sometimes, the tourists sing the song they learnt in the minibus. Sometimes they choose a song they are familiar with. One or two representatives will be selected to answer the song. I heard some middle-aged tourists chant:

> There is no new China without the Communist Party.
> There is no new China without the Communist Party.
> Communist Party works very hard for the nation.
> Communist Party intends to save China.
> He showed the way for the people's liberation.
> He leads China to the enlightenment.

I also heard a young man chant the song he had learnt during his childhood:

> I picked up a one cent coin at the roadside,
> Immediately I delivered it to the police uncle's hand,
> The police uncle took the money and nodded at me.
> I joyfully said to him, 'Goodbye, uncle!'

Figure 4.2 Obstruction of songs between the tourists and the Miao girls, Gouliang, China
(source: Y. Hua).

Some popular songs concerning love are also chanted to get the tourists past
the obstruction. For example:

There is a girl named *Xiaofang* in the village,
She looked lovely and beautiful,
A pair of bright large eyes,
A long and thick hair braid.

The songs chanted by the tourists in Mandarin are popular songs in mainstream
Chinese culture. The Miao girls chant the welcoming song in the Miao language,
which is unintelligible to tourists from other areas in China and abroad. They
sing in Miao to demonstrate their ethnic identity and construct for the tourists a
sense of an ethnic and exotic place. Thus, obviously, they did not construct a
dialogue with the Miao girls in terms of semantic meaning, nor did they fit into
the ethnic Miao context. The tourists chanted a song in Mandarin with more
interest in fitting into the genre of a dialogue rather than the meaningful dialogue
in the obstruction ritual. Though the tourists' songs are not a direct response to
the Miao girls' welcoming song in content, they show their cooperation and
sincerity in this communication genre. The welcoming Miao girls and the

tourists are involved in a communication without fully understanding each other. And they are still communicating with each other in a pleasant way. The ritual performance helps provide a strong interaction with tourists at local community events (Schein 2000). In this case, it is the genre of the obstruction ritual that has provided an interactive space for the tourists and the local cultural performers to meet and communicate.

Sometimes, when tourists are reluctant to sing, the girls still unfurl the red silk band and invite them to have a small bowl of rice wine, which is called the second obstruction of alcohol. Meanwhile, four local boys in blue Miao attire played the bass drum in their local style, which is termed Miao Flower-Drum. After a few seconds of drum performance, they invite the tourists to strike once on the drum, saying that 'play the drum once and you will have a safe and sound life for a whole lifetime'. After the three obstructions, the tourists are invited into the village.

During the drumming and songs, most tourists took out their cameras and captured the moment with the Miao girls and boys. Afterwards they put these pictures on their blogs and wrote about their exciting, romantic or disappointing experiences in Gouliang. The pictures of these singing girls, drumming boys and drinking tourists dominated their memory of this village tour. The value of the 'three obstructions' lies more in its fabricated symbolic meaning and depiction of ethnicity for tourists to consume and enjoy rather than the revival of ritual in the form of 'reified tradition' (Oakes 1993; Wood 1984).

The appropriation of the traditional rituals into tourism brought to the locals a sense of pride in their traditional life and culture. The manager of a Miao restaurant said:

> Through tourism, we realized the value of our culture, including our customs, our attires and silver decorations. Many tourists are willing to travel afar and pay a lot of money to see our old mud houses. In the past, we dare not wear Miao clothes to go to the town, because others would laugh at us. But now, we are so proud to wear Miao attire, even to the city.
>
> (interview notes 2009)

Ethnic tourism also creates job opportunities for youths. A mother of four children, who set up a stand to sell Miao snacks to tourists, said: 'The development of tourism retains some young Miao to stay in the village, acting as tour guide and actors. A very good thing to keep children around.' For the locals, the appropriation of rituals in tourism has not only enhanced their ethnic pride but also kept many young people in the village to inherit the ritual performance both in the secular context of tourism and the sacred context in everyday life.

Discussion and conclusion

This chapter attempts to construct the genealogy of the meanings of ritual, especially wedding ritual, in Fenghuang town and its village Gouliang. Wedding ritual in Fenghuang town and neighbouring Miao villages was recorded by the Qing officials from the perspective of Confucian ritual classics in early modern China. The ethnography of the ritual in Qing dynasty was intended to explore the nature of the 'Other' people, govern the ethnic groups and legitimise the expansion of the empire. Later the ritual practices as a whole were demonised as 'feudalism' and 'superstition' in the Cultural Revolution during the Mao period in China. The officials as well as the villagers have been involved in an ideological struggle and a rupture from the past. With the opening-up policy in the 1980s, villagers were still in the shadow of accusations of superstition and carried out the wedding ritual in a simple but proper Miao way. The state's control over the ritual practices loosened during this period. Involved in the bidding process of the intangible heritage movement and the development of ethnic tourism, wedding ritual has been segmented and used in a different context for different purposes in post-Mao China. A wedding, as the transitional life ritual in everyday life, is still performed in the traditional Confucian way. The traditional meaning of the wedding is expressed in the act of offering sacrifices to the ancestors and the chanting of Miao songs throughout the wedding.

To explore diversified uses of ritual in the modern world in this chapter, we selected the ritual of 'obstruction of songs' in the present practice of the traditional wedding and the appropriation of it in a tourism context. In the contemporary practice of traditional wedding in the life domain, the antiphonal songs chanted in the obstruction ritual in the traditional wedding ceremony construct a dialogue between the bride's *Geniang* and the groom's *Geshi*. The two sides of the chanters' dialogue revolve around the rituals in the initial meeting, compliments to others, self-humility and blessings for the new couple. Unless the answers chanted in the songs are satisfactory, the obstruction will not come to an end. The improvised and fluid content of their antiphonal songs is woven in an attempt to initiate a good relationship between the two families in a ritual way.

In comparison, the obstruction of songs in a tourism context appropriates the genre of the antiphonal songs without taking in its content. The content of the songs chanted by the tourists are randomly selected without considering the meaning of the song in front of the Miao girls. It can be irrelevant what the Miao girls are chanting. According to Cohen (1988), old meanings of ritual do not thereby necessarily disappear in tourism, but may remain silent on a different level. As a response to Cohen, our case shows that old meanings can be replaced by new ones without affecting the communicative function and relationship-building effect of the traditional ritual. The genre of the ritual of obstruction can embrace any songs, regardless of their semantic content. Either meaningful or meaningless in the communication, the ritual of obstruction still constructs a joyous and jovial atmosphere for the further interaction between the tourists and the Miao.

As a welcoming ritual for the two sides to meet for the first time, the ritual of obstruction in the wedding context and the tourism context shares some similarities as well. In either context, this ritual is to establish a relaxed and friendly relationship between the two who are to establish some relationship for the first time. The content of the antiphonal songs are mostly based on the chanters' own repertoire. And the ritual of obstruction at the gate, either for the locals in the wedding or for the tourists, has always involved a continuous process of social recognition, imagination and construction of Miao culture and identity.

Ultimately, this chapter presents the transforming interpretations of ritual from early modern China to contemporary China, appreciating the messiness of the state with its internal contradictions (Oakes and Sutton 2010). Transcending the dichotomies of modernity and tradition, state and private, secular and sacred, the thick description and detailed analysis of ritual performances in a different context open up a space to understand ritual as a living organism that can accommodate transforming discourses in a flexible manner.

Acknowledgements

Many thanks to Anthony Buccitelli for his valuable comments, arguments and encouragement.

Unless otherwise noted, all translations presented in this chapter were done by the authors.

References

Cohen, E. (1988) 'Authenticity and commoditization in tourism', *Annals of Tourism Research*, 15(3), 371–386.

Ebrey, P. (1991) *A Twelfth-Century Chinese Manual for the Performance of Cappings, Weddings, Funerals, and Ancestral Rites*, Princeton, NJ: Princeton University Press.

Gernet, J. (1985) *China and the Christian Impact*, trans. J. Lloyd, Cambridge: Cambridge University Press.

Hall, D. and Ames, R. (1998) *Thinking from the Han: Self, truth, and transcendence in Chinese and Western culture*, Albany, NY: State University of New York Press.

Hostetler, L. (2000) 'Qing connections to the early modern world: Ethnography and cartography in eighteenth-century China', *Modern Asian Studies*, 34(3), 623–662.

Huang, W.H. (2012) 'West Hunan intangible cultural heritage project arrangement and protection research', *Journal of Central South University*, 18(3), 171–176.

Hu, J. (2011) *Chinese Confucian History: Volume of modern China*, Beijing: Peking University Press.

Kinkley, J. (1987) *The Odyssey of Shen Congwen*, Stanford, CA: Stanford University Press.

Legge, J. (trans.) (1885) *Sacred Books of the East*. Online: http://ctext.org/liji/hun-yi?searchu=two%20surnames&searchmode=showall#result (accessed 15 December 2013).

Ling, C.S. and Rui, Y.F. (2003) *An Ethnographic Report on the Miao People in West Hunan Area*, Beijing: The Ethnic Publishing House (first published 1940).

Ministry of Culture of the People's Republic of China (2013) *Tujia and Miao Cultural Ecological Preservation Area in Wuling Mountainous Area*. Online: www.ccnt.gov.

cn/sjzz/shwhs_sjzz/shwhs_ssmzwhjs/201312/t20131210_424740.htm   (accessed   15 December 2013).

Oakes, T. (1993) 'The cultural space of modernity: Ethnic tourism and place identity in China', *Environment and Planning D: Society and Space*, 11, 47–66.

Oakes, T. and Sutton, D. (eds) (2010) *Faiths on Display: Religion, tourism, and the Chinese state*, Lanham, MD: Rowman & Littlefield.

Peng, Z.R. (2008) *Heritage: Rethinking and interpretation*, Kunming: Yunnan Education Publisher.

Rawski, E. (2001) *The Last Emperors: A social history of Qing imperial institutions*, Berkeley: University of California Press.

Schein, L. (2000) *Minority Rules: The Miao and the feminine in China's cultural politics*, Durham, NC: Duke University Press.

Wang *et al.* (2013) *Study on West Hunan Minority Ethnic Intangible Cultural Heritage Protection and Exploitation*. Online: www.mzb.com.cn/html/Home/report/447559-1. htm (accessed 15 December 2013).

Wood, R. (1984) 'Ethnic tourism, the state, and cultural change in Southeast Asia', *Annals of Tourism Research*, 11, 353–374.

Wu, Z.J. and Hu, M.X. (2010) 'Ritual hermeneutics as the source of meaning: Interpreting the fabric of Chinese culture', *China Media Research*, 6(2), 104–113.

Yu, H. (2013) *Interweaving Ritual Meanings in Gouliang Miao Village*, dissertation, Zhejiang University.

Zhao, Y.Y. (2008) *Fear, Tourism and Cultural Reproduction: The opening course of the Miao people in Shanjiang Western Hunan*, Lanzhou: Gansu People Publishing House.

5 Re-creation of traditional ritual into festival

The case of the Kangnung Danoje festival in South Korea

Sunny Lee and Aise Kim

Introduction

In many cultures festivals are closely associated with religion and rituals pre-scribed by the traditions of the community (Getz 2010). Rituals typically involve special gestures and words, performance of special music, songs or dances, pro-cessions, manipulation of certain objects, use of special costumes and consump-tion of particular food or drink with a special meaning or history. Some of these activities are exclusively and privately performed but in many cases the ritual involves community members and guests sharing sacred and spiritual experi-ences and these naturally take on the character of an event. They may include *rituals of affliction*, performed to placate or exorcise preternatural beings or forces believed to have afflicted community members with illness, bad luck, gynaecological troubles, severe physical injuries and the like (Turner 1973).

In the modern world, many traditional ritual performances such as rites of affliction are re-created into a form of touristified cultural festival that is used for tourism purposes. These events are religious and traditional in origin or theme, and incorporate rituals into event programming, but also include non-ritual or non-tradition-related activities to attract not only people who seek sacred and cultural experiences related to the particular ritual in the community, but also non-local visitors who are looking for secular festival experiences to enjoy.

Such original rituals that form part of a community's traditional culture are becoming commoditised *cultures on display* as theatrical ritual-like perform-ances at touristified cultural festivals. One criticism is that through this process they lose a sense of their true and original meaning. Authenticity and commodi-fication have been, therefore, issues of concern with respect to such tourism development, particularly cultural tourism. Tourism development has been viewed as a destroyer of culture as it has been argued that tourism development turns culture into a commodity, packaged and sold to tourists, resulting in a loss of authenticity. Although there are numerous discussions about how mass tourism and tourism development negatively impact on traditional cultures, it has also been argued that traditional cultures can be preserved through tourism development (Esman 1984; McKean 1973; Xie 2003) and cultural reproduction in festival settings (McCabe 2006; Quinn 2005).

This chapter aims to illustrate how traditional rituals are re-created into a form of cultural festival that is being adopted for tourism purposes, using the case of Kangnung Danoje festival in South Korea (hereafter Korea). The chapter outlines the key processes involved in the re-creation of a traditional ritual into a cultural festival and discusses how such re-creation generates new meanings for culture and community in a modern society using the concept of *cultural involution*.

The Kangnung Danoje festival

The annual Kangnung Danoje festival is a traditional local ritual festival held in the town of Kangnung, situated east of the Taebaek mountain range on the Korean peninsula, to celebrate Dano on the fifth day of May in the lunar calendar, one of the three major national holidays in Korea. This festival is rooted in traditional purification and shamanistic rituals, Danoje, praying to the mountain deities and tutelary deities and asking to remain unaffected by potential natural disasters and to keep residents peaceful and prosperous (Jeong and Santos 2004). Although there are a number of Danoje rituals held in different regions in Korea, the Danoje ritual in Kangnung is the most symbolic among them, and has been designated as important intangible cultural heritage in Korea, added to the UNESCO (United Nations Educational, Scientific and Cultural Organization) Representative List of the Intangible Cultural Heritage of Humanity in 2005.

The history of the Kangnung Danoje festival is not clearly recorded, but it is thought that it started about 2,000 years ago, and was established into its current format in 1966 (Jeong and Santos 2004); that is, a 'touristified' cultural festival format. The process of re-creation of a traditional ritual festival for local residents into a touristified cultural festival involves three main aspects, as shown in Figure 5.1: the people involved (key stakeholders of festival), the festival activity/programme and the scope of the festival.

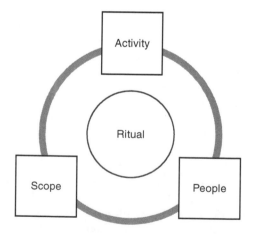

Figure 5.1 The process of re-creation of a traditional ritual into a touristified cultural festival.

People: key stakeholders of the festival

The traditional Kangnung Danoje festival was a local festival for residents to attain the community's continuing blessing. Rites involved in the traditional festival were performed by local shamans with local residents assembled at the Taebaek Mountains and the presentation of offerings (foods) to village guardian spirits who live in the mountain. Shamans worshipped and danced during the rites to make the guardian spirits happy so they would take care of local residents and provide a suitable climate for a year. After the rites, the local people shared foods and entertainment such as traditional games and activities. Traditionally, the festival was organised by local people voluntarily for their own benefits and desires without a structured programme or organisation.

Today the festival involves a mixed group of people including locals, sponsors and tourists. It has become an eight-day-long festival that attracts more than one million non-local visitors. Due to its large size, a festival committee organises and manages the festival, and the Kangnung City Council has also become involved as a festival organiser. The festival also attracts corporate sponsorship for financial and in-kind support. The festival creates entertainment for visitors by offering dance, music and touristified rites that are a representation of traditional Danoje rites without the original meanings. Local and national media actively promote the festival to attract non-local visitors by depicting it as a cultural festival as well as a family-oriented festival, a getaway opportunity from the cities, and associate it with other tourism attractions near Kangnung. Although different stakeholders may have different interests and try to use the festival for their own benefit, sustaining the Danoje tradition and rituals is central to their involvement as a key stakeholder.

Festival activity/programme

The traditional Kangnung Danoje festival includes rites of purification at a mountain and river aimed at mitigating spirits that may inflict misfortune on local residents and providing offerings to the guardian spirits of villages. It includes a parade to shepherd the guardian spirits to the villages, and other traditional cultural activities that are also for cleaning or the chasing away of evil such as bathing in water infused with calamus (sweet flag), which was believed to cast out evil spirits, so they could be healthy for a year. These traditional activities still remain in the current festival, but today it includes more than these traditional ritual-related activities.

The festival offers a diverse ritual-related programme that includes ritual performances and exorcisms encompassing traditional folk songs and traditional cultural activities, but it no longer has the original meanings of these rites. The festival still provides visitors opportunities to participate in traditional recreational activities that are not commonly practised in daily life, such as *Ssireum* (Korean wrestling) and *Neolttwigi* (Korean jumping game similar to see-sawing), and observe traditional rites performed in the public space that do not necessarily contain the original meaning of the rites. However, it also offers some spectacle-oriented and entertaining activities that are not related to Danoje, such as dance competitions, an outdoor market and other contemporary performances such as pop culture, hip-hop dance and rap music in order to attract a large number and broad range of interstate or international visitors.

Scope of the festival

Different stages of cultural presentation (e.g. front-stage and back-stage) are arranged in the Kangnung Danoje festival in terms of different types of settings, time and performance based on the intended audience. The notion of front-stage and back-stage in the presentation of culture has been developed and used in the context of *staged* authenticity research (Connell 2007; MacCannell 1976). The front-stage is where a host meets guests and the patron interacts with service providers, and could be seen as a *false reality* for show and performance, while the back-stage is the *real reality* for performers. Providing access to the front-stage of a cultural presentation becomes as important as the back-stage today in the context of the experience economy (Pine and Gilmore 1999), in order for visitors to have unique, memorable and engaging experiences associated with a particular culture, ritual or cultural festival. In the case of today's Kangnung Danoje festival, there are a few traditional rites that are specifically performed by local shamans in a private place, the back-stage for the locals, while most of the other events, such as a parade, are arranged in a public place (e.g. the Dano market and the river side) within the city that could be seen as the front-stage for a broad range of tourists (Jeong and Santos 2004).

The traditional Danoje rites are performed at a holy site in the mountains that is not known to tourists and is not open for tourists in order to protect the local nature of Confucian symbolic and ritual identity. Those rites that are only for local residents follow the traditional way of Danoje rites before the actual festival begins, and contain the original meaning of the rites. For the front-stage of the festival, non-local shamans and tourists are invited to perform the opening ceremony (i.e. a parade) and other traditional performances at the public place that are not holy rites, but rather amusing attractions for tourists (Jeong and Santos 2004). In particular, the opening ceremony of the festival marks an important symbolic transition between the private, sacred ceremonies and the public festival, the transferring of a holy spirit from the private sacred temples to a ceremonial public place (Jeong and Santos 2004). Falassi (1987) conceptualises opening ceremonies as the rite of valorisation that opens the festival and modifies the daily function and meaning of time and space. The opening ceremony of today's Kangnung Danoje festival particularly realigns the scope of the festival, in a transferral from the authentic back-stage of ritual to the front-stage touristified festival.

It seems that the Kangnung Danoje festival controls the symbolic boundaries of ritual performance and spatial division that are drawn by the local group in order to maintain control over the identity of the festival and sense of place it creates. Such symbolic boundaries of the festival help the local community to be strict about keeping the authentic traditions from commodification, although the public performances of rituals have received some criticism because of their closeness to the authentic rites.

Discussion: cultural involution

Clearly, such a shift from local ritual to spectacle or festival has led to criticism about the loss of certain traditional elements of the ritual. Nevertheless, the social significance of this festival cannot be underestimated as it plays an important role in generating new meanings of the culture and community (Cole 2007). The phenomenon of the re-creation of traditional cultures or rituals into commodified or touristified festival settings has been seen as another form of cultural expression and presentation that creates new meanings. Shepherd (2002) argues that it is more important to look at how people create meanings through cultural commodification rather than examine what has been commodified and compare it with cultural authenticity. Shepherd (2002) sees cultural commodification as a social fact in modern society, so that the management of commodification is needed to create the desired meanings, rather than not accepting cultural commodification at all.

The concept of *cultural involution* has been used to understand culture preservation within the development of tourism, with the argument that instead of development being conceptualised as the pollution of authentic ethnic cultures, it is fully incorporated within local culture and potentially used to preserve cultures with new or additional meanings (McKean 1973). Although the original meaning of cultures can be reshaped by tourism development and commodification, as shown in the case of Dragon Boat Races (McCartney and Osti 2007), the touristified cultural presentation can be another form of cultural expression that generates new meanings of culture and community (Xie 2003). Many tourism research studies have been undertaken to understand the positive power of the commodification of cultures, and the new meanings that tourism development injects into cultures and communities, using a range of diverse cases from traditional dance (Henry 2000; Magowan 2000; Xie 2003) to a specific community (Croes *et al.* 2013), which demonstrate a process of cultural involution. Through examining the key literature relevant to cultural involution, a range of cultural involution events are identified as occurring at three different levels: individual, community and societal levels, and these are also found in the case of the Kangnung Danoje festival. The summary of these processes of cultural involution at different levels is presented in Table 5.1.

Individual level of cultural involution

First, cultural involution occurs at the individual level by providing new meanings to individuals including local people who present the culture, and others who are local people but not directly involved in the activities, for example the

Table 5.1 The level of cultural involution

Levels	Cultural involution
Individual level	• Cultural transmission • A revival of individual interest in traditional culture • Material benefits
Community level	• A sense of community (social cohesion/local pride) • Community identity
Societal level	• Ongoing dialogue with the general public (through promoting and recapturing the culture) • An increased public interest in traditional culture and issues related to the meanings and effects of the culture • Cultural education

local younger generations. It has been argued that tourism development generates individuals' interest in traditional culture that ultimately promotes the continuation of culture (Cole 2007). It is also identified that cultural tourism development provides the local actors involved in the tourism initiatives with access to financial benefits that are used to preserve culture. For example, Henry (2000) argues that Aboriginal dances, presented at a festival, theatre and museum, support the continuity of cultural transmission to the younger generations by showcasing it to their young dancers and displaying cultural vitality. It also found that tourism provides financial resources to create jobs (Xie 2003) and enhances the quality of life of residents (Croes, Lee & Olson 2013), and preserves the truly authentic back-stage elements of the real original culture for locals (McKean 1973).

In the case of the Kangnung Danoje festival, local young people are motivated to maintain and inherit the community's traditional culture, Danoje ritual, as they are naturally exposed to their traditional culture from their early years through the touristified festival and perceive their traditional culture as fun and interesting, rather than old or boring. The Danoje rites, praying to the mountain deities and tutelary deities to keep residents peaceful and prosperous, in particular, can be seen as non-rational or 'unscientific' acts by the younger generation in a modern society. The festival that attracts a huge number of tourists helps them realise the value of their traditional culture and see the preservation of culture as an enjoyable task, not as a tedious duty that they need to do as a local. Although the festival is a free event for tourists, the material benefits provided by tourists to local businesses and people involved are obvious, given that tourists spend money not only on food and beverages at the festival, but also to have their personal prayers incorporated into the rituals. The financial resources created by the festival, particularly for the preservation of the back-stage of culture, have not been clearly identified, but it could be argued that such tourism development using traditional rituals generates local people's interest in their culture.

Community level of cultural involution

At the community level, the touristified festival built on traditional rituals continues to assert a sense of community identity, internally and externally. The community can strengthen its identity internally by redefining culture, and externally by presenting their culture to external viewers.

The traditional culture presented in the form of commodification can still strengthen the local sense of community through promoting social cohesion and bonds by practising rituals. Carnegie and McCabe (2008) argue that due to the current times of great change, the present cannot be linked to the past through the continuity of lifestyle. Thus, new creations of cultural representation about the past in the present are helpful to reaffirm and re-establish community identity and to remind locals of the role of traditional culture in shaping the present and creating who they are. Hicks (2010) supports this view, claiming that a community can maintain its cohesion by collectively performing rituals. McCabe (2006) points out that a sense of place can be created through not only the practice of a historical festival, but also in a community's effort to continue the festival. McCabe (2006) also comments that authenticity is not the issue, but a sense of belonging and a sense of ownership are more important for community. Community rituals, even in a re-created form in a modern society, thus provide individuals with the feeling they are part of a community, and such a feeling can strengthen the bonds uniting individuals.

A community could also build identity through presenting traditions to an external audience. Henry (2000) highlights the importance of cultural performance or representation for strengthening community identity, claiming that identities are not given but are made through social action such as cultural performances. It could be powerful particularly when the cultural performance or representation continuously occurs in specific locations (Jeong and Santos 2004). The re-creation or representation of tradition can be seen as a social action that shows the locality of the community (Crain 1998) and creates a symbolic association between a place, and stories or traditions connected with the past and the local people (Bird 2002), in turn strengthening community identity.

The touristified Kangnung Danoje festival mainly involves profane festival activities based on a theme of Danoje rituals, but it still presents community identity through a symbolic presentation associated with traditional rites and the place of Kangnung. Local people who are not directly involved in the back-stage of authentic Danoje rites can still feel a sense of community; they are part of the Kangnung community. Externally, the community re-establishes its identity associated with Danoje rituals through putting on the festival every year, attracting media attention and tourists. Without the recognition of the Danoje rituals and Kangnung's community identity connected to the rituals by external people, the rituals and tradition could disappear due to acculturation (Esman 1984) and the community could lose its cultural and social sustainability.

Societal level of cultural involution

Lastly, cultural involution has also been recognised at the societal level. It has been discussed in the literature that tourism development enables locals and non-locals to engage more interactively and tangibly with traditional cultures (Carnegie and McCabe 2008; Costa 2002). A touristified cultural representation has therefore been seen as an effective vehicle for ongoing dialogue with a broader society and cross-cultural understanding (Davies 2011; Xie 2003) through promoting and recapturing the culture. Costa (2002) supports this function of cultural festivals, describing a traditional cultural festival as a field of interaction between tradition and modernity, establishing an expressive and emotional collective dialogue of recognition with the public.

It is also identified that a cultural representation is helpful to raise public interest in traditional culture and issues related to the community or culture. For instance, Magowan (2000) claims that indigenous dance performed in non-ritual settings and/or presented as a national spectacle of Australia can be seen as a new process of indigenous identity formation and as a performative dialogue with the nation, as well as one means by which reconciliation can be manifested between indigenous and non-indigenous performers and spectators.

The cultural involution of the Kangnung Danoje festival also occurs at the societal level as a communication channel about traditional culture to an external audience. The traditional Kangnung Danoje rituals were meaningful enough to maintain and preserve and their cultural value has been recognised by non-locals. The touristified Kangnung Danoje festival has been additionally helpful to create public awareness about the significant meanings of rituals and its impact issues (e.g. political and socio-cultural agenda) through the enormous media attention on the festival, which results in the increased public interest and attachment to the traditional culture after experiencing the festival. For example, when the Korean government tried to have the Kangnung Danoje festival and rituals recognised on the UNESCO Representative List of the Intangible Cultural Heritage of Humanity, there was a claim by China that the Danoje rituals originated in China. Although after UNESCO's review on the Danoje rituals, Korea's Kangnung Danoje festival was added to the list in 2005, the development of the festival sparking renewed discussion about the origin of the Danoje rituals. It received enormous support and attention from the general public at a national level. The re-creation of rituals into a festival reminded a broader society beyond the local community of the value of tradition and the importance of preserving and practising these traditions.

Moreover, Dano is one of the three major national holidays in Korea, together with Lunar New Year's Day (commonly known as Chinese New Year's Day) and Korean Thanksgiving Day (*Chuseok* in Korean), which are associated with traditional rituals. As Danoje rituals only occurred at a specific location associated with a myth, which distinguishes it from the other two national holidays, it is difficult for everyone in Korea to celebrate, practise or appreciate Dano. The annual Kangnung Danoje festival is, therefore, meaningful in offering an educational opportunity for non-locals to learn more about Korean traditional rituals and culture.

Conclusion

This chapter provides an analytical perspective on the process of cultural involution through examining the case of the Kangnung Danoje festival in Korea. The Kangnung Danoje festival is rooted in the Korean traditional ritual of affliction, and re-created into a form of touristified cultural festival incorporating ritual and non-ritual activities. This chapter has critically examined the process of the re-creation of the traditional Kangnung Danoje ritual into a touristified cultural festival, particularly focusing on three aspects of the festival – the people involved (key stakeholders of festival), the festival activity/programme and the scope of festival.

Through this review, cultural involution occurring at three levels was identified – individual, community and societal levels. This demonstrates that a re-created ritual in a form of a touristified festival generates new meanings to the tradition, which helps to preserve the culture, although the original meanings of the ritual might be reshaped. Cultural involution occurs at the individual level in the form of supporting cultural transmission, reviving local interest in traditional culture and providing local access to financial resources. At the community level, cultural involution occurs to re-establish and strengthen the local sense of community and build a strong community identity associated with the traditional culture that is recognised by non-locals. Cultural involution at the societal level occurs through providing the regional culture and community with a communication channel for cultural education, and a revival of public interest in traditional cultures and related issues.

These cultural involutions are particularly important for a traditional ritual of affliction like the Kangnung Danoje festival, as the original meaning and aim of the ritual could not be fully understood by a new generation in a context of modern society and, in turn, it could be discontinued and disappear. Re-creation of traditional ritual through a festival offers a stage for communities and the general public to experience and engage with the traditional ritual so that they can respect the practices of the past and better understand the original meaning attached to the ritual.

It was also identified from the case of the Kangnung Danoje festival that if appropriate control and management are implemented, the authentic back-stage elements of ritual can be practised with the original meanings, and can benefit from the front-stage touristified festival. Authenticity and commodification are common concerns for such cultural tourism development, and many studies have been conducted to identity the true authentic cultural tourism experiences and to minimise the extent of cultural commodification. It was suggested in this chapter that the commodification of culture, however, is a social fact in a modern society (Shepherd 2002), so the re-creation of culture needs to be carefully packaged (Quinn 2003). Further research on suitable control and management of cultural tourism development is essential to understand how commodification has helped to preserve culture, how it continues to help and how it can be better shaped to create more valuable benefits and meanings at the individual, community and societal level.

References

Bird, S.E. (2002) 'It makes sense to us: Cultural identity in local legends of place', *Journal of Contemporary Ethnography*, 31(5), 519–547.

Carnegie, E. and McCabe, S. (2008) 'Re-enactment events and tourism: Meaning, authenticity and identity', *Current Issues in Tourism*, 11(4), 349–368.

Cole, S. (2007) 'Beyond authenticity and commodification', *Annals of Tourism Research*, 34(4), 943–960.

Connell, J. (2007) 'The continuity of custom? Tourist perceptions of authenticity in Yakel Village, Tanna, Vanuatu', *Journal of Tourism and Cultural Change*, 5(2), 71–86.

Costa, X. (2002) 'Festive traditions in modernity: The public sphere of the festival of the "Fallas" in Valencia (Spain)', *The Sociological Review*, 50(4), 482–504.

Crain, M.M. (1998) 'Reimaging identity, cultural production and locality under transnationalism', in F. Hughes-Freeland and M.M. Crain (eds), *Recasting Ritual: Performance, media, identity* (pp. 135–160), London: Routledge.

Croes, R., Lee, S.H. and Olson, E.D. (2013) 'Authenticity in tourism in small island destinations: A local perspective', *Journal of Tourism and Cultural Change*, 11(1–2), 1–20.

Davies, K. (2011) 'Cultural events as a catalyst for increased intercultural communication and understanding', *Journal of Tourism and Peace Research*, 2(1), 70–79.

Esman, M.R. (1984) 'Tourism as ethnic preservation: The Cajuns of Louisiana', *Annals of Tourism Research*, 11(3), 451–467.

Falassi, A. (1987) 'Festival: Definition and morphology', in A. Falassi (ed.), *Time out of Time: Essays on the festival* (pp. 1–10), Albuquerque: University of New Mexico Press.

Getz, D. (2010) 'The nature and scope of festival studies', *International Journal of Event Management Research*, 5(1), 1–47.

Henry, R. (2000) 'Dancing into being: The Tjapukai Aboriginal Cultural Park and the Laura Dance Festival', *The Australian Journal of Anthropology*, 11(2), 322–332.

Hicks, D. (2010) *Ritual and Belief: Readings in the anthropology of religion*, Lanham, MD: AltaMira Press.

Jeong, S. and Santos, C.A. (2004) 'Cultural politics and contested place identity', *Annals of Tourism Research*, 31(3), 640–656.

McCabe, S. (2006) 'The making of community identity through historic festive practice: The case of Ashbourne Royal Shrovetide Football', in D. Picard and M. Robinson (eds), *Festivals, Tourism and Social Change: Remaking worlds* (pp. 99–118), Clevedon: Channel View.

MacCannell, D. (1976) *The Tourist: A new theory of the leisure class*, New York: Schocken.

McCartney, G. and Osti, L. (2007) 'From cultural events to sport events: A case study of cultural authenticity in the Dragon Boat Races', *Journal of Sport and Tourism*, 12(1), 25–40.

McKean, P. (1973) *Cultural Involution: Tourists, Balinese, and the process of modernization in an anthropological perspective*, PhD thesis, Brown University, USA.

Magowan, F. (2000) 'Dancing with a difference: Reconfiguring the poetic politics of Aboriginal ritual as national spectacle', *The Australian Journal of Anthropology*, 11(2), 308–321.

Pine, B.J. and Gilmore, J.H. (1999) *The Experience Economy: Work is theatre and every business a stage*, Boston MA: Harvard Business School Press.

Quinn, B. (2003) 'Symbols, practices and myth-making: Cultural perspectives on the Wexford Festival Opera', *Tourism Geographies*, 5(3), 329–349.

Quinn, B. (2005) 'Changing festival places: Insights from Galway', *Social and Cultural Geography*, 6(2), 237–252.

Shepherd, R. (2002) 'Commodification, culture and tourism', *Tourist Studies*, 2(2), 183–201.

Turner, V.W. (1973) 'Symbols in African ritual', *Science*, 179(4078), 1100–1105.

Xie, P.F. (2003) 'The bamboo-beating dance in Hainan, China: Authenticity and commodification', *Journal of Sustainable Tourism*, 11(1), 5–16.

6 Wishing you good health, prosperity and happiness

Exploring the rituals and traditions of Chinese New Year

Leanne White and Daniel Leung

Introduction

Chinese New Year rituals and traditions are celebrated annually by Chinese communities around the world. This 'festival of the year', with its emphasis on renewal and a fresh start, is widely acknowledged as the most important festivity in the traditional Chinese calendar with a history that dates back centuries. Each year Chinese communities around the world joyfully exchange the signature greeting in the customary manner – Kung Hei Fat Choi!

As a time to honour deities and ancestors, Chinese New Year is accompanied by various rituals, traditions, customs and taboos. Some of them are carryovers from the ancient practices of Taoism, Confucianism and Buddhism (Bennett 1986). According to Yeung and Yee (2010), these traditions originated during the early Xia Dynasty (twenty-first to sixteenth centuries BCE) and have persisted over time. The enduring rituals and traditions in the Chinese community can be explained by two key thoughts from Confucianism. As the most influential way of thinking in the Chinese community, Confucianism advocates that certain virtues (namely propriety, humanity, righteousness, wisdom and faithfulness) are essential for ensuring a stable and orderly society (Martinsons 1996). In terms of propriety, for example, conforming to the customs and traditions put in place by ancestors is important for sustaining a stable and orderly society (Martinsons 1996). As such, while many modern Chinese may not necessarily believe in all of the traditional rituals, many are still performed by families before and during the celebration.

As with many traditions, the sometimes curious rituals of Chinese New Year incorporate complicated historical antecedents that have specific cultural implications. While regional customs and traditions vary somewhat throughout the world, similar symbolic meanings are shared among some common rituals or practices throughout the celebration such as: diligent cleaning of the house to sweep away any bad luck from the preceding year; the displaying of red decorations on doors and windows; the hanging of red lanterns; a family feast (often consisting of fish, pork, chicken, duck, dumplings and sticky cake) attended by all family members; red fireworks and firecrackers to ward off evil spirits; the giving of red envelopes containing money to junior members of the family and the exchanging of small gifts among friends as a form of blessing; receiving a haircut and the wearing of new clothes and shoes to symbolise a new start; and lion and dragon dances that are thought to bring rain and good luck.

In this chapter we consider the role of Chinese New Year in sustaining social cohesion in the Chinese community – an area that has received limited scholarly attention to date. Drawing on a thorough examination of these rituals, this chapter explores the concepts in a holistic manner and examines how particular rituals built on tradition have helped develop distinctive identities and ways of thinking for those who engage in these sometimes peculiar rituals.

Falassi argues that festivals modify our normal sense of time with various ritualistic movements that are carried out from the beginning to the end of the festival. This modification creates a so-called 'time out of time' – with a respectfully observed temporal dimension devoted to each key activity (Falassi 1987: 4). The Chinese New Year celebrations indeed place our *normal* sense of time in something of a holding pattern while festival (*atypical*) time is taken to focus on others – particularly the family. Festivals usually consist of a number of ritual acts or rites. The rites that form key functions in the Chinese New Year festival are: the rites of purification, rites of conspicuous display, rites of conspicuous consumption and rites of exchange (Falassi 1987). Having introduced our approach in this chapter, some further background on this festival that is so critical to Chinese identity will now be explored.

Background

Chinese New Year, also known as the Lunar New Year or the Spring Festival, is a traditional festival that marks the end of winter and welcomes the spring (and a good harvest). Yeung and Yee (2010) argue that the celebration became more of a tradition from the Han Dynasty (206 BCE–220 CE). Although considered a traditional Chinese festival, it is popularly celebrated in Asian and non-Asian countries including Hong Kong, Taiwan, Singapore, Thailand, Malaysia, Australia, the United Kingdom and the United States.

The exact date of the celebration differs each year as the event is calculated by the Lunisolar calendar as opposed to the Gregorian calendar. However, it normally begins between late January and the middle of February. For instance, the first day of Chinese New Year in 2013 was 10 February, whereas the corresponding day in 2014 was 31 January. Despite the varied commencement date, festivities generally run from Chinese New Year's Eve – the last day of the last month of the Lunisolar calendar, to the Lantern Festival, which is celebrated on the fifteenth day. While this is the longest festival in the Chinese calendar, the first three days are the main focus of the celebration.

Each Chinese New Year is named in honour of one of 12 Chinese symbolic creatures. Depending on the year of our birth, the sages of Chinese astrology proposed that we are governed by one of the 12 zodiac (animals). For example, people who are born in the years 1925, 1937, 1949, 1961, 1973, 1985, 1997 and 2009 are born in the Year of the Ox. It is thought that the all-important order of the animals was decided by the Jade Emperor (ruler of Heaven and Earth). He organised a race across a river where the rat, having crouched on the back of an ox, then jumped across to the river bank at the last moment, winning the race (Wang 2010).

Chinese believe that their personality traits, along with their physical and mental attributes, are reflected in the horoscope. Those born in the Year of the Rat are said to be charming and smart with lots of friends; the ox is thought to be dependable, calm and honest; tigers are brave, determined and generous; rabbits are happy, gifted, thoughtful and make the best friends; dragons are leaders who like to be among the action; snakes are wise and charming; horses are independent, popular and hardworking; goats (sometimes referred to as rams) are artistic and caring; monkeys are creative, successful and mischievous; roosters are clever and brave; dogs are intelligent, kind and loyal; while pigs are said to be popular and tolerant (Chambers 1997). Hence, understanding the 12 animals (six wild and six domestic – yin and yang) of the Chinese zodiac apparently helps people understand the personality and character of others.

The Chinese also share a superstitious belief that a person may encounter more obstacles if the zodiac of the year in which they were born clashes with the current year. For instance, China experienced a turbulent year in 2008 with some political upheaval and natural disasters – the Tibetan unrest and the Sichuan earthquake. Some feng shui masters argued that these events were caused as a result of the incompatibility between the Chinese animal for that year (the horse) and the birth year of the Chinese leader, as Hu Jintao was born in 1942 and his affiliated zodiac sign is the rat. As the compatibility with the zodiac of the year may affect one's fortune throughout the year, checking the Chinese zodiac for the forthcoming year is a 'must-do' task in most families prior to each celebration. This example provides a glimpse into the strong belief in astrology and the highly superstitious nature of the Chinese.

Our chapter aims to explore some of the ways in which Chinese heritage is imagined and celebrated. By examining some of the rituals surrounding this time of the year, we can rethink our understanding and awareness of Chinese New Year's significant heritage and tradition. For the individual celebrating the festival, heritage becomes somehow embodied and personified by their own experiences and those of others – along with the many photographs of the experiences that may be taken and shared. If we understand heritage as a process that constructs meaning about the past, then the construction of the related rituals and traditions is illustrative of this process. It is, essentially, a construction of Chinese heritage based on stories, memories, reports and photographs that have been documented and passed down through the ages by family and friends. Having outlined some background information, a variety of rituals that take place in the time leading up to Chinese New Year will now be explored.

Rituals leading up to Chinese New Year

After China adopted economic reform and opened its doors to the outside world in 1978, the Chinese economy began to grow at a significant rate. Since the

Chinese government constantly encourages people to move to cities for supporting its continuous economic growth, more people migrate to urban areas (*South China Morning Post* 2013). Though members of most Chinese families are now dispersed and settled in different territories, this geographical limitation has limited impact on people's interest and passion to celebrate the Chinese New Year with their family. Before the beginning of every Chinese New Year, adults who live away from home travel back to their home towns for family reunions. The Chinese government estimated that more than 3.4 billion individual journeys were made during the festival in 2013 (Chen 2013). Despite the advancement of communication technologies, many Chinese people believe that attending family reunions and personally catching up with older family members at this time of year is important. The mass migration of people for the celebrations reveals the cohesive function of the festival.

Preparations for Chinese New Year festivities begin well in advance of the actual date of the holiday. As the festival signifies the passing of the old year, people normally purchase new clothes, new shoes and get their hair cut to symbolise a fresh start. As one might expect, organisations such as shoe manufacturers and retailers are keen to capitalise on the annual tradition (see Figure 6.1). Importantly, families usually give their home a thorough spring cleaning. In Chinese society, a spring clean at this time is not merely an excuse for making the home clean and tidy. The cleaning represents sweeping away any ill fortune

Figure 6.1 Shoe sales generally increase prior to Chinese New Year (source: L. White).

from the preceding year and preparing the home for future good luck. Hence, a thorough cleaning is conducted for ushering out the old and welcoming in the new. For example, all linen such as bed covers, sheets and pillow cases are washed.

For families who follow the philosophy of Buddhism or Taoism, home altars and statues are meticulously cleaned. The old decorations on the altars are generally replaced with new ones. After the spring clean, all brooms and dust pans are put away so that the newly arrived good luck cannot be swept away. It is thought that any sweeping on New Year's Day would brush away good luck, and that scissors or knives used on this day would also snip and cut away the good luck. The teachings of feng shui (meaning wind and water) advocate that people living in a harmonious environment gain maximum inner peace, health and prosperity (Too 1996). Since a thorough spring clean can help create a clean and comfortable living environment for family well-being, the spring clean thus aligns with the principles of feng shui.

Following the methodical clean, the house is decorated with vases of plum or peach blossoms, narcissus flowers and tangerines. The ritual of selecting and decorating the house with these plants reflects the superstitious nature of the Chinese. These flowers and fruits are chosen due to their bright colours and also for the literal meaning of the Chinese characters of the words. For instance, the sound of the Chinese word for tangerine is similar to the Chinese word for prosperity. Flowers also represent abundance. Related superstitions include that if the narcissus flower blooms on Chinese New Year, extra wealth and good fortune will come to the family throughout the year. Some Chinese even believe that decorating the home with peach blossoms assists those looking for love, due to the association of the face of the potential beloved with the beauty of that particular flower. While peaches are a sign of longevity, oranges are purchased for good luck as they are thought to attract wealth.

In keeping with the theme of bright colours, banners with short poems and positive greetings, such as good luck, happiness, wealth and longevity, are displayed in and around the home in order to bring good luck and blessings (see Figure 6.3). Red and gold are the colours of good fortune in the eyes of Chinese (Lambert 2013). Hence, decorations are usually made of red and gold paper. The greetings of happy and uplifting messages are written in Chinese characters. Kung Hei Fat Choi, which literally means 'may you prosper in all your activities', is obviously one of the most common greetings found on decorations. Others such as xin nian kwai le (happy new year), tsao hai ching bao (bring money) and san tai kin hong (wishing you good health) are commonly used. Special poetic couplets that often describe a theme such as good luck or happiness are known as chun lian. If the sign 'fu' (prosperity) is displayed, it should be hung upside-down so that the good luck does not flow out. Some families also hang pictures of the Door Gods outside the front door. It is thought that these two gods (Qin Qiong and Yuchi Gong) serve to guard the house against any bad luck (Chambers 1997; Pirotta 2006). Traditionally, new decorations must be put up before Chinese New Year and remain displayed in the home for the first month. The decorations are usually taken down after the Lantern Festival.

Chinese New Year is a time for the family to reunite, enjoy each other's company and eat well. As a symbol of family solidarity, a reunion dinner is usually arranged prior to the New Year (see Figure 6.2). Being the principal event of Chinese New Year, the reunion dinner is comparable to a Christmas dinner in terms of significance. In general, families partake in eight or nine dishes because those numbers are considered lucky and also represent prosperity, longevity and good luck. The number four is considered unlucky because the word sounds like 'death' in Chinese. As such, it is a word that should not be uttered at this time. All cuisines prepared and eaten during the dinner have a special meaning as well. For example, in northern China, steamed dumplings (jiao zi) symbolise wealth and prosperity as their shape resembles a Chinese tael (a weight measure) and a money bag, while in southern China, a sticky cake or rice pudding (nian gao) is popular as it represents progress and continual improvement. A sea vegetable known as facai, often consumed with dried oysters, is another preferred dish. This is because the Chinese pronunciation of the word facai sounds like a phrase meaning 'to become wealthy', while dried oysters symbolise good business. A whole fish, representing abundance and togetherness, is also part of the reunion dinner menu. The ritual is that the fish should not be eaten completely during the dinner. The remainder of the fish is stored overnight to signify that the year will indeed reap a surplus.

Figure 6.2 The reunion dinner reinforces the strong family bonds of the Chinese (source: D. Leung).

The superstitious nature of the Chinese is also reflected by a number of religious rituals. Kiernan (2008) has described some religious customs that take place in families where Buddhism or Taoism is prevalent. For example, Taoists send the Kitchen God (Tsao-Wang – the observer of family functions) to heaven and report the family's activities to the Jade Emperor. In order to ensure the cooperation of the Kitchen God in providing a glowing reference to the Jade Emperor, Chinese families offer sweet cakes, lollies and sometimes smear honey on the lips of the statue of the god. The belief behind this act is that he would then only report sweet things about the family to the emperor. The Chinese recognise that there are both beneficial spirits (Shen) and evil spirits (Kuei). Equally, the negative forces in nature are the yin, while the positive forces are the yang. With the exception of just a few objects such as the sun, everything else is a combination of yin and yang (Hopfe and Woodward, 2012). When the two forces work in harmony, life is balanced.

What has effectively become a global media event for the people of China and the wider Chinese community around the world is the state-run Chinese Central TV's *Spring Festival Gala*. The four-hour media extravaganza has become compulsive viewing as many families tune in to watch the programme after their reunion dinner (Orgad 2012). At midnight on Chinese New Year's Eve, red firecrackers are normally lit at the entrance of the home (see Figure 6.3). The loud noise and the colour are thought to prevent evil spirits and bad

Figure 6.3 Red firecrackers herald the new year and ward off evil spirits (source: D. Leung).

luck from entering the house. Fireworks also serve as a noisy welcome to the new calendar year. It is important that the remains from the spent firecrackers are not cleaned up as the red paper represents good luck. As one might expect, the use of firecrackers can sometimes lead to accidents involving burns for the user. As a result, some governments have enacted laws that ban private fireworks displays.

Rituals during Chinese New Year

The first day of Chinese New Year is a time to honour ancestors and elders. Incense sticks (also known as joss sticks) are usually burnt when remembering those who have died. Traditionally, the order of the visits begins with the most senior member of the family or extended family. It is customary to visit the paternal family relatives first, followed by a visit to the maternal relatives on the second day. The order of visiting tends to both reflect the patriarchal nature of Chinese society and reinforces the accepted world view of social relationships and hierarchy. Chinese people typically wear new clothes from head to toe to symbolise a new beginning in the New Year. Newly cut hair should not be washed on New Year's Day as it is thought that any good luck would be washed straight down the drain. Any broken furniture is also discarded to avoid possible accidents as it is considered highly unlucky to break anything on the first day of the year (Pirotta 2006).

Clothing featuring the colour red is commonly worn throughout the Chinese New Year period for two reasons. First, red is the colour of joy. The Chinese pronunciation for the word red sounds like the word prosperous. Red is therefore regarded as an auspicious colour. Second, Chinese myths and legends feature a mythical beast (monster) called Nian who is known to attack at this time of year. The beast does not discriminate and can eat any creature – including small children. It is thought that that the beast was once scared away by a small child wearing red clothes. As a result of this myth and similar tales, the Chinese believe that red scares away evil spirits.

A glutinous rice cake (nian gao) is normally served to family members and guests in certain parts of China (see Figure 6.4). Lotus seeds and bright red melon seeds, symbolising fertility, are another signature snack during this time of year. The lotus is particularly significant as Buddha is normally depicted enthroned on a lotus in full bloom (Cooper 1992). Snacks such kumquat (prosperity), lychee nut (strong family relationships), melon (happiness and good health), lotus (fertility), coconut (togetherness) and peanuts (many sons) are eaten from a special tray known as a 'tray of togetherness' (Fox and Fox 2007). Because of their resemblance to gold bars and ingots in terms of the shape, spring rolls and dumplings are usually consumed as well.

Apart from eating traditional cuisine, the giving of red packets (envelopes) is another signature activity of Chinese New Year. Members of the family who are married normally give red packets containing money to junior family members. These red envelopes (lai-see hong bao) which contain 'lucky money' are given

Figure 6.4 Glutinous rice cakes symbolising aspiration are a popular treat (source: L. White).

as a form of blessing and to assist with the financial challenges to be faced in the year ahead. To express respect and appreciation to the giver of the packet, it is customary that children wish elders a happy and healthy life before accepting the gift. Should younger people ask for an envelope, elders would generally not turn down any request as it would mean that he or she would be out of luck during the forthcoming year. Apart from elders, business managers give red packets to employees for good luck, good health and wealth creation. In Chinese society, sending gifts can symbolise good luck for future research, a successful conclusion to an endeavour or simply returning a favour (Yau *et al.* 1999). Among those who run businesses, gifts are exchanged with business partners to represent the willingness to sustain a harmonious business relationship. This traditional ritual reinforces the significance of 'guanxi' (the special connection between two people whereby one prevails upon another for a favour) in Chinese culture.

In Chinese society, odd numbers are associated with the cash that is given for funerals. Hence, the amount of money in the red packet should be either even numbers or lucky numbers such as eight. The number eight is considered the luckiest as the word sounds similar to the Chinese word for 'wealth'. As the visual representation of 88 is similar to the characters for double joy, more eights are even better. When Australia's national airline advertised flights with the heading 'Celebrate the New Year with Qantas' in January 2013, return flights from Melbourne to Hong Kong were alluringly advertised for the lucky price of $888. At around the same time, Singapore Airlines advertised flights from Melbourne to Hong Kong for an almost as lucky $1088.

Along with the traditional family rituals outlined above, many people also actively partake in public events to celebrate the festival. For example, in Hong Kong, visiting the flower markets is a compulsory activity at this time of year. Along with stalls selling flowers and floral decorations, the flower markets feature stalls serving hand-held windmills, toys and other quirky souvenirs. The International Chinese New Year Parade is another signature event during the celebration in Hong Kong. Featuring an array of brightly coloured floats as well as professional dancers and performers from more than 20 countries, this event transforms the waterfront area of Hong Kong into a giant street party venue. On the second evening of Chinese New Year, the skyline of Hong Kong is set ablaze with fireworks and laser displays over Victoria Harbour – an area well-known for its regular 'Sound and Light' show throughout the entire year.

On the final day of the celebrations, the Lantern Festival is celebrated. Lanterns are hung up in many Chinese cities and towns, while children dressed in red carry lanterns in street parades. This festival marks the first full moon of the New Year and sees the appearance of mythical animals such as the phoenix and dragon. The lion dance is normally an important part of the festival as lions indicate good luck and their fierce nature scares away evil spirits. Being the king of the jungle, the lion has long been a popular representation of stateliness and bravery, and is a symbol of strength. Since lions are believed to have powerful mythic protective powers, statues of guardian lions have traditionally stood at the entrance of palaces, government offices, temples and commercial buildings. Some families and businesses invite a lion dance troupe to usher in the New Year. The lion is constructed with cloth and papier mâché over a bamboo or wicker frame. The lion costume is normally operated by two men and accompanied by musicians who loudly pound a large drum, symbols and a gong.

Chinese people believe that the deafening sounds from the instruments, the face of the lion and the burning of incense sticks are highly effective in casting out unwanted mythical beasts such as Nian. Dancers in monkey and clown costumes often accompany the lion. Even more spectacular than lion dances are dragon dances where as many as 40 men may operate the long and winding display.

The Lantern Festival is celebrated under the light of the full moon with lantern displays. The inside of the lantern is lit to represent long life, energy and good luck. The lantern also serves as a guide for any wayward spirits to return to their home. Regarding the cuisine eaten during this time, the Chinese believe that every family should prepare tangyuan, a glutinous rice ball brewed in a sweet soup, to worship the God of Fire. Since the round shape of the tangyuan and the bowls are a symbol of family togetherness, it is believed that eating this food brings family happiness in the forthcoming year and provides a perfect conclusion to the celebration.

Conclusion

Many rituals such as the mass migration of people every New Year (regardless of the geographical limitation) demonstrates the pivotal role of this festival in sustaining the solidarity of families. Moreover, many of the rituals and traditions such as the spring clean reveal the superstitious nature of the Chinese. As to the question of whether or not these rituals and traditions will continue, Low (1995) has argued that a natural loss of Chinese New Year rituals and traditions could happen as younger Chinese are less in favour of these older traditions. Nevertheless, the rituals are expected to persist for some time as the Chinese people are renowned for their strong family solidarity. As was also discussed, the five virtues and basic human principles of Confucianism place strong behavioural forces on Chinese people.

This chapter examined some of the fascinating rituals surrounding the celebration of this significant event. The enduring traditions of the Chinese hold an important place in the heritage, culture and identity of billions of people around the world. This chapter has also attempted to reveal how intangible and tangible Chinese traditions are experienced and imagined by many people today. Chinese New Year rituals are a key component of Chinese identity. When partaking in these rituals, the heritage experience and appreciation of that identity is heightened. The heritage moment can be savoured by partaking in activities such as those outlined in this chapter – and of course capturing some of these memories with the all-important photographs that are readily shared with friends and family via social media. It would appear that Chinese New Year traditions and rituals will continue to be a source of strength for Chinese people and their sense of identity.

References

Bennett, O. (1986) *Festival: Chinese New Year*, Houndmills: Macmillan.
Chambers, C. (1997) *A World of Festivals: Chinese New Year*, London: Evans.

Chen, S. (2013) 'Lunar New Year travel scramble gets under way', *South China Morning Post*. Online: www.scmp.com/news/china/article/1136872/lunar-new-year-travel-scramble-gets-under-way (accessed 25 October 2013).

Cooper, J.C. (ed.) (1992) *Brewer's Book of Myth and Legend*, New York: Cassell.

Falassi, A. (1987) 'Festival: Definition and morphology', in A. Falassi (ed.) *Time out of Time: Essays on the festival* (pp. 1–10), Albuquerque: University of New Mexico Press.

Fan, Y. (2000) 'A classification of Chinese culture', *Cross Cultural Management*, 7(2), 3–10.

Fox, M. and Fox, O. (2007) *Time to Celebrate: Identity, diversity and belief*, Melbourne: Curriculum.

Hopfe, L.M. and Woodward, M.R. (2012) *Religions of the World*, Upper Saddle River, NJ: Pearson.

Kiernan, J. (2008) *China: A cultural perspective*, Hobart: Davies Brothers.

Lambert, C. (2013) 'Spring into New Year', *Herald Sun* (Melbourne), 4 February, p. 36.

Low, C. (1995) *Ritual and Community in Chinese New Year Traditions*. Online: www.oocities.org/lionscave1/Articles/Ritual.html (accessed 1 December 2013).

Martinsons, M.G. (1996) 'Cultural constraints on radical re-engineering: Hammer and Lewin meet Confucius', *Journal of Applied Management Studies*, 5(1), 85–96.

Orgad, S. (2012) *Media Representation and the Global Imagination*, Cambridge: Polity.

Pirotta, S. (2006) *We Love Chinese New Year*, London: Wayland.

South China Morning Post. (2013) 'China's urbanisation push needs land reform, freer residency rights in cities'. Online: www.scmp.com/business/economy/article/1353204/urbanisation-push-needs-land-reform-freer-residency-rights-cities (accessed 1 December 2013).

Too, L. (1996) *Feng Shui*, New York: Barnes and Noble.

Wang, G. (2010) *The Race of the Chinese Zodiac*, Melbourne: Black Dog.

Yau, O.H.M., Chan, T.S. and Lau, K.F. (1999) 'Influence of Chinese cultural values on consumer behaviour: A proposed model of gift-purchasing behaviour in Hong Kong', *Journal of International Consumer Marketing*, 11(1), 97–116.

Yeung, R.M.W. and Yee, W.M.S. (2010) 'Chinese new year festival: Exploring consumer purchase intention at the flower market in Macau', *International Journal of Hospitality Management*, 29(2), 291–296.

7   Catholic processions in Macau

Ubaldino Couto

Introduction

Macau, an ex-Portuguese colony, was the first and last European outpost in Asia. It was the centre of sea trade, and was also a stepping stone to China for missionaries who travelled from Europe (Cheng 1999). After the establishment of the Catholic Diocese of Macau in 1576, a number of religious groups used Macau as their gateway to the Far East. With full Portuguese influence in the administration and political environments in Macau, the Catholic Church gained much power, dominance and popularity, even – though slowly – among the local Chinese. Architectural marvels like baroque churches and seminaries become today's much-prized UNESCO World Heritage sites, which were inscribed onto the list in 2005 (Du Cros 2009).

Throughout much of its colonial history, Macau was a premier centre of Catholic festivals and events in Asia. The unprecedented economic prosperity primarily brought about by the liberalisation of the gaming industry brought in 28 million visitors in 2012, a 144 per cent increase in visitors compared to 2002 data (DSEC 2012b). Even after the transfer of sovereignty from the Portuguese to the Chinese in 1999, the festive atmosphere appears to be undeterred. For instance, Catholic events are encouraged to continue, alongside a number of Buddhist festivals such as the feast days of gods and deities. Indeed, Article 34 in the Basic Law of Macau clearly stipulates the freedom to practise religious activities, thus encouraging the coexistence and practice of different religions and celebration of religious festivals and events in Macau.

Among some of the vibrant festivals and events celebrated in Macau, the Catholic street processions are unique in the region, and possibly the only ones to take place in Asia other than those in the Philippines. Catholic processions can be ordinary rituals celebrated by the Church but they can also be extraordinary, where they are organised for a particular cause or according to the local customs of the church. In general, a Catholic procession is seen as an 'organized body of people advancing in formal or ceremonial manner as an element of Christian ritual or as a less official expression of popular piety' (Thurston 1911). Figure 7.1 shows one of the Catholic processions celebrated in Macau, dedicated to mark the beginning of Lent, demonstrating its colourful pageantry and devotion to Jesus Christ.

Figure 7.1 The Procession of Our Lord, the Good Jesus (source: U. Couto).

This chapter examines extensively these dynamic and rare events, their ritual-istic characteristics and significance to the people of Macau, in five broad aspects, using a framework developed by Crespi-Vallbona and Richards (2007). The data in the form of photographic evidence and field diaries were collected over a number of years and are used to support the discussions in this chapter. As most text on processions in Macau has been published in Portuguese and Chinese, the official languages of Macau, this literature is drawn upon exten-sively to offer a background to the study. This is then followed by an application of Crespi-Vallbona and Richards' framework to these vibrant events. The chapter concludes with an examination of the implications of these processions for Macau, and beyond.

Macau's Catholic processions

Out of the 2.2 billion Christians in the world, the Roman Catholic Church is the largest denomination with 1.2 billion followers worldwide (Pew Research Center 2012). Traditionally not an Asian religion, the Catholic Church, and to a lesser degree the other branches of the Christian community such as Protestants, have acquired a large following in the region, accounting for 13.2 per cent of Chris-tians worldwide. In Asia, only two countries name the Christian faith as the majority religion – the Philippines and Papua New Guinea – while many other Asian countries are Buddhist, Muslim, atheist or not affiliated with any religion.

Like many other metropolitan Asian cities, however, Macau has a diverse mix of religious backgrounds.

Besides the extraordinary tourist arrivals in Macau, the population mix has also changed significantly over the last decade due to economic reforms and relaxation of immigration policies. As shown in Table 7.1, of the 552,503 population in Macau according to the census in 2011 (DSEC 2012a), less than half were born in Macau; in fact, over half of the total population was born in Mainland China, with Hong Kong, the Philippines and Taiwan China the major countries of birth.

These statistics offer critical background information for the analyses of the significance of Catholic processions to the people of Macau – because there is no such thing as the 'people of Macau' and these events are only spiritually meaningful to those who are affiliated with the Catholic and, to a wider extent, Christian religion. Indeed, the Catholic population of Macau is 5.3 per cent of the total population, with less than half comprising local people and just over half expatriates, mostly dominated by Filipino domestic workers in Macau (Macao Yearbook 2013). Macau has long departed from a homogeneous societal structure. In fact, most visitors to Macau are bewildered by some interesting statistical facts – more than half of the population was not born in Macau, and there is no official religious affiliation, with only a minuscule portion of the population being Catholics, yet the ratio of churches to the number of Catholics appears to be over-proportional. Still, most services are packed with devotees, no matter whether they are delivered in Chinese, Portuguese, English, Tagalog or other languages. That does not mean, however, that Catholic events like processions are irrelevant to the general population of Macau. These events are held in public roads, occupy the time and space of the local people and cause them inconvenience. Yet the peculiarity is that the non-Christian population appears not to be hostile towards these processions (Couto 2010).

Though Catholics constitute only a small fraction of Macau's population, their importance and significance to the community is relatively prodigious. For instance, there are a number of Catholic festivals designated as public holidays in Macau. Apart from the usual Easter and Christmas, the people of Macau enjoy traditional Catholic celebrations on All Soul's Day on 2 November and on 8

Table 7.1 Population of Macau by place of birth

Place of birth	Population	%
Mainland China	255,186	46.2
Macau	226,127	40.9
Hong Kong	19,355	3.5
Philippines	14,544	2.6
Taiwan China	2,221	0.4
Portugal	1,835	0.3
Other Asian countries	27,401	5.0
Others	5,834	1.1
Total	552,503	100.0

December, the Immaculate Conception of the Virgin Mary. The latter two are celebrated and made public holidays in very few countries, even where the majority of the population are Catholics.

Historically the centre of the Catholic Church and the gateway to elsewhere in Asia (Cheng 1999), Macau celebrates a number of processions each year. Fundamentally, the reason that the people of Macau celebrate these processions is to commemorate various incidents as recorded in the Bible or recognised by the Church. However, they also serve as a platform for believers to show devotion and to pray in unison asking for God's blessings and penance. In Macau, the largest processions are the Procession of Our Lord, the Good Jesus, celebrated during Lent, and the Procession of Our Lady of Fátima in May.

According to Li (2009), the Procession of Our Lord, the Good Jesus in Macau is a large and solemn ritual that dates back to at least 1857, according to official government correspondence between Macau and Portugal. Apart from its purpose in serving the Catholics in Macau, this is also a traditional religious and cultural showcase for tourists. The Procession of Our Lord, the Good Jesus is actually a series of two processions celebrated over the first weekend of Lent. On the first day of the procession, a Saturday, the statue of the Passion of Jesus is carried from St Augustine's Church to the Cathedral on the 9.3-km^2 Macau island, roughly a 450-m downhill trek. On the second day, colloquially known as 'the big Jesus procession', a longer 3-km return trip occurs as it takes a detour around the city (hence the 'bigger' procession) in a city-wide Way of the Cross, a ritual that commemorates the final hours of Jesus' suffering leading to his death. During the procession, the congregation marches in silence, while examining their conscience and their distance from God. The recognition and support from the government is clearly apparent. Not only are the local authorities tolerant of these events blocking major roads and causing a number of traffic disruptions, but large numbers of police are also called to assist in dealing with congestion and maintaining road diversions. The police brass band traditionally joins the processions to play solemn funeral-style music.

The other major procession of the Catholic Church in Macau is the Procession of Our Lady of Fátima, celebrated each year on 13 May. The reason for the specific dedication to Our Lady of Fátima is the historical association with Macau's Portuguese heritage. Since the apparition of the Virgin Mary in the Portuguese town of Fátima on 13 May 1917, the Portuguese declared the permanent consecration of the day to the Virgin Mary. Like Portugal, since 1929, Macau has celebrated the day with an annual large-scale procession (Beja 2011). The apparition in Fátima was widely publicised for two reasons. The apparition was about three closely guarded secrets that the Virgin Mary told the three children, one of which has been widely speculated to be the apocalypse, and the second, which is in fact the third secret, was the attempted assassination of Pope John Paul II on 13 May 1981 – which coincidently occurred on the anniversary of the apparition of Our Lady of Fátima.

Similar to the Procession of Our Lord, the Good Jesus, the Procession of Our Lady of Fátima is about 2.5 km in length, and takes the form of a detour around the city rather than a direct route. The congregation parades around the city from the St Dominic's Church to the Chapel of Our Lady of Penha, strolling slowly behind the statue of Our Lady of Fátima, which is carried by women in white garments, signifying purity, while holding a lighted candle in one hand and rosary beads in the other. Unlike the other processions where participants reflect and pray silently, the congregation in this procession prays the Holy Rosary in three languages – Portuguese, Cantonese and English – and sings hymns devoted to the Virgin Mary. The procession concludes with the Bishop of Macau celebrating mass and giving a blessing to the city of Macau, at which the congregation gathers and joins in.

Apart from the two large processions, Macau also celebrates a number of smaller ones. As they are more colloquial and restricted to the local vicinity of parish churches, these processions receive significantly less attention than the bigger ones. The first small-scale procession, which is a short 45-minute procession around the vicinity of the Cathedral, is celebrated on Good Friday during Lent. Like the Procession of Our Lord, the Good Jesus, this event is supported by the government, not just in the form of emergency services and logistical support by the police brass band playing funereal music to the procession. Indeed, interviews with participants after the procession reveal that many participants see similarities between this procession and state funerals, which are held only to honour national figures of great importance and significance.

The other smaller processions are restricted to the vicinities of the parish churches of St Lazarus and St Anthony. One of the lesser known is the Procession of St Roch in the St Lazarus parish in Macau. It is held yearly and also supported by the police brass band to honour the spirit of St Roch, which is to love and care for others. The devotion to this saint grew when Macau was hit by a plague and the residents at that time were praying to him for help. The other, and more famous procession is that dedicated to St Anthony, often considered to be the saint of finding lost items and protection against danger. The Catholic community in the St Anthony parish honoured the saint by organising a yearly procession commemorating his good works. Like the Procession of Our Lord, the Good Jesus, the government, through emergency and traffic diversion services, supported this procession as well as providing a brass band playing music (it used to be composed of fire services personnel before the police brass band was introduced). However, the St Anthony procession was cancelled a few years after the handover of sovereignty from Portugal to China in 1999 (Lu and Huang 2009). In the old days, the procession was essentially a community event; it was complemented by street fairs and games. Homes in the neighbourhood would open their doors and welcome guests to visit and savour Macanese-style delicacies (Macanese is a name given to the specific group of Eurasians, who are mixed Chinese and Portuguese). In his novel, *The Bewitching Braid*, Henrique de Senna Fernandes wrote a little about this historical, never to be seen again procession, which was so important to the community (Brookshaw 2004).

The majority of Christian activities, including the processions, are restricted to the peninsula of Macau and not the islands of Taipa and Coloane, reflecting the major urban areas during colonial times. The first bridge connecting Macau and Taipa was opened only in 1974, thus encouraging the population to move to more rural areas. While the Catholic community has had a long-standing presence in the outlying islands since in the early 1900s, this is much later than those on the Macau peninsula, which date back to the mid-1550s (Lu and Huang 2009).

A people's event

Catholic processions are obviously not exclusive to the people of Macau, but are extremely rare even in more traditionally Christian communities. They are even rarer when the processions are taken out to the city streets, as many processions, such as the Our Lady of Fátima procession in Portugal, are entirely conducted within the Sanctuary. However, in Asia, there are very few Catholic processions. Some Catholic communities in post-colonial cities like Singapore and Hong Kong do celebrate processions but they are often, if not all, restricted to within the compound of their respective churches. The Philippines stands out as the only destination other than Macau that takes Catholic processions to the streets. The most famous is the Black Nazarene, celebrated on 9 January every year (Zialcita 2013). In his article, Zialcita (2013) examines the process of changes towards an imported artefact – the image of the Black Nazarene that the infamous procession is supposed to be commemorating – by modern Filipinos. He argues that the Black Nazarene image, which is black in colour as a result of a fire that broke out on the ship to Manila over 400 years ago, has a special meaning to the Filipinos, hence their devotion and attachment. Indeed, Catholic processions are often held as a manifestation of not just their religious attachment but the cultural identity of the celebrants. Seales (2008) discusses the changing cultural and political attachments of a religion and its public display in Siler City, North Carolina. He explains that the arrival of Latino workers into the area brought with them Good Friday processions. Predominantly a white Protestant community, the vitality of the celebrations of Fourth of July parades were overshadowed by the success of the Catholic processions, in part due to the falling economic power of the local whites.

Analysis of the Macau processions

Crespi-Vallbona and Richards (2007) found that there were five important stakeholder perspectives or concerns of the role of cultural festivals, which are useful to structure this analysis of Catholic processions in Macau.

Identity

Macau appears to be a place without a consistent, agreed and uniform identity. Cheng (1999) calls Macau 'a cultural Janus'. The reasons for this are twofold. First, the historical background of Macau being ruled by the Portuguese for well over 400 years while peoples from all corners of the world walked and lived peacefully alongside each other made it impossible for Macau to have a consistent identity. Second, economic prosperity in recent years has led Macau to employ large numbers of imported labour, and this is further fuelled by the new immigrants by investment. With over half of the population being born not in Macau but in Mainland China, there is not a strong local identity. However, the processions do occupy an important place in Macau's identity mix.

Community and participation

The nature of the procession, being exclusively related to the Catholic religion, somewhat frames the audience mix. One is unlikely to see a non-Catholic or somebody not interested in the religion at all participating wholeheartedly in the processions. However, observations suggest that those who are not seen as the target audience still appear to be very supportive of the event. Indeed, there are no known complaints or voices calling to stop these processions from going ahead, even though all of these processions occupy public space and take up publicly funded resources, for example, police. Figure 7.2 shows part of the scale of these processions, with the audience taking up the majority of a main road through the centre of Macau. In addition, tourists who are coincidentally in the area also find that they are presented with an authentic cultural spectacle, which is very different from those found in their home countries (the top five inbound markets to Macau are from non-Catholic countries). Crespi-Vallbona

Figure 7.2 The crowds taking up the whole of the street during the procession (source: U. Couto).

and Richards point out the importance of community participation in festivals in building social cohesion. Indeed, conceptual (Arcodia and Whitford 2006) and empirical (Couto 2010; Van Winkle *et al.* 2013) research does suggest that by attending a festival, people get closer to each other, and thus achieve a sense of community.

Integration

Cultural festivals can bring different people together and encourage toleration of different cultural backgrounds. It is thus hoped that the processions can have the potential of heterogeneous groups within society accepting each other and appreciating these differences. Similar to the work of Crespi-Vallbona and Richards (2007), one of the major issues faced by the people of Macau is the number of immigrants and the huge visitor arrivals. Macau society generally does not feel that the government is biased towards a particular group – the Western, Catholic side or the Chinese, Buddhist community. In fact, the government supports a wide variety of festivals by 'both' sides, financially and with a variety of resources. For example, support is given to the Chinese festivities honouring gods and deities, the Portuguese festivals that celebrate its culture and ethnic events of the Filipino and Burmese communities. Whether or not this has a positive effect on integration remains to be seen but it seems the government is not doing anything that may impede integration, particularly the acceptance of minorities into the society.

Globalisation and localisation

Though increasingly these processions receive international attention and are widely publicised by the local tourist office, they are still ritualistic and traditional, and practised only to satisfy the historical needs of the Catholics in Macau. In recent years, the language used in the procession has grown from Portuguese only to bilingual Portuguese and Chinese, and now Portuguese, Chinese and English. Rather than seeing this as globalisation, it appears that the inclusion of the English language in the procession arises from a needs basis, that is, the mix of Catholics in Macau. Given that half the Catholic population of Macau consists of expatriates, English is the most logical language to adopt. Indeed, this is probably evidence of efforts towards integrating minorities into the mainstream.

Commercialisation

All processions are open to the public and freely accessible. The nature of the processions, being carried out entirely on city streets and involving devotees walking solemnly behind the sacred statues, avoids any possibility of putting the processions under the business spotlight. Besides, the government also – probably out of respect – has not turned certain rituals of the processions into a performance that they could sell. This is in contrast to the national listed Intangible Heritage Drunken Dragon Dance, where the government organises dance performances for tourists all year round at key touristic spots so as to offer a more varied programme of tourist attractions. This lack of commodification is important for the event attendees who participate in the processions – no matter how graciously or reluctantly they accept tourists in the vicinity, they do not wish to re-create, sell or modify any part of the procession for commercial purposes.

Conclusion

Though Catholics make up only a minority of the population, the historical significance of the Portuguese heritage and Catholic attachments to Macau is still evident today. The processions are largely seen as 'Western' celebrations and are accepted by the general public (Couto 2010). On a political level, the Portuguese language is used and people who are of Portuguese heritage are still in power, though much less than before. Preventing the processions would mean a violation of the Basic Law, which clearly stipulates the religious freedom of the people of Macau, and would be a direct challenge to the Portuguese power still present in Macau. Finally, Macau positions itself as the premier tourism and entertainment destination in Asia, fuelled by the gaming business as its dragonhead industry and supported by heritage and events. The touristic value of these processions will not be undermined, though to the Catholic community these processions are still a manifestation of their religion rather than a tourist attraction (Beja 2011).

The future remains optimistic for these Catholic processions. Their nature almost certainly guarantees that the ritualistic elements of the events will not be modified or taken out in any way, as they are backed by strict Vatican protocols. The business interest of the Macau government in offering a varied list of tourist attractions also safeguards the continuity of the event. Though the population is becoming more and more 'non-Christian', it appears that the people in Macau have lived through and grown from a strong foundation of understanding and respect for each other's culture. To this end, these processions, even though sometimes disruptive, are tolerated and supported across the broader Macau community.

References

Arcodia, C. and Whitford, M. (2006) 'Festival attendance and the development of social capital', *Journal of Convention and Event Tourism*, 8, 1–18.
Beja, H. (2011) 'The journey of faith', in *Macao* (pp. 50–57). Macao: Government Information Bureau.
Brookshaw, D. (2004) *The Bewitching Braid*, Hong Kong: Hong Kong University Press.
Cheng, C.M.B. (1999) *Macau: A cultural Janus*, Hong Kong: Hong Kong University Press.
Couto, U.S. (2010) 'Catholic processions: Festivals that cause disturbance to the city – an

exploratory study through observations', in B. Wu (ed.), *Mega Events and Urban Tourism* (pp. 140–152), Beijing: China Travel & Tourism Press.

Crespi-Vallbona, M. and Richards, G. (2007) 'The meaning of cultural festivals: Stakeholder perspectives in Catalunya', *International Journal of Cultural Policy*, 13(1), 103–122.

DSEC. (2012a) *2011 Population Census*, Macao: Direcção dos Serviços de Estatística e Censos (Statistics and Census Service).

DSEC. (2012b) *Yearbook of Statistics 2011*, Macao: Direcção dos Serviços de Estatística e Censos (Statistics and Census Service).

Du Cros, H.L. (2009) 'Emerging issues for cultural tourism in Macau', *Journal of Current Chinese Affairs*, 38, 73–99.

Li, C.M. (2009) *Conhecer bem Macau*, Macau: Editora Arte da China Contemporânea.

Lu, Z.P. and Huang, J.W. (2009) *Igrejas Católicas de Macau*, Hong Kong: Joint Publishing (Hong Kong) Company.

Macao Yearbook (2013) *Macao Yearbook 2013*, Macau: Government Information Bureau of the Macao Special Administrative Region.

Pew Research Center. (2012) *The Global Religious Landscape: A report on the size and distribution of the world's major religious groups as of 2010*, Washington, DC: Pew Research Center.

Seales, C.E. (2008) 'Parades and processions: Protestant and Catholic ritual performances in a Nuevo New South Town', *Numen*, 55, 44–67.

Thurston, H. (1911) 'Processions', in *The Catholic Encyclopedia*, New York: Robert Appleton.

Van Winkle, C.M., Woosnam, K.M. and Mohammed, A.M. (2013) 'Sense of community and festival attendance', *Event Management*, 17, 155–163.

Zialcita, F.N. (2013) 'The Burnt Christ. The filipinization of a Mexican icon', *Cuaderno internacional de estudios humanísticos y literatura: civilización Filipina y relaciones culturales Hispano-Asiáticas*, 19, 67–75.

Part II
Europe

8   Christmas traditions

Pagan roots, invented rites

Jennifer Laing and Warwick Frost

There never was such a goose. Bob said he didn't believe there ever was such a goose cooked. Its tenderness and flavour, size and cheapness, were the themes of universal admiration. Eked out by apple sauce and mashed potatoes, it was a sufficient dinner for the whole family ... Mrs Cratchit left the room alone – too nervous to bear witnesses – to take the pudding up and bring it in ... In half a minute Mrs Cratchit entered – flushed but smiling proudly – with the pudding, like a speckled cannon-ball, so hard and firm, blazing in half of half-a-quartern of ignited brandy, and bedight with Christmas holly stuck into the top ... At last the dinner was all done, the cloth was cleared, the hearth swept, and the fire made up. The compound in the jug being tasted, and considered perfect, apples and oranges were put upon the table, and a shovel-full of chestnuts on the fire. Then all the Cratchit family drew around the hearth.

Charles Dickens, *A Christmas Carol*, 1843

Introduction

This extract from Charles Dickens eulogises the Christmas meal and the gathering together of the family around the fire. Many of these traditions that we associate with a European Christmas became widespread thanks to the pen of Dickens, who wrote five Christmas Books and Christmas-themed stories for his own periodical (Ackroyd 1991). The sentimental world Dickens created in *A Christmas Carol* was not overtly Christian, yet sinners like Scrooge could be redeemed, and love, symbolised by the Cratchit family, triumphed over all. It appears that Dickens was trying to escape the memories of a troubled childhood with a father who was sent to debtors' prison, by conjuring up an idealised family setting. He remembered his early family Christmases in Rochester, where it snowed at Christmas six years out of nine (Jamieson 2008). Dickens was born in 1812 at the end of the Little Ice Age and in 1813/1814, the last Frost Fair was held on the frozen surface of the River Thames. There is thus a strong link made between snow and a Dickensian Christmas, illustrated by the emphasis of the Rochester Dickensian Christmas Festival on a 'guaranteed [fake] snowfall' (Enjoy Medway 2013). Even in Australia, Sovereign Hill, a recreation of the Ballarat goldfields, provides fake snow for its Christmas in July celebrations (Figure 8.1).

Figure 8.1 Christmas in July celebrations at Sovereign Hill, Ballarat (source: B. Harvey).

In recent times, it has become fashionable to deride Christmas as an over-commercialised paean to excess consumption, largely devoid of meaning and divorced from its religious, let alone pagan roots. Yet Christmas is deeply infused with ritual elements, some with ancient origins and others invented in more recent times (Hobsbawm 1983). These rituals resonate deeply, whether those who celebrate Christmas recognise their origins or not. Despite the popularity and ubiquity of this celebration around the globe, there is a paucity of research in the emerging field of events studies focusing on Christmas. Miller's (1993) edited work *Unwrapping Christmas* is over 20 years old, and more recent studies have tended to concentrate on an *aspect* of Christmas, such as Christmas street lights (Edensor and Millington 2009), Christmas-themed festivals (Winchester and Rofe 2005), Christmas markets (Haid 2006) and Christmas-themed tours (Janiskee 1996; Terry 2008). This chapter aims to fill this gap by considering Christmas more holistically, exploring some of the rituals underpinning this festival, and how they have mutated and been transformed over time.

It should be acknowledged up-front that the celebration of Christmas is a long-standing rite, which extends further back than the birth of Christ and the creation of the early Christian Church. Its timing, around the time of the winter solstice, was a pagan period of festivity that heralded the return of summer and fertility. Apart from the pagan festival of *Natali Sol Invicti*, the birthday of the unconquered Sun (Rowell 1993), other festivals said to have been replaced by Christmas are the Roman festival of the *Kalends* and *Saturnalia*. In these we can see the origins of traditions such as giving presents, generosity and indulgent eating and drinking, as well as the inversion of social norms (Miller 1993).

The early Christian Church took Jesus' birthdate to be 25 December and thus cemented Christmas within the traditional period of midwinter celebrations. This helped the conversion to Christianity, in that people were used to taking part in festivities around this time of year. In the same way, the Celtic festival of *Samhain*, celebrating the cycles of life, including the start of the long, cold winter, was appropriated by Christians into the feast of All Hallows' Eve, which honoured the dead through the saints. This later became the secular holiday of Halloween (Santino 1994).

Despite its popularity in contemporary times, there were periods when Christmas looked to be on shaky ground. The English Reformation brought with it a Puritan distrust of holidays that were not grounded in Scripture, and made celebrating Christmas an offence (Miall and Miall 1978; Restad 1995). It was only with the restoration of Charles II to the throne that Christmas regained its status as a legitimate event for Christian worship (Lalumia 2001; Rowell 1993). It was a low-key and mostly private affair throughout the seventeenth and eighteenth centuries, and some commentators and writers, such as Washington Irving, voiced concerns that the observance of Christmas might die out (Rowell 1993).

The Victorian era, however, saw a phoenix-like revival of Christmas, exemplified by Dickens's cosy family vignettes and the example set by Queen Victoria herself (Belk 1993; Kuper 1993; Miall and Miall 1978). The ritual of the Christmas tree is generally linked to the influence of her husband Prince Albert, who brought his German customs with him to England on his marriage in 1840. While other German-born royals such as Queen Charlotte and Queen Adelaide had also displayed Christmas trees in the royal palaces (Miall and Miall 1978; Weintraub 1997), it was Albert who 'turned the royal family's Christmases into semi-public events. The fashion caught on, popularized by the new illustrated papers' (Weintraub 1997: 114). New traditions were introduced, such as Christmas cards and crackers, while old rituals became popular again, such as carol singing and the resurgence in patronage of the pantomime (Miall and Miall 1978).

Lalumia (2001) argues that Christmas in the 1840s became

> a life raft of familiarity in changing times ... a festival of family and kinship
> ... The Christmas-makers of the early-nineteenth century were attempting to
> create a festival – to reflect a society – that was better, morally and socially,
> than the immediate past.

This was done through the blending of old and new rituals and the examples set
by opinion leaders such as Victoria and Albert, and Charles Dickens. There was
a greater focus on children than before (Lalumia 2001), which we take for
granted today. This Victorian version of Christmas is still influential on today's
society, although many of these rituals and traditions have been modified to suit
modern, multicultural tastes.

In this chapter, we consider four key rituals associated with Christmas – displays and decorations, gift giving and benevolence, family activities and the
Christmas meal. While we focus largely on English, American and Australian
examples, the wide sweep of the chapter assists in exploring the continued
importance of these rituals, their changes over time and the contradictions inherent in the festivities.

Christmas displays and decorations

Home decorations are an intrinsic part of the Christmas ritual. The Victorians
used greenery, like ivy, mistletoe and holly, both in their homes and their
churches, but their lineage goes back far beyond this, to pagan times (Miall and
Miall 1978). They were thought to promote abundance and the continuity of life
(Barber 2013). Poorer people had to make do with paper decorations (Pimlott
1978). Kissing under the mistletoe was a tradition in many households, and
ostensibly 'owes something to the use of the plant in ancient Celtic fertility rites'
(Pimlott 1978: 139). Pimlott also argues that this rite was 'popular [in Victorian
times] because it provided an outlet for impulses which had at other times to be
restrained' (1978: 140). Presumably because of its sexual connotations, many
churches banned mistletoe as a Christmas decoration (Brasch 1994; Pimlott
1978). Holly was used to create wreaths on doors, but the origin of this practice
is contentious (Pimlott 1978). Holly berries were believed to guard against
witches in the Middle Ages, and thus protect the home from harm (Brasch 1994).
Others contend that the shape of the wreath symbolises the crown of thorns worn
by Jesus at the Crucifixion, or link it with the Roman god Bacchus, 'whose worshippers were thought to have worn circular ivy crowns' (Brasch 1994: 24). The
use of wreaths still persists in the modern era, with a variety of materials used to
create them, both natural and handmade.

Home-made paper chains made by children, paper lanterns and candles in the
window have given way in contemporary times to mass-produced items that are
more glitzy and showy, such as sparkling tinsel, and strings of electric lights,
both inside and on the facade and roof. There are numerous books and television

shows on Christmas decorating, which generally emphasise understated and minimalist designs. This school of thought, associated in particular with the United Kingdom, views excessive displays of Christmas lights as vulgar, wasteful and crass (Edensor and Millington 2009). In contrast, those who display these lights see themselves as generous, giving something back to their communities, and providing 'a sense of family togetherness and enjoyment, particularly for child family members' (pp. 113–114); closer to the Dickensian ideal than their detractors would allow. Edensor and Millington (2009: 116) describe this ritual as producing 'a sense of worth and local form of cultural capital', arguably a social good in neighbourhoods where hopelessness and powerlessness might otherwise hold sway. In Australia and the United States, street lighting is not necessarily seen as evidence of a lack of class or taste. Certainly in the United States it is a more mainstream tradition, which can also be seen in the external decorating of houses and gardens for festivals like Halloween and Thanksgiving.

The ritual of putting up and dressing the Christmas tree still remains the centrepiece of many family Christmases (Figure 8.2), and has been extended to public spaces. Most workplaces are graced with a communal tree, often in the foyer or public areas, while retail stores compete to have the most lavish trees on display, particularly the large department stores. The lighting of a Christmas tree in some of the great cities of the world has become an event attended by thousands. Famous Christmas trees include the 76-foot giant at the Rockefeller

Figure 8.2 Decorating the family Christmas tree (source: J. Laing).

Center in New York, a tradition since 1933 (*Daily News* 2013), with a lighting ceremony and pop concert which is broadcast on NBC TV, and the Christmas tree in Trafalgar Square, which has been an annual gift from the city of Oslo to the people of London since 1946 (Pimlott 1978).

Public street decorations are part of the Christmas ritual, usually found along shopping streets and concourses. The annual turning on of the Christmas lights in London's Regent Street attracts thousands of onlookers and the task is usually given to royalty or a celebrity guest. Princess Diana turned on the lights in 1981, her first Christmas as a member of the Royal Family. Many retail shops make a special effort to decorate their windows, as well as interiors. The decorating of shop windows at Christmas can be traced back to the Victorian era. The journalist and writer George R. Sims noted in an essay titled *Christmas London* (1902: 152): 'Now on the eve of the great day, there is not a street in the capital containing a shop, from its broadest thoroughfare to its narrowest by-way, that has not decked its windows for the Christmas market'. The Myer department store in Melbourne has had an annual animated window display since 1956, often linked to a particular children's book or film, such as *Peter Pan*, *The Water Babies*, *The Wizard of Oz* and modern favourites like *Olivia Helps with Christmas*.

Department stores saw Christmas as an opportunity to entice shoppers inside with attractions aimed at children, and parades in the streets. As far back as the 1870s, Lewis's Bon Marché in Liverpool created an annual Christmas Fairyland (Pimlott 1978). Famous seasonal parades championed by department stores include Macy's Thanksgiving Parade in New York, started in 1924, which features huge helium-filled balloons; the Toronto Santa Claus Parade, a 1905 innovation by Eaton's department store; and Adelaide's Christmas Pageant, an initiative started by John Martin's department store in 1933. The film *Miracle on 34th Street* (1947) featured Christmas scenes set in Macy's and its Parade, with a Santa Claus (Edmund Gwenn) who directs shoppers to other stores when they can't find what they want. This act of altruism is ultimately endorsed by Macy's management as good business practice (Belk 1993). In Melbourne, Myer's Lonsdale Street store had an annual rooftop carnival with rides, accessible from the sixth-floor toy department, which we both visited as children. The other tradition associated with department stores was the visit to Santa to sit on his knee, often accompanied by a commemorative photograph (Figure 8.3). Belk (1993) argues that the presence of Santa 'helps sacralize these retail sites'; a 'god of materialism ... [in a] cathedral of consumption' (p. 91).

Another site of public display is the Christmas market, which is a popular tourist attraction in Europe, particularly Germany and Austria (Haid 2006). There are more than 50 Christmas markets in Berlin, and other popular examples can be found in Nuremberg, Vienna, Prague and, more recently, London (Figure 8.4).

Figure 8.3 Posing with Santa Claus in Grace Bros department store, Sydney (source: J. Laing).

Figure 8.4 Tourists wander through London's Christmas market (source: S. Laing).

Gift giving and benevolence

C.S. Lewis (1970) argues that

> The interchange of presents was a very small ingredient in the older English festivity ... [and] the idea that not only all friends but even all acquaintances should give one another presents, or at least send one another cards, is quite modern and has been forced upon us by the shopkeepers.

Despite this view, which comes perilously close to Scrooge's 'Bah Humbug', the association of gift giving with the modern Christmas is so strongly intertwined that it is hard to see how they could ever be separated. Even the commodification of Christmas presents is not a twentieth-century notion. Certainly by Victorian times, Christmas catalogues and advertisements in the December issues of English magazines beguiled would-be purchasers with the latest wares as potential gifts, and most toys given to children were store-bought, such as china dolls, toy soldiers, model trains and games (Miall and Miall 1978). Many people of the time, however, made their own presents (Miall and Miall 1978; Waits 1993), with the assistance of articles in magazines such as *Cassell's Household Guide*.

The roots of gift giving can be found in the legend of St Nicholas. He was the Bishop of Myra in the fourth century CE and loved to share his riches with those who needed them. He was said to have given a gift of three bags of gold to a man of modest means, whose three daughters lacked a dowry to be married. This is the origin of the three golden balls that symbolise a pawnbroker (Miall and Miall 1978). Another story refers to a bag of gold being dropped down a chimney into a stocking drying by the fire. The Dutch particularly revered St Nicholas, whom they called Sinter Klaas (Brasch 1994), later Anglicised to Santa Claus. The ritual spread to Germany, and then to other parts of Europe and the United States (Brasch 1994). On St Nicholas' Day on 6 December, children traditionally hang up stockings (a link to the original stocking) or put out their shoes for St Nicholas to fill with a gift. A second ritual associated with St Nicholas' Day was the choice of a choirboy to be the *boy bishop*, a rite of inversion (Nissenbaum 1996), and 'a symbol of the lowly taking authority, even as Christ had done' (Nettel 1957: 46). This inversion essentially

> filled a psychological need, whether it was as an outlet for youthful high spirits constrained by the normally severe discipline of medieval religious and educational institutions, or as an assertion of human equality at the season when universal good will was supposed to prevail.
>
> (Pimlott 1978: 25)

Another rite of inversion in medieval times at Christmas was *mumming*, where people wore masks or blackened their faces, donned costumes, and went from house to house, performing music and dancing for the occupants (Pimlott 1978).

The St Nicholas' Day traditions were not without their critics, who, apart from outrage at the revelry and tomfoolery that accompanied these celebrations, felt that this emphasis on the saint overshadowed the Christian story. German Protestants at the time of the Reformation therefore 'substituted the *Christkind* [the infant Christ] as the gift-bringer' (Nettel 1957: 28), in a bid to diminish the role of St Nicholas in Christmas festivities. Others took a half-way approach, providing the *Christkind* with a messenger, often dressed as an angel (Nettel 1957). Jennifer's stepfather was told as a child growing up in Hungary in the 1920s that the gifts were provided by 'the angels'.

In the Victorian era, the story of St Nicholas was fused with the idea of the *Spirit of Christmas*, *Jolly Old Christmas* or *King Cheer*,

> who was seldom depicted without a glass in his hand. This jovial figure was the one most often seen in Victorian Christmas pictures. He was shown as the founder of the Christmas Feast, the purveyor of jollity, as well as the children's present-giver. Half pagan and half Christian, he inspired awe as well as love.
>
> (Miall and Miall 1978: 87)

In England he became known as Father Christmas, while Dutch-Americans called him Santa Claus. The famous children's poem by Clement Clark Moore in 1822, *A Visit from St Nicholas*, better known by its opening line ''Twas the night before Christmas', immortalised 'St Nick' as chubby, white-bearded and merry, riding a sleigh with eight reindeer and 'dressed all in fur from his head to his foot'. This morphed into the popular image of Santa as a jolly plump man with a red jacket and hat, broad belt and black boots, which some argue can be traced back to the Christmas advertisements produced for Coca-Cola by Haddon Sundblom, beginning in 1931 (Belk 1993; Pendergrast 1993). The European St Nicholas, by contrast, wore variously coloured clothing and was often portrayed as 'tall and gaunt' (Pendergrast 1993: 181), although Brasch (1994) notes that the Bishop of Myra's vestments were red and white. Other fictions were created around Santa Claus during the nineteenth century, which parents ever since have kept alive for their children:

> Winter meant snow, snow suggested the Arctic, the Arctic suggested reindeer; they were all in character, and by making Santa Claus' headquarters the North Pole (which is a real geographical location) fictional belief was strengthened, but it was nineteenth century fiction.
>
> (Nettel 1957: 44)

For Lévi-Strauss (1993), the Santa myth is an *initiation ritual*, which keeps young children in order and gives them licence to demand presents at this time of year in exchange for good behaviour. In time, they will grow up to tell the same stories to their children and later grandchildren. Adults keep the secret from children 'until an opportune moment, thus sanctioning the addition of the younger generation to the adult world' (Lévi-Strauss 1993: 44). Santa himself is a mythic figure, and even Christ-like in his omniscience and ability to work miracles, except that he brings material gifts rather than gifts of the spirit (Belk 1993).

Sometimes the rites associated with gift giving are reversed. In European countries with Germanic roots, St Nicholas is accompanied on the evening of 5 December by an alter ego, *Krampus*, who punishes naughty children by hitting them with birch rods and stowing them in a sack, rather than rewarding them with presents. In some places it is St Nicholas rather than Krampus who brings a birch bundle, but in this case it is often decorated with sweets, and was supposed to scare away evil spirits and bring abundance to the household. Birches or willows are the first trees to recover their green foliage in spring, and thus symbolise new life and fertility (Barber 2013).

Krampus is also known as *Perchten* in some regions, and is essentially a *barteln* or pagan monster, with links back to the Feast of Fools held during the Roman Saturnalia festival (Barber 2013; Nettel 1957). The importance of Krampus appears to be increasing in parts of Europe, perhaps in an attempt to build Christmas-related tourism (Haid 2006). In Neustift im Stubaital, Austria, a new event called *Krampusnacht* was celebrated on 30 November, when 16 groups, including over 200 Krampuses, descended on the town, dressed in hand-carved wooden masks with animal horns and suits of sheep or goat skins. Other characters who might be seen with St Nicholas are a Fool (the Lord of Misrule), a Witch (acted by a man, in a rite of inversion) and Death. As Nettel (1957: 12) observes: 'Here are the elements of the great drama of life; this is more than mere horse-play.' The Netherlands has a different tradition, where St Nicholas is accompanied by Black Peter, who threatens to take naughty children back to Spain (Nettel 1957), presumably a reference to the Moors. Originally the role was played by 'immigrants from the colonies, West Indian descendants from the slave trade preferably' (Van Tiggelen 2013). These days, the (usually) white man or woman blackens their face, a ritual that the UN human rights commissioner, Verene Shepherd, labelled offensive, leading to rallies by the Dutch in support of maintaining Black Peter (Van Tiggelen 2013).

The exchange of presents at Christmas can be understood an example of a rite of consumption (Falassi 1987), in particular *conspicuous consumption*. This often 'causes months of financial anxiety [and] generates sheaves of bills that are paid off over subsequent months' (Waits 1993: xix) or contribute to an endless cycle of debt. C.S. Lewis (1970) is correct when he argues that the scale of gift giving in the current era has gone way beyond what it used to be, and expectations of recipients have accordingly soared, whetted by media images of the latest gadgets and trinkets, and the guilt trip carefully laid by commercial interests, which associates the amount of money spent with the amount of love that is bestowed. Yet the argument that Christmas presents have been forced on an unwilling public by the business sector is somewhat spurious. Pimlott (1978) observes that this ritual was already established by the nineteenth century, and the fact that Christmas cards took a while to catch on was evidence of the failure of market forces to make the public do what it didn't intrinsically want to do.

Waits (1993: 5) argues that gifts convey symbolic messages about 'the relationships between the exchanging parties' and this may lead to feelings of pressure to choose the right gift for the right person, adding to the stress of Christmas. The ritual of shopping turns products into gifts, assisted by devices such as gift wrapping to make them special, and is hard work (Carrier 1993). The home-made Christmas gift in modern times might be deemed 'unsatisfactory because it denies [this] ritual' (Carrier 1993). Similarly, adopting a 'rational approach to Christmas gift-giving' runs the risk of destroying 'the myth and mystery needed for sustaining a key contemporary ritual in the home' (Belk 1993: 96). Thus the recent trend for donating a practical item like a pig or a water purifier to someone in need in the name of the recipient raises strong feelings. Some appreciate the association with benevolence at Christmas, while others might question the appropriateness of dictating generosity and giving a present that is in effect a present to another. Some families adopt the *Kris Kringle*, drawing a name out of a hat and buying a relatively expensive present only for that family member, often a gift that the recipient has selected or recommended in advance. Again, this might appear clinical, and detract from the joy of present-giving. Giving cash rather than a present at Christmas is often seen as cold or impersonal (Waits 1993), unless it is between parent and child or is 'likely to be memorialized in a durable object', such as a major purchase (Carrier 1993). This has led to the production of Christmas-themed wallets to enclose the notes; a way to make the gift seem less of a transaction. Gift certificates or vouchers could be seen in the same light, despite their convenience. Some people enjoy the ritual of present-buying, which might bestow a sense of identity on the buyer or feelings of self-worth, and find these shortcuts do not provide the same warm glow, even when they are unsure whether the recipient wants what they have bought.

Cheap tat in the form of Christmas novelties also comes in for criticism in an age of greater environmental awareness and concern about recycling and a more careful use of resources. Georges Monbiot, a journalist and political activist, bemoans the junk that accumulates at Christmas, designed for fleeting entertainment and then consigned to landfill. He declares: 'This is pathological consumption: a world-consuming epidemic of collective madness, rendered so normal by advertising and by the media that we scarcely notice what has happened to us' (Monbiot 2012). The desire to divest unwanted Christmas presents has led to the sneaky practice of *re-gifting*, which can lead to hurt feelings and great embarrassment if a present ends up back in the hands of the original giver (Meagher 2013).

One is struck in contrast by the simplicity of Christmases of the nineteenth century. As a child, Jennifer was in awe at the altruism of the March girls in *Little Women* (1868), who gave their Christmas meal away to the poor and spent all their pocket-money on small gifts for their mother. The subtext was that giving was better than receiving (Miall and Miall 1978). Another example she vividly remembers from childhood is the frontier nineteenth-century Christmas written about so eloquently by Laura Ingalls Wilder in *Little House on the Prairie* (1935). There is no snow for Santa Claus to travel with his reindeer, nor can the Ingalls children see how Santa can cross a creek in flood to bring them presents. Their mother suggests that Santa Claus might not come this year, but encourages them to hang their stockings. That night, their neighbour, Mr Edwards, braves the swollen creek to bring the children gifts from Santa Claus, who he says 'had the longest, thickest, whitest set of whiskers west of the Mississippi' (p. 370). The children are desperate to look at what he has brought. They draw out a tin mug, a striped candy cane and a heart-shaped sugar cake for each child. We are told that 'Laura and Mary never would have looked in their stockings again. The cups and the cake and the candy were almost too much. They were too happy to speak' (p. 371). Ma encourages them to check them again, and they find a shiny penny in the toe. Laura writes:

> They had never even thought of such a thing as having a penny. Think of having a whole penny of your very own. Think of having a cup and a cake and a stick of candy *and* a penny. There never had been such a Christmas.
>
> (p. 372)

The last comment is a tribute to Dickens, the idea that each Christmas is more memorable than the last. But it is heartfelt. For Laura and her sisters, unaccustomed to great wealth or possessions, these small items are treasure indeed. But the adult Laura also recognises and rejoices in the love that inspired Mr Edwards to risk his life to bring Christmas cheer to the Ingalls family, particularly the *children*. That was the greatest of the gifts they received that year.

In the Victorian era, the association of Christmas with munificent acts, rather than mere conviviality, began to take hold. Lalumia (2001) attributes this to the influence of Dickens's *A Christmas Carol*. Scrooge learns the benefits of helping others and we are told that Christmas was a 'good time; a kind, forgiving, charitable, pleasant time'. It also accords with the Christian origins of the festival, notably Jesus' commandment of 'doing unto others as you would have them do unto you'. Priests distributed the contents of the poor box known as *Christ's Mass box* (Brasch 1994) and the Victorians gave Christmas 'boxes' to the needy on the day after Christmas (Miall and Miall 1978), the origin of the Boxing Day celebration. Americans similarly gave baskets to the poor, illustrated by the March family in *Little Women*, and a Santa Claus Association was set up in 1904, aimed at giving every poor child a Christmas present (Waits 1993). In the same vein, the charity Samaritan's Purse Australasia has run a campaign since 1993 known as Operation Christmas Child, which provides shoeboxes filled with gifts to children in South-East Asia and the South Pacific. Over 308,000 boxes were donated in 2012 (Operation Christmas Child 2013). Shopping centres, malls or retail or department stores may have Christmas trees where shoppers can donate a present, or buy an ornament representing a gift for a child.

This notion of benevolence underpins such acts as Christmas bonuses to employees, the granting of clemency to prisoners and the temporary cessation of warfare. The most famous example of the latter occurred during the First World War, where soldiers on opposite sides famously played football between the trenches around Ypres on Christmas Day in 1914. This temporary and unofficial truce began with a ceasefire to recover the dead, and turned into a game of football when a ball was kicked by the British into 'no man's land'. This 'universal language' helped to overcome communication barriers. The soldiers also sang their favourite carols to each other; *Stille Nacht* (*Silent Night*) by the Germans and *O Come All Ye Faithful* by the British. James Taylor, a historian at the Imperial War Museum, described it as 'the last bit of chivalry of the First World War' (*Telegraph* 2012).

While a number of accounts of the event exist, a common ground appears to be the sense of comradeship across cultural and battlefield boundaries, connected to Christmas festivities, and a sense of optimism that the war would not continue for long, given this shared brotherhood (*Telegraph* 2012). This event has been honoured over the past three years, with an annual Christmas Truce Tournament held in Ypres involving young Under-12 footballers from England, Belgium, France and Germany and an announcement in 2013 of a new all-weather pitch, funded by the English Premier League (Diaz 2013). The UK Sports Minister, Helen Grant, who is also the Minister for the First World War Centenary, observed: 'As we count down to the start of our WW1 commemorations, the Premier League's initiative will use football to help forge lasting links and bonds of friendship as we come together to remember' (Department for Culture, Media and Sport 2013).

An annual Christmas party for children is another act of benevolence. The courtyard of the Monegasque palace has been the location for an annual Christmas party, where the royal family distribute gifts to local children, since 1956, the year Grace Kelly became Princess Grace of Monaco. It was her idea. Many aristocratic families hosted similar functions for their local children at Christmas, with gifts and party food. Fiona the Countess of Carnarvon (2013: 57) notes that her husband's grandfather was enthusiastic about maintaining this ritual: 'Continuity of tradition was important to him and he knew that it was essential to Highclere's position as the centre of a community that such occasions be upheld.'

Family activities

Christmas is a way of marking the calendar and the cycles of life, and thus functions as a *rite of passage*. It is a time for families to get together and reminisce about the past, including memories of different Christmases over the years. The *family* is in fact the axis around which Christmas rituals are generally organised (Miller 1993). This is still the case, even in an era where the nuclear family is less the norm, and blended families, same-sex relationships and single people are far more common. Christmas becomes an 'alternative reality of a world in which the family retains its central presence and by extension those values which are associated with this core of our sociality' (Miller 1993: 15). Even if pronouncements of the death of the family are premature, the fact that it is often held to be the case makes Christmas even more important, as the one day when the strength of family bonds is affirmed and championed (Miller 1993).

The Victorian family Christmas involved the opening of presents, visits to church on Christmas morning and a festive lunch or dinner. Shops still traded, however – it was not a universal holiday in those days – illustrated by Scrooge's ability to purchase a turkey for the Cratchits on Christmas morning (Miall and Miall 1978). Games were played after dinner, like Blindman's Buff and Charades, along with songs or recitations, before the children headed off to bed.

The invention of many of the Christmas traditions in the Victorian era does not mean that it has stayed fossilised since that time; although it is true to say that much of it remains unchanged. However, as Pimlott (1978: 182) notes: 'Within the general pattern there is fortunately great scope for individual variations, and each family has its own ritual.' The modern Christmas still involves a visit to church for many people, although more would gather around the television than the pews these days. This is mainly a British tradition, the result of families cooped up inside on a cold winter's day, once the meal is over. A Christmas version of popular television shows would be eagerly awaited, with one of the most famous being the *Morecambe and Wise* Christmas special, which ran from 1969 to 1980 (with the exception of 1974). Current examples include the annual Christmas-themed episodes of *Doctor Who*, *Downton Abbey* and *Mrs Brown's Boys*, as well as the *Strictly Come Dancing Christmas Special*, all screened on Christmas Day in the United Kingdom in 2013. *Doctor Who* featured the regeneration of Matt Smith into the new Doctor, Peter Capaldi, and attracted 8.3 million viewers (BBC 2014).

The Queen's televised Christmas speech was slightly less popular with 7.5 million viewers (BBC 2014). The tradition of an annual speech by the British monarch to their subjects began in 1932 with a radio broadcast by George V, at the instigation of the BBC, who wished to inaugurate the Empire Service, now the BBC World Service. The speech would also give members of the empire the sense that the king was speaking directly to them, and thus boost feelings of solidarity around the monarch. The 1932 speech was written by Rudyard Kipling, a measure of the importance given to it and the king's concerns about the new technology and the challenges of making a personal speech. He didn't plan to deliver the speech the following year, but its popularity made him feel that it was his duty as the sovereign to do so, a sentiment shared by subsequent monarchs. While there were breaks in 1936 and 1938, the outbreak of war in 1939 saw the speech take a central role in maintaining public morale in grim times. The struggles of the next king, George VI, to record the speech live given his stuttering have been immortalised in the Oscar-winning film *The King's Speech* (2010). His daughter, Queen Elizabeth II, continues the tradition, and even uses the same desk that her father and grandfather sat at to record their speeches. Her speeches generally include references to the birth of Christ and affirm the values that are popularly associated with Christmas such as kindness and love; highlighting that the Royal Family is essentially a *family* just like us (Kuper 1993). Since 1957, the speech has been broadcast annually on television, except for 1969, due to a scheduled repeat of the documentary *Royal Family*. This innovation was met with a public outcry, and the queen was forced to reassure people that the speech would return the following year (British Monarchy 2014).

Cusack (1966: ix) suggests that the Australian Christmas 'picnic to beach or bush did represent a departure; a first, tentative recognition of sun and summer. Boxing Day Sports went a step further'. The backyard or beach cricket match laid the foundations for the Boxing Day Test cricket match at the Melbourne Cricket Ground. First held in 1950, with the third day's play coinciding with Boxing Day, there was a hiatus until the 1974–1975 Ashes series, when a Test match starting on Boxing Day was scheduled to accommodate six Test matches over the summer. This has been a tradition ever since in Melbourne and attracts large crowds, with a record attendance of 91,092 occurring in 2013. This success has been adopted by other countries, which has led to controversy over who might host this event. Cricket Australia refuses to play a Boxing Day Test in South Africa, and cites a reciprocal agreement between the two countries not to host each other over Boxing Day (ABC 2009). The other well-known Australian sporting event on Boxing Day is the Sydney to Hobart Yacht Race. Families who don't watch sport on Boxing Day often attend the retail sales, sometimes queuing overnight to be the first to enter a store and snap up the bargains. The growth of web shopping is changing this tradition, with some Internet sites opening up their sales online as early as Christmas Day. Thus commercial interests are intruding into the family celebrations, supporting the perception that commerce is eroding 'the spirit of Christmas celebrated by Dickens' (Miller 1993: 4).

No Victorian Christmas was complete without a visit to the pantomime, which started their run on Boxing Day (Miall and Miall 1978). A rite of inversion can be seen in the tradition of a man playing the old woman's part, such as the Widow Twankey in *Aladdin*, and the fact that the title role in *Peter Pan*, the boy who never grew up, is normally played by a young woman. The origins of its bawdy humour might be traced back to the rites of Saturnalia, and it can also be viewed as an example of the *carnivalesque* (Miller 1993). This English tradition, however, has not been preserved in its former colonies, such as Australia, although many Australian soap actors in recent years have appeared as guest stars in English pantomimes.

The traditional meal

Food associated with Christmas lunch or dinner, whether enjoyed on Christmas Eve as in many European countries, or on the day itself, is an example of a rite of consumption (Falassi 1987). In the United Kingdom, one thinks of roast meat (often turkey or beef) and vegetables, a flaming plum pudding, mince pies and Christmas fruitcake. Yet in the medieval period, it was the boar's head that was traditional Christmas fare, a 'link with the pagan past ... thought to have originated in primaeval rites involving the actual sacrifice of a mock king whose place was subsequently taken by an animal substitute' (Pimlott 1978: 22–23). The meat of choice when Queen Victoria ascended the throne was beef in the north of England and goose in the south, like the Cratchits enjoyed in *A Christmas Carol* (Miall and Miall 1978). Many working-class families contributed a proportion of their wages each week to a Goose Club, to spread the cost over the whole year (Miall and Miall 1978). Turkey, by contrast, was expensive, and did not come into favour in Victorian England until the late nineteenth century. North America was replete with wild turkeys, and they were popular as a Christmas meal long before the English adopted the trend (Miall and Miall 1978).

In France, the favoured Christmas dessert is the *Bûche de Noël*, a chocolate roll that resembles the Yule log of medieval times, while in Italy, it is the dome-shaped sweetbread studded with raisins and dried candied fruit, known as *panettone*. Germany has *lebkuchen*, a type of ginger and honey biscuit covered in icing, whose antecedent is the milk and honey cake (*libum* in Latin) given as an offering to the Roman gods (Barber 2013), as well as *stollen*, a cake of dried fruit and marzipan.

The Ingalls family in *Little House on the Prairie* enjoy roast wild turkey, with sweet potatoes brought by their neighbour Mr Edwards and a dessert made of stewed dried blackberries and cakes made with brown sugar. It was simple but festive, because it was superior to their normal fare. The expeditioners engaged in the race to the Poles used the Christmas meal as a way to keep up morale, overcome boredom and mark the passing of time, similar to the rituals undertaken in modern times at the Antarctic stations (Suedfeld and Steel 2000; Wood *et al.* 2000). Apsley Cherry-Garrard writes of a meal with jokes, whistles and pudding in *The Worst Journey in the World* (1922), while Shackleton gave his team en route to the South Pole a cigar and a sip of crème de menthe (Worsley 2011).

Even in parts of the world where Christmas is celebrated in summer, a hot meal (lunch or dinner) is customary, although there is a growing emphasis in Australia on seafood, particularly prawns, fruits in season such as mangoes and cherries, and the meringue-based pavlova as an alternative to heavy pudding. This reflects the Australian climate, but still retains the quality of being *special* and thus appropriate for a festive meal. The introduction to *The Australian Christmas*, edited by Cusack (1966), notes that early Christmases in Australia, pre-Dickens, were 'something of a duty'. Cusack argues that Dickens's writings imparted a spiritual gloss on these festivities, a reason for all the carousing, which was able to accommodate 'prevailing custom, whatever its origin' (p. viii).

Some of the Christmas traditions lovingly transported to these far-away shores are captured in novels of the period. In *The Mystery of a Hansom Cab* (1886), Hume writes (p. 198):

John Bull, Paddy, and Sandy [i.e. Englishman, Irish and Scot], all being of a conservative turn of mind ... [have] strong opinions as to the keeping up of old customs. Therefore, on a hot Christmas day, with the sun one hundred odd in the shade, Australian revellers sit down to the roast beef and plum-pudding of Old England, which they eat contentedly as the orthodox thing.

Similarly, several chapters of *We of the Never Never* (1908), by Mrs Aeneas Gunn, are devoted to preparations for the Christmas meal. Jeannie Gunn writes of her life on a cattle station in the remote, dry and harsh Northern Territory at the turn of last century, and there are allusions to Dickens in her prose ('[he] asked us if there ever was such a ham') and a direct reference to *A Christmas Carol* in the following vignette about the pudding (p. 249):

> Only Cheon [the Chinese cook and gardener] was worthy to carry it in to the feast; and as he came through the leafy way, bearing the huge mottled ball, as big as a bullock's head – all ablaze with spirits and dancing light and crowned with mistletoe ... We held our breaths in astonishment, each feeling like the entire Cratchit family rolled into one, and by the time we had recovered speech, Cheon was soberly carrying one third of the pudding to the missus.

Plum pudding was originally a savoury dish in medieval times, and its plums were gradually replaced by raisins and currants (Miall and Miall 1978). The pudding was often doused with alcohol, usually brandy, and set alight, in a rite of purification (Falassi 1987). Pimlott (1978) makes a connection between the brandy and the flaming punch of Victorian times, which has essentially died out as a ritual. In the vignette above, poor Cheon nearly chokes on the three-pence buried in the pudding, which is another ritual that seems to have gone out of favour, although as children, we remember the excitement of being the person to find a coin in our slice of plum pudding. This ritual dates from medieval times and was said to bring the recipient prosperity, symbolising the gifts given to the infant Christ by the Three Wise Men. Pimlott (1978) associates the coins with the bean and pea hidden in the Twelfth Night cake, with those who found them allowed to preside over the night's festivities. Hiding money in the pudding may have been phased out due to concerns about swallowing the coin, which was smaller than its pre-decimal equivalent. They also had to be inserted into the pudding just before it was served, to avoid the copper and nickel content in the coin turning it green during the cooking process. These days, one can buy a small pack of silver pudding coins to overcome this problem. Another ritual associated with Christmas pudding is for every member of the family to stir the mixture 'from East to West in honour of the Three Kings' (Miall and Miall 1978: 119).

Any Christmas meal is unthinkable without pulling crackers, wearing the paper hats they contain and reading out the type of joke that is accompanied by a groan at their direness. The popular explanation behind the cracker is that Tom Smith, an English confectioner, visited Paris in 1844 and discovered the French *bon-bon*, a wrapped sweet (Pimlott 1978). The idea to convert it into a cracker came when he heard a log on the fire crackle and pop. He found out how to make the characteristic bang by a small explosive (Brasch 1994). The Christmas cracker was introduced in 1846, with the sweet replaced by a small trinket, jokes or sayings and a paper hat as a surprise inclusion (Brasch 1994; Pimlott 1978).

The paradoxical nature of Christmas

Christmas as a ritual has a number of *paradoxes* that surround it. The first concerns its religious origins. Christmas is often seen as a Christian festivity, yet it has never shaken off its pagan roots. According to Waits (1993: 3), elements, such as present giving and the family meal 'have dwarfed its religious aspects in resources spent and in concern given'. Christmas is both 'the greatest religious holy day and the greatest commercial holiday in the Christian world' (Belk 1993: 75). It might be argued that Christianity has always faced an uphill battle in privileging the Christian elements of Christmas over the secular (Nissenbaum 1996). Some Christians, recognising its tenuous link with Christianity, have pushed to stop Christmas altogether, as evidenced by the Puritan efforts during the Reformation.

The second paradox concerns the perceived age of most of the rituals central to a modern Christmas. While many of us think of Christmas as a 'rite of considerable antiquity' (Miller 1993: 3), most of our modern traditions only date from the mid nineteenth century, albeit often an amalgam of disparate elements that can be traced back in time, as we have outlined in this chapter. For reasons of nostalgia, people overlook the recent origin of many of these rituals (Miller 1993). The desire for tradition in fact 'leads to the intense creation of new traditions' (Löfgren 1993: 231). It is also the case that Christmas is both a barometer of change and an agent for change (Nissenbaum 1996).

Third, Christmas is a global festival, yet it has its greatest significance in the home and the rituals of the domestic (Miller 1993). Thus, while there are rituals in common on an international scale, a number of Christmas rituals are local and specific to a particular culture or place. It is therefore represents both 'the epitome of globalisation' and 'the triumph of localism' (Miller 1993: 24–25).

Fourth, it is a holiday that is both serious and playful (Löfgren 1993). There are 'norms and taboos' (p. 232) about how to celebrate Christmas and what it means to have an *authentic* Christmas experience (Löfgren 1993). Nostalgia demands that it be treated reverently. Yet rites of inversion and bacchanalian rites are still rife within Christmas festivities, in a throwback to medieval times and possibly a legacy of the carnivalesque elements of Saturnalia (Miller 1993). Office parties are an example, which 'tend to break down barriers of hierarchy and sexual constraint between colleagues, and are associated with tolerated drunkenness' (Kuper 1993: 165). These symbolic inversions help to 'demarcate a sacred time and place' (p. 164), being the Christmas period.

Fifth, the Christmas moral economy, with its gift giving and the temporary cessation of work, subverts 'the economy of everyday life' (Belk 1993: 167). Thrift is no longer seen as virtuous in the context of Christmas (Miller 1993; Nissenbaum 1996), and we have licence to throw caution to the wind and spend lavishly on our family and friends, if not ourselves. Yet a hiatus from work may be illusory, and many people, particularly women, carry the burden of catering for large numbers and catering for multiple whims. Even shopping can be considered a form of work (Carrier 1993; Miller 1993), with the common refrain of getting the present ritual 'over and done with', and having to battle crowds of shoppers and the fear of not meeting the expectations of the intended recipients of the gifts. We do it for the social value we place on it, which outweighs its onerousness. It also makes us feel good, to undertake something that is partly unpleasant, yet bestows benefits on those we love and care about. Thus, it can be understood as a 'moral act' (Miller 1993: 21).

Sixth, commercialisation of Christmas and materialist sentiments might be seen as antithetical to family values celebrated at Christmas (Miller 1993), yet the reality is less straightforward. Gift giving may assist in building family relationships (Carrier 1993). Christmas might also be seen as a time when those who feel moral compunction over their wealth can assuage their guilt through the exchange of gifts and public and private benevolence, and thus might 'ameliorate [the] negative consequences [of materialism] for society' (Miller 1993: 20). It can also provide an opportunity for high creativity, where people have 'a chance to tinker, to decorate, to create, with an energy which can almost make the traditional peasant seem paralysed' (Löfgren 1993: 232). Others argue that the cry that Christmas has become over-commercialised due to the dominance and persuasiveness of business interests is almost a cliché, given that gift giving can be traced back to the Roman celebrations of Kalends and Saturnalia (Miller 1993) and there is a long tradition of people musing nostalgically about a less commercial Christmas in the past (Nissenbaum 1996).

Finally, Christmas is a time to be happy and joyful, yet some people get depressed, perhaps conscious of their loneliness at a period when families come together (Löfgren 1993; Miller 1993). It is almost seen as a pathological condition not to like Christmas (Pimlott 1978). However, arguments are often rife at this time, given 'family togetherness brings out divisions' (Löfgren 1993: 232). Many movie plots are constructed around the awkward Christmas family gathering, with people telling lies to get out of their obligations, exemplified by *Four Christmases* (2008). Those who work hard to prepare for and host a Christmas occasion may be disappointed at the result, or find it hard to relax and enjoy the festivities (Löfgren 1993).

The importance and diffusion of Christmas ritual

Miller (1993: 5) is effusive about the success of Christmas as a global event. It has spread far beyond those countries that would regard themselves as nominally Christian. How did this happen and more importantly why? The rituals discussed in this chapter must be meaningful to the vast majority of people, given the amount of time, money and effort that goes into this festival, its international impact, and more importantly the 'consistency which has marked the celebration of Christmas' (Pimlott 1978: 174), with these rituals repeated annually in an endless cycle. Known as *cyclical time*, this repetition allows people to look forward to the 'return to the special festive atmosphere of the holiday, a return that promised escape, of a sort, from everyday problems' (Waits 1993: 7). Each new cycle allows a fresh start. Christmas time is a juncture between the old year and the new and becomes idealised and mythologised in the minds of those who anticipate it. It is an 'alternative world' (Kuper 1993: 171), in contrast to the normal, historical time we experience, which is linear, and will never be returned to again.

It is the *re-enactment* of rituals at Christmas that helps us to escape the feeling that linear time is rushing on, and running out, and to see it more in cyclical terms. Thus, despite Christmas representing a new beginning, people like to do things in the same way, and often to celebrate with the same people:

> The ritual gathering of the same family members each year helped create the sense that they were once again back at the time when they all lived together. Symbolically, this served to mitigate the pains that separation had brought, and also helped to reassure family members that they could re-create the gathering again in the future.
>
> (Waits 1993: 10)

Another reason advanced for the importance of Christmas in our lives is its relationship to the winter solstice (Waits 1993). The latter marked the gradual return of the power of the sun from the depths of midwinter. It is a time of hope, a promise of renewal. While winter is associated with death, spring is associated with new life, and

> this powerful life-over-death message inherent in the change of seasons has exerted a strong – almost irresistible – appeal for humans concerned about their own individual paths toward death and about the continuance of the societies in which they live.
>
> (Waits 1993: 9)

While this premise does not hold sway for those living in the southern hemisphere, where Christmas falls around the summer solstice, it arguably fulfils a role for them much like midsummer in pagan times, a celebration of warmer weather and a time of plenty.

Pimlott (1978) argues that the main reason why Christmas rituals have remained essentially unchanged since the nineteenth century, aside from the fact that they suit 'powerful vested interests' such as the business sector, is that 'the values which the celebrations express and the institutions they support show no signs of losing public acceptance' (p. 177). While he wrote this back in 1960, nearly 20 years before his book was published, there is little to suggest that this assertion is no longer correct in the early twenty-first century. Lévi-Strauss (1993) makes a similar assertion, observing that 'customs neither disappear nor survive without a reason' (p. 46) and that the resilience of Christmas rituals is due to a 'desire to believe in boundless generosity, kindness without ulterior motives, a brief interlude during which all fear, envy, and bitterness are suspended' (p. 50). Kuper (1993) goes further, arguing that rituals like Christmas help to balance out perceived shortcomings in the social fabric, thus having a 'homeostatic role' (p. 162). When Christmas was abolished in the Soviet Union during the Communist era, they saw fit to create their own version of Santa Claus, *Ded Moroz* – translated as Grandfather Frost or Father Frost – an example of a rite that they felt should endure, albeit under a different name.

Connected to the values discussed above is the desire for fantasy and magic in a prosaic world. These sentiments are encapsulated in the famous 1897 editorial in the *New York Sun*, titled 'Yes, Virginia, There Is a Santa Claus', which includes the words: 'Alas! How dreary would be the world if there were no Santa Claus. There would be no childlike faith then, no poetry, no romance to make tolerable this existence.'

The spread of Christmas around the globe is an example of what Lévi-Strauss (1993) terms a *diffusion* of rites. This may occur either by the assimilation of a tradition or practice, or where the latter acts as a catalyst for the development of an identical custom. Either way, there are subtle differences between countries, although the essential elements remain the same. The variety of names given to Santa Claus 'shows that it is a result of a process of convergence and not an ancient prototype preserved everywhere intact' (Lévi-Strauss 1993: 42). It seems we all need a Santa Claus, as the *New York Sun* put it so eloquently nearly 120 years ago.

References

ABC (2009) Australia refuses to play a Boxing Day cricket test in South Africa, *ABC PM*, 9 January. Online: www.abc.net.au/pm/content/2008/s2462665.htm (accessed 28 January 2014).

Ackroyd, P. (1991) 'Introduction', in C. Dickens (1843), *A Christmas Carol*, London: Mandarin, 1991 edn.

Alcott, L.M. (1868) *Little Women*, London: Penguin Books, 1989 edn.

Barber, E.W. (2013) *The Dancing Goddesses: Folklore, archaeology and the origins of European dance*, New York; London: W.W. Norton.

BBC (2014) 'Doctor Who regeneration tops Christmas Day TV ratings', *BBC News*, 26 December. Online: www.bbc.co.uk/news/entertainment-arts-25518352 (accessed 7 January 2014).

Belk, R. (1993) 'Materialism and the making of the modern American Christmas', in D. Miller (ed.), *Unwrapping Christmas* (pp. 75–104), Oxford: Oxford University Press, 1995 edition.

Brasch, R. (1994) *Christmas Customs and Traditions: Why we do what we do at Christmas*, Sydney: Angus & Robertson.

British Monarchy (2014) *A History of Christmas Broadcasts*. Online: www.royal.gov.uk/imagesandbroadcasts/thequeenschristmasbroadcasts/ahistoryofchristmasbroadcasts.aspx (accessed 5 January 2014).

Carnarvon, F. (2013) *Lady Catherine and the Real Downton Abbey*, London: Hodder & Stoughton.

Carrier, J. (1993) 'The rituals of Christmas giving', in D. Miller (ed.), *Unwrapping Christmas* (pp. 55–74), Oxford: Oxford University Press, 1995 edn.

Cherry-Garrard, A. (1922) *The Worst Journey in the World*, London: Vintage Books, 2010 edn.

Cusack, F. (ed.) (1966) *The Australian Christmas*, London; Melbourne: Heinemann.

Daily News (2013) 'Rockefeller Center Christmas tree lights up New York City', 4 December. Online: www.nydailynews.com/new-york/rockefeller-center-christmas-tree-lights-city-article-1.1537918 (accessed 3 January 2014).

Department for Culture, Media and Sport (2013) 'First World War Christmas Truce football match commemorated', 9 December. Online: www.gov.uk/government/news/first-world-war-christmas-truce-football-match-commemorated (accessed 5 January 2013).

Diaz, A. (2013) 'Premier League to donate new football pitch at Ypres to commemorate "Christmas Truce" match during First World War', *The Independent*, 7 December. Online: www.independent.co.uk/sport/football/news-and-comment/premier-league-to-donate-new-football-pitch-at-ypres-to-commemorate-christmas-truce-match-during-first-world-war-8990357.html (accessed 5 January 2013).

Edensor, T. and Millington, S. (2009) 'Illuminations, class identities and the contested landscapes of Christmas', *Sociology*, 43(1), 103–121.

Enjoy Medway (2013) *Dickensian Christmas*. Online: www.visitmedway.org/events/dickensian-christmas (accessed 8 November 2013).

Falassi, A. (1987) 'Festival: Definition and morphology', in A. Falassi (ed.), *Time out of Time: Essays on the festival* (pp. 1–10), Albuquerque, NM: University of New Mexico Press.

Gunn, A. (1908) *We of the Never Never*, London: Hutchinson, 1971 edn.

Haid, O. (2006) 'Christmas markets in the Tyrolean Alps: Representing regional traditions in a newly created world of Christmas', in D. Picard and M. Robinson (eds), *Festivals, Tourism and Social Change: Remaking worlds* (pp. 209–221), Clevedon: Channel View.

Hobsbawm, E. (1983) 'Introduction: Inventing traditions', in E. Hobsbawm and T. Ranger (eds), *The Invention of Tradition* (pp. 1–14), Cambridge: Cambridge University Press.

Hume, F. (1886) *The Mystery of a Hansom Cab*, Melbourne: Currey O'Neill, 1982 edn.

Ingalls-Wilder, L. (1935) *Little House on the Prairie*, New York: Library of America, 2012 edn.

Jamieson, A. (2008) 'Dreaming of a white Christmas? Blame the nostalgia of Charles Dickens' snowy childhood', *The Telegraph*, 24 December. Online: www.telegraph.co.uk/topics/christmas/3933091/Dreaming-of-a-white-Christmas-Blame-the-nostalgia-of-Charles-Dickens-snowy-childhood.html?fb (accessed 29 December 2013).

Janiskee, R.L. (1996) 'Historic houses and special events', *Annals of Tourism Research*, 23(2), 398–414.

Kuper, A. (1993) 'The English Christmas and the family', in D. Miller (ed.), *Unwrapping Christmas* (pp. 157–175), Oxford: Oxford University Press, 1995 edn.

Lalumia, C. (2001) 'Scrooge and Albert', *History Today*, 51(12). Online: www.historytoday.com/christine-lalumia/scrooge-and-albert (accessed 3 January 2014).

Lévi-Strauss, C. (1993) 'Father Christmas executed', in D. Miller (ed.), *Unwrapping Christmas* (pp. 38–51), Oxford: Oxford University Press, 1995 edn.

Lewis, C.S. (1970) 'What Christmas means to me', in *God in the Dock* (pp. 304–305), Grand Rapids, MI: William B. Eerdmans Publishing Co.

Löfgren, O. (1993) 'The great Christmas quarrel and other Swedish traditions', in D.

Miller (ed.), *Unwrapping Christmas* (pp. 217–234), Oxford: Oxford University Press, 1995 edn.

Meagher, D. (2013) 'Nothing wrong with a little give and take', *The Australian*, Weekend A Plus, p. 7.

Miall, A. and Miall, P. (1978) *The Victorian Christmas Book*, London: Dent.

Miller, D. (1993) 'A theory of Christmas', in D. Miller (ed.), *Unwrapping Christmas* (pp. 3–37), Oxford: Oxford University Press, 1995 edn.

Monbiot, G. (2012) 'On the 12th day of Christmas … your gift will just be junk', *The Guardian*, 11 December. Online: www.theguardian.com/commentisfree/2012/dec/10/on-12th-day-christmas-present-junk (accessed 3 January 2014).

Nettel, R. (1957) *Santa Claus*, Bedford: Gordon Fraser.

Nissenbaum, S. (1996) *The Battle for Christmas*, New York: Knopf.

Operation Christmas Child (2013) *Operation Christmas Child*. Online: http://operation-christmaschild.org.au (accessed 3 January 2013).

Pendergrast, M. (1993) *For God, Country and Coca-Cola: The unauthorized history of the world's most popular soft drink*, London: Phoenix.

Pimlott, J.A.R. (1978) *The Englishman's Christmas: A social history*, Hassocks, UK: The Harvester Press.

Restad, P. (1995) *Christmas in America: A history*, New York; Oxford: Oxford University Press.

Rowell, G. (1993) 'Dickens and the construction of Christmas', *History Today*, 43(12). Online: www.historytoday.com/geoffrey-rowell/dickens-and-construction-christmas (accessed 3 January 2014).

Santino, J. (1994) 'Introduction: Festivals of death and life', in J. Santino (ed.), *Halloween and Other Festivals of Death And Life* (pp. xi–xxviii), Knoxville: University of Tennessee Press.

Sims, G.R. (ed.) (1902) *Living London: Its work and its play, its humour and its pathos, its sights and its scenes*, Vol. 1, London; Paris; New York; Melbourne: Cassell.

Suedfeld, P. and Steel, G.D. (2000) 'The environmental psychology of capsule habitats', *Annual Review of Psychology*, 51, 227–253.

The Telegraph (2012) 'Britons started WWI Christmas football match with ball kicked from trench', *The Telegraph*, 23 December. Online: www.telegraph.co.uk/history/9763539/Britons-started-WW1-Christmas-football-match-with-ball-kicked-from-trench.html (accessed 31 December 2013).

Terry, A. (2008) 'Claiming Christmas for the tourist: "Living history" in Dundurn Castle', *Journal of Heritage Tourism*, 3(2), 104–120.

Van Tiggelen, J. (2013) 'Stomping through the tulips', *The Saturday Age*, GoodWeekend, 30 November, p. 38.

Waits, W.B. (1993) *The Modern Christmas in America: A cultural history of gift giving*, New York; London: New York University Press.

Weintraub, S. (1997) *Albert Uncrowned King*, London: John Murray.

Winchester, H.P.M. and Rofe, M.W. (2005) 'Christmas in the "Valley of Praise": Intersections of the rural idyll, heritage and community in Lobethal, South Australia', *Journal of Rural Studies*, 21, 265–279.

Wood, J., Hysong, S.J., Lugg, D.J. and Harm, D.L. (2000) 'Is it really so bad? A comparison of positive and negative experiences in Antarctic winter stations', *Environment and Behaviour*, 32(1), 84–110.

Worsley, H. (2011) *In Shackleton's Footsteps: A return to the heart of the Antarctic*, London: Virgin, 2012 edition.

9 Beyond the masks

Continuity and change in a Sardinian rite

Monica Iorio and Geoffrey Wall

Introduction

The endurance of collective rituals and the revitalisation of local folklore throughout Europe since the 1970s provides evidence that rituals, traditions and festivals have an important place in contemporary societies (Boissevan 1992). Indeed, rituals continue to be important occasions for communities, families and individuals to express in public their identities, lifestyles, social relation and sense of belonging. While doing so, they experience *time out of time* through the interruption of daily activities to participate in activities that may be extra-ordinary in many ways (Falassi 1987). In this sense, participation in or attend-ance at a ritual is likely to be a liminal experience that takes people out of their workaday world, while also offering opportunities for socio-cultural affirmation and personal transformation (Picard and Robinson 2006). Rituals may also be a means to build social capital and to nurture resilience through the sharing of values, with both insiders and outsiders, interests and traditions that are central to the community and how it is represented (Adger 2000; Derrett 2009).

Traditionally, rituals and festivals have strong relationships with religious beliefs, moral codes, long-held customs and culturally shared myths (Falassi 1987; Sofield and Li 1998; Turner 1982). Such belief structures are expressed and celebrated with varying degree of frequency as festivals and special events. Some are regularly occurring celebrations whereas others are rare, one-off or occasional, even intermittent, events. Some are of very brief duration whereas others may last for days. Some spring seemingly spontaneously from long tradi-tions and are rooted in the local culture, whereas others are modern, even newly invented, having a limited association with the cultural traditions and the place in which they now occur (Ma and Lew 2011). Furthermore, they take place in very different settings, from major cities to remote rural areas, which have implications for how they are performed and can be experienced.

Whether religious or secular, traditional or modern, rituals and festivals are rich in meanings for the community celebrating them, the individuals that perform them and for the wider audiences that experience them. However, as performances, they may evolve and their significance often changes (Picard and Robinson 2006; Robinson *et al.* 2004). Similarly, the meanings communicated through them are subject to reconfiguration and reinterpretation as the form and content of a festival is remoulded in response to cultural changes and the processes of modernisation.

A major trend in recent decades has been the opening up of what were previously internally consumed rituals and festivals to tourist audiences as part of a wider process of the consumption of culture (Robinson *et al.* 2004). In many parts of the so-called developed world, as important markers of *pre-modern* tradition, they have become popular cultural tourism attractions (Arnold 2001). This has impinged upon the form, function and meaning of rituals within the local communities in which they are rooted and produced. However, changes in the way that festivities are enacted are not merely linked to tourism intervention; rather, they are bound up in wider social, cultural and economic processes and pressures emanating from both within and outside the community (Burke 1997). This is especially the case when rituals date back to ancient times, and their origins and original meanings have vanished over time, so that the current form, although providing a link between the past and present and potentially the future, does not find a full reference in the changed and changing society.

This chapter examines the development of the masked rite performed by the *Mamuthones* and *Issohadores* during the Sant'Antonio festival in the rural village of Mamoiada, Sardinia (Italy). The island still preserves and presents a rich and varied heritage of rituals, ceremonies and festivals, some of which are linked to the shepherds' economic and social system that has long characterised the inland area of the region. Here, the agro-pastoral world has remained largely intact over the centuries, as have the identities that have been associated with it, but now the rituals are part of a rapidly evolving world where such traditions do not have an obvious place.

Drawing upon various texts, photographic documentation and narratives, collected both on-site by the authors and from videos available through the Internet, the chapter traces the way in which the festival has developed in relation to an increasingly significant tourist audience. In doing so, it emphasises the present meaning of the festival for the local people and the way the community is using its mask heritage to open itself to a globalising world, without renouncing its own identity.

Sant'Antonio's Day: setting and attractiveness

Mamoiada is a rural village of around 2,600 inhabitants located in the mountainous centre of Sardinia, in the so-called *Barbagia* region (Figure 9.1). Romantic interpretations, often found in tourist brochures, travel books and videos (Iorio and Wall 2012), depict this region as being suspended in an archaic state untouched by time. The area is portrayed as having a traditional pastoral economy and shepherds are described as the custodians of ancient cultural practices and tradition. Mamoiada is a typical Barbagian village, once isolated and relying on agriculture and sheep farming (Le Lannou 1941). The village has become more accessible in recent years through the construction of fast roads

Figure 9.1 Mamoiada (source: M. Iorio and G. Wall).

traversing western Sardinia, although it still takes several hours to reach Mamoiada from the main city of the island, Cagliari. Farming is still an important activity, though tourism is growing and provides, directly and indirectly, new economic opportunities. Moreover, some of the residents commute to the city of Nuoro (the capital of the province to which Mamoiada belongs) where they are employed mainly in the service sector.

Mamoiada is becoming famous because it is home to a mask tradition that is not replicated elsewhere. Although some other places in Sardinia possess a mask tradition, that of Mamoiada is the most distinctive, with its *Mamuthones* (from uncertain etymology, though according to some linguists the term comes from *mommoti-motu*, which means the death; Dedola 2004) and *Issohadores* (the man with the lasso) masked male figures. The former wear black masks with distorted faces, caps secured under the chin by a headscarf, dark sheepskins, black pants and heavy hiking boots (Figure 9.2). They are festooned with numerous bells of great weight and they march rhythmically so that their bells sound in unison. They exude a sense of mystery, strength and evil.

They are escorted by the *Issohadores* who have a contrasting appearance with white masks, red jackets, white pants with a fancy scarf tied at the waist, and tall, black shiny boots. They also march rhythmically with the *Mamuthones*, giving guidance and direction to their pace. Moreover, there is a chief *Issohadore*, who plays a key role and, once all participants have dressed up, establishes the positioning of both the *Mamuthones* and *Issohadores* and leads them along the whole procession.

Figure 9.2 Mamuthones (source: M. Iorio and G. Wall).

The *Issohadores* carry lassos, which they use to 'capture' unsuspecting observers – preferably pretty girls (Figure 9.3)! Together the *Mamuthones* and *Issohadores* create a vivid spectacle and their performances are colourful and
rhythmic to both eyes and ears. A number of presentations or performances are
available on YouTube and should be consulted to gain a better appreciation of
the spectacle.

The *Mamuthones* and *Issohadores* masks are worn by Mamoiada's inhabitants in a celebration that is held on 16 and 17 January to celebrate Sant'Antonio's

Figure 9.3 Issohadores (source: M. Iorio and G. Wall).

Day, the most important feast in the village. This ceremony opens the carnival of Mamoiada, during which *Mamuthones* and *Issohadores* continue to perform their routine. Every year, on 16 January, bonfires are built throughout the village and form the foci of neighbourhood festivities. The procession of the *Mamuthones* and *Issohadores* from bonfire to bonfire can be interpreted as a rite of purification. The fire, indeed, has a purifying value: the old and negative is burned to make way for the new and the positive. The fires are scattered throughout the village in small spaces among the houses – a phenomenon facilitated by the irregular street pattern and the fact that structures are made from brick and stone rather than wood. The fires are lit in the late afternoon and are tended for several days until they eventually expire after the festival is over. The first bonfire is lit by the priest, after the Mass in honour of Sant'Antonio. Every bonfire is blessed by the *Mamuthones* and the *Issohadores* who dance around it honouring with their presence the inhabitants of each neighbourhood. After the awaited blessing, they are the first to be offered wine and traditional sweets (called *pobassinos*). These are then offered to the spectators.

While Christianity has absorbed and transformed most of the pagan rites, in this case an inverse process can be noticed, a paganisation of the Christian rite. This event highlights the coexistence of two distinct worlds, the pagan and the Christian, that, rather than overlapping, complement each other – the first seems to lead the second towards it. This is a sign of the endurance of tradition, of a ritual that has survived continuously across generations. The keepers of the sacred fires that are lit in Mamoiada also wear its colours: the *Mamuthones* wear black, the colour of soot which is returned to the earth and linked to it with their heavy steps, while the *Issohadores* wear costumes that have the colour of flames that rise with the upward movements of the *soha* (lassos) (Gregu 2014).

The first night of festivities is predominantly for local people and very few outsiders attend the event. It is an occasion to renew and reinforce social relationships. People gather around the fires, talking, singing, occasionally dancing, eating snacks and drinking red wine. Participants walk from fire to fire where they are greeted with more conversation and more red wine. This involves people of a wide variety of ages and both genders and extends late into the night – or into the early hours of the morning.

On the second day, 17 January, the community opens itself to visitors. Most visitors come from Sardinia, particularly from neighbouring villages, although the number of foreign visitors is growing (according to the head of the cultural district, in 2013, around 2,000 spectators from outside Mamoiada followed Sant'Antonio's celebration) and there is considerable media presence. The crowd builds during the day until the *Mamuthones* and *Issohadores* are ready to appear. People jostle for a good position to take photographs and follow one of the two groups of *Mamuthones* and *Issohadores* (one for the upper village and one for the lower village) as they move from bonfire to bonfire performing their routines (Figure 9.4). After each performance, wine and *pobassinos* are freely offered to

Figure 9.4 The Masked Rite (source: M. Iorio and G. Wall).

all present and there is a pause for conversation while the *Mamuthones* rest and recover from their exertions, before moving on to the next bonfire, always guided by the chief *Issohadore*. The evening and night, by which time most visitors have departed, follow the pattern of the previous night with conversation, music, dancing and local food and red wine, all generously provided by local residents.

During the festival, visitors also take the chance to buy local products (wine, bread, cheese, traditional sweets) and handicrafts (in particular souvenirs related to the masks) and to visit the Museum of Mediterranean Masks, which was established in 2001 and celebrates the mask tradition of the Sant'Antonio festival and places it in a broader context. The mask museum provides an additional focal point for those interested in masks in Mamoiada. The mask event occurs only on a couple of days annually, but, while there are not performances, the museum can be visited throughout the year and provides a reason for tourists to visit the village that is not constrained by the very limited performance schedule.

The growing audience of the festival and the activities held by the *Pro-Loco* and the museum are helping to stimulate the local economy and generate pride in a place that was formerly losing its young people, needed enhanced economic opportunities and suffered from a bad reputation resulting from a history of family feuds that lasted for most of the second half of the past century and resulted in numerous deaths (Iorio and Wall 2011, 2012). Mamoiada was not a place that many tourists would visit. Nowadays, there are around 150 beds for tourists (though on the occasion of the festival, when accommodation is not enough, local families informally host tourists). New economic activities have been established, such as bed and breakfast accommodation, restaurants, cafes, a tourism agency, workshops that produce typical bread, wineries that produce excellent wine and craftsmen that produce the masks for sale as high-quality souvenirs (Iorio and Wall 2012). Also, *Mamuthones* and *Issohadores* masks have been proposed for inscription in the World Heritage List, in an application that contains all the traditional masks of Sardinia.

The origin and the recent evolution of the rite

The origins and original meanings of the event are lost in antiquity. Marchi (1951) suggested that the danced procession could originally have been a commemorative ceremony for a local historical event: the victory that the Sardinians enjoyed over their Muslim assailants. The *Mamuthones* represent the Muslim invaders, captured and dressed to resemble oxen and paraded through the village by the local shepherds who are themselves *veste di turco*, i.e. dressed as Turks or as Muslim invaders. Thus the Muslim invaders were subjugated and underwent the ritual of *imbovamentu*, the reduction of man into beast.

Atzori *et al.* (1989) based their interpretation of the procession on the Sardinian ritual of *imbovamentu* and see the ritual as the enactment of the self-irony of the peasants. According to them, since the animals they raise are the peasants' main source of income, peasant life is dominated by this man–beast relation.

Atzori *et al.* (1989) therefore saw this ritual as the exorcism of the man–beast relation through ironic beast–man inversion.

In another of his hypotheses, Marchi (1951) goes back to the time of the civilisation of the *Nuraghe* in Sardinia, between 1600 and 600 BCE. He identified the danced procession as one of the numerous rituals carried out by the Nuraghic people to honour their agricultural and pastoral deities and to celebrate the fertility of the earth and the transformation of a wild animal, the bull, into a domesticated animal, the ox. Turchi (1996) came to a similar conclusion and asserted that the procession derives from ancient agricultural rites performed by the Sardinians in pagan times when, according to her, they were followers of a mysterious Dionysiac cult.

Later interpretations agree on seeing in this danced procession a sort of propitiatory rite of the shepherd world. Rites are usually made at the beginning of the agrarian season to promote a better harvest and a successful year. Indeed, the sound made by the *Mamuthones'* bells is believed to have an apotropaic function, a kind of magic intended to turn away harm or evil influences from the community (Mamuthones 2013). Local people also believe that the rite celebrates the rhythm of life for humans – the death (represented by the *Mamuthones*) and the birth (represented by the *Issohadores*). Together the *Mamuthones* and *Issohadores* celebrate the renewal of a life cycle. Indeed, they announce to the community that the new age has come, and the community responds by joining in the procession. Observers hope to be caught by the rope of he who celebrates life (the *Issohadore*) rather than to follow in the footsteps of those who, silently, slide to the end (the *Mamuthones*). The throwing of the *soha* (symbol of virility) by the *Issohadores* to capture young women symbolises the wish for fertility. It is through the woman that the new age, the transition from the old to the new, can be accomplished. So, women, who at first may seem marginal in the ritual, are in fact being honoured, becoming, perhaps, the main recipients of the whole rite. Their presence is also clearly evoked in some elements of the *Mamuthon*es' dress (the scarves that cover their heads) as well as the *Issohadores'* scarves that cover their waists. The feminine items in their clothing testify to the androgynous and sacred element that characterises the rite (Gregu 2014). Referring to Falassi's (1987) classification of rites, it is possible to assert that *Mamuthones* and *Issohadores* perform a polymorphic rite – purification and passage.

The ancient ritual of *Mamuthones* and *Issohadores* has seen numerous changes over time. An analysis of studies by Sardinian scholars, videos (Mamuthones 2013; Sardegna Digital Library 2013; Sardegna Visuale 2013) and photographs of past performances (Associazione Culturale Atzeni-Beccoi 2013; Associazione Turistica Pro-Loco Mamoiada 2013; Mamoiada.org 2013; Sardegna Digital Library 2013), as well as information gathered by the authors through interviews with elderly residents, reveals some of the changes that have occurred over recent decades. The costumes and the masks have changed somewhat, and so has the organisation of the festivities. While in the past the *Mamuthones* used to be elderly shepherds and peasants, today there is a greater variety in age and occupation among the participants, and organised groups of young children dressed as mini *Mamuthones* and *Issohadores* also parade.

The most important change is in the organisation of the ritual. Once a spontaneous local celebration that depended largely on improvisation and limited resources, it is now more formally organised and has become a tourist attraction. According to interviews collected from local people, participants used to provide the costumes personally, sometimes just arranged in a simple way by poor people, so that they had no homogeneous appearance. The bells were taken directly from their own sheep or borrowed from the shepherds, and this took a lot of time for preparation. The moment of dressing up was a rite in itself. It was held in the courtyard of some of the participants and the presence of external observers was prohibited. The pace of the procession was quite slow in rhythm and the participants stayed silent and aloof. They very rarely used to take off their masks. However, according to some interviewees, there was not, and still is not, a definite rule for the rhythm of the procession, which very much depends on the leadership of the chief *Issohadore*.

In addition to women, the *Issohadores* also used to capture key people that represented the wealth of the community, like land owners, the mayor and the local head of the police. This no longer occurs. However, short stops of the *Mamuthones* and *Issohadores* in front of the houses of sick people or people who had lost beloved relatives, in order to share a word of sympathy and express good wishes, are moments that still occur during the procession.

The rite used to be held only for Mamoiada's inhabitants. The number of non-local spectators was very few. The late photographer Pablo Volta, who was the first to document the procession, asserted that in 1957 he was the only non-local to attend the event, while later on, in 1981 and in particular in 2008, when he came back a third time, there were thousands of tourists: 'It seems to me that the protagonists of the rite are the tourists and that the rite, once propitiator of a good harvest, now propitiates the tourist season' (Sardegna Visuale 2013).

Nowadays, much of the organisation is carried out by two voluntary bodies called *Pro-Loco* and *Associazione Atzeni-Beccoi*. The first has existed since the 1950s, although it formalised its statute in the middle of the 1970s. It now has some 250 members. Its building is one of the two headquarters of the *Mamuthones* and *Issohadores* and it is here that costumes and mask are kept, and participants now dress for the occasion. People can visit it to see the costumes of *Mamuthones* and *Issohadores*. The Pro-Loco is particularly active for the preservation of the rite, as well as for its promotion. The Associazione Atzeni-Beccoi, established at the end of the 1980s, is the second headquarters of *Mamuthones* and *Issohadores* with some 200 members.

Both associations are responsible for planning and coordinating the various activities related to the Sant'Antonio celebration and the carnival. They provide the costumes, bells and so on, and select among members those who will perform the rite. They try to choose talented people since the procession must be as perfect as possible, otherwise it might affect Mamoiada's reputation as well as that of the participants themselves. The procession is somewhat staged nowadays, it is more spectacular and participants interact more with observers. The performers take off their masks from time to time, in part to breathe more easily and, in part, to salute the spectators while making them recognisable. In contrast, according to some interviewees, tradition dictates that performers should stay unidentifiable. However, there is some uncertainty in this regard, since other interviewees reported that even in the past, at times, performers removed their masks.

The dressing up is opened to the public and there are thousands of spectators. To some extent, the rite has become staged and its attendance turned into a liminal experience, more than a sacred, intimate one, especially for the young-sters. No admission fees are charged and refreshments are still distributed freely so it is not fully commodified but, on the other hand, the performances are now a commodity that is consumed by visitors, masks are sold and images are dupli-cated on calendars, postcards and even on mouse pads, although not all of these items are readily available in the town.

The two associations now also organise performances of *Mamuthones* and *Issohadores* outside of Mamoiada, in Sardinia, the rest of Italy and internation-ally. Throughout the summer, *Mamuthones* and *Issohadores* perform in the tourist villages of Sardinia, where they are an additional attraction. Both the associations have bought a bus and provide the performers with suitcases and other accessories decorated with the *Mamuthones* and *Issohadores* logo, which make them to look like a football team going to a game (Sardegna Visuale 2013)!

While these initiatives are criticised by some people, believing that they con-stitute commodification of the rite and a loss of its authenticity, the associations argue that funds are necessary to guarantee the endurance of the rite, its success and its attraction as a tourist resource, both for Mamoiada and the rest of the island. Also, according to a member of the *Pro-Loco*, performances held in Mamoiada always have a deeper meaning compared to those held outside, which are purely touristic.

The meaning and the enduring importance of the rite

People from Mamoiada are very attached to the masks and this is demonstrated by the fact that around 500 local men are members of the two associations that run the *Mamuthones'* and *Issohadores'* headquarters. Passion and sacrifice are needed to be a good *Mamuthone* or *Issohadore*. Indeed, carrying the 25–30 kilos of bells requires great strength, for the sequence of performances around numer-ous bonfires is long and tiring. Also, it requires great ability to lasso spectators successfully.

Wearing the mask and performing the dance generate special feelings that in some cases have been described to the authors as a sort of metamorphosis:

> When I wear the mask, I become another person, I see things and people with other eyes ... I feel an energy coming to me that makes me strong, that

brings me into another dimension, almost as if I was a beast living in another time.

(Salvatore)

I have a feeling that my personality splits. I become full of mysticism and bustle, go into a trance, it is like entering a person of another era. I also feel a sense of inner freedom, I see the world around me in a different way, detached from reality, this is the magic of the mask.

(Francesco)

There is also a sort of fusion of the self with the role that is played. There is an extension of one's self thanks to the mask that hides the person's identity, and which is lost and rediscovered within the same process. By continuously entering and exiting one's self, the person who wears the mask becomes stronger. He takes upon himself the soul of the *Mamuthone* or that of the *Issohadore* who, for centuries, have performed the same gestures. Protected by the mask, the individual gains more awareness of himself (Gregu 2014). He follows the same paths that his ancestors followed, while introducing new memories, emotions, worries and pains and, behind the mask, he gains strength to move towards recovery:

Every year I walk the same streets, it brings memories of when I was a child ... I think of my father who is no longer with us, he loved this procession so much ... To wear the mask gives me strength and courage to continue along the path of life.

(Gregu 2014)

The depth of personal significance of the rite was revealed to the authors by Rafael who, on showing a picture of himself in his regalia, said: 'When I die, I want to be buried as a Mamuthone', which we understood to mean in his complete outfit including mask, bells and boots.

Performing the procession gives participants the opportunity to test their skills and endurance, and to receive praise from observers. The *Mamuthones* are expected to move in an appropriate way throughout the procession, despite the heavy weight of the bells, and the *Issohadores* are expected to lasso the spectators successfully, thereby demonstrating their skill. The successful lassoing of spectators is acknowledged by the crowd who cheer, while unsuccessful attempts are met with reactions of disappointment and the *Issohadores* themselves may feel slightly embarrassed. Most importantly, in such instances, the wish for fertility is thwarted.

Sant'Antonio is also an occasion for the locals to stay together, especially on the first day, and to build and reinforce social relations. On the backstage of the procession, local women prepare *pobassinos* and men collect their best wine to be offered to visitors. Many people from Mamoiada who now live elsewhere use the opportunity to drop by the village to attend the procession and to meet their relatives and friends again. However, the first day really is for people with strong local ties. Indeed, when the second author visited a bonfire on the first day, he was approached by a local man, whom he subsequently learned was a *Mamuthone*, and was firmly informed: 'You cannot come here.... This is for us!' However, once 'rescued' by the first author, wine was offered and a long friendly discussion ensued that ended with 'Come back next year – but learn to speak Sardinian: Italian is not so important!'

The festival provides an opportunity for residents to show off their village to outsiders. Their participation in the celebration is even considered a duty that they have towards their village. Being a *Mamuthone* or an *Issohadore* is an honour and a responsibility, and it has both a personal and a cultural significance that is displayed at multiple scales. It means carrying on the tradition, keeping Mamoiada's distinct culture and, at the same time, representing the distinctiveness of Sardinia:

> Mamuthones and Issohadores masks mark our identity as people from Mamoiada; they also represent ancestral Sardinia. When Mamuthones and Issohadores perform outside they become ambassadors of Sardinian culture ... The danced procession of Saint Antonio brings diversity in a world that tends to be globalised and homogenous.
>
> (Fabrizio)

Performers, as well as ordinary people from Mamoiada, seem to be proud that the danced procession is a tourist attraction and that a Museum of Mediterranean Masks has been created. They both contribute to a form of development based on local culture.

The growing interest in Sant'Antonio's Day and in the masks, demonstrated by the number of spectators and visitors to the museum (in 2012, the museum registered around 17,500 visits, over a regional average of about 10,000 visitors), is perceived by local inhabitants positively as a sign that Mamoiada has a bright future and renews and reinforces their place attachment. Indeed, Mamoiada's reputation has been improved substantially. In the words of a local resident:

> We have forgotten the bad time we lived over the faida (*feuds*), now our village is a safe place to live in and visitors enjoy spending time here, you see foreigners walking here and there and we are proud of it.
>
> (Ruggero)

Although the rite has been somewhat commodified and some people complain about this, suggesting that it is losing its intimate sense, the tradition is still there, moulding itself to the new needs of Mamoiada's people. After all, as stated by the director of the museum:

> The dance is still a propitiatory rite – in the past, it propitiated the good harvest, today it propitiates a good tourist season. To live, we need to work

and the dance and the masks bring work to us, so it propitiates our lives and the prosperity of our village, exactly like it was in the past.

Conclusion

All rites and festivals undergo some degree of change. Over the years, the procession of *Mamuthones* and *Issohadores* held for the Sant'Antonio celebration has experienced some transformations, mainly related to an increased number of observers, both from elsewhere in the region and outside it, and it has also gained a great media audience. The partial reconfiguration of the rite as a tourist attraction, and its partial commodification, matches the changes in the Mamoiada community that, due to internal and external forces, has opened itself to the outer world. If in the past the Sant'Antonio festival was a low-key but very intimate and meaningful event, nowadays it is an occasion of spectacle; a statement from a peripheral village and culture that they too are involved in the process of development and modernisation. In particular, Sant'Antonio's Day and the wider tradition of *Mamuthones* and *Issohadores* masks have become the catalyst for local development: cultural events are increasing and tourism is bringing new economic initiatives. This constitutes a noteworthy reversal in the well-being of a community that was stagnant or even in decline. Moreover, the territorial image of Mamoiada has changed. As deduced from informal conversations with stakeholders and local residents, the *faida* has been forgotten, it belongs to the past, while nowadays Mamoiada is for everybody 'the village of the *Mamuthones* and *Issohadores*'.

Although there have been critics that the rite of the *Mamuthones* and *Issohadores* is facing commodification, we believe that Mamoiada people are using their culture, no matter whether commodified or not, as a way of affirming their identity and telling their own story, which brings pride and a positive attitude to the future and builds empowerment. A key part of this process of managing and sharing culture are the new institutions that have been put in place and are under local control that now organise the rite itself and share it with interested outsiders, namely the two associations and the Museum of Mediterranean Masks, respectively.

Despite the increased tourist audience at Sant'Antonio, it would be wrong to assume that the meaning implicit to the rite has been wiped out. For the local people, the event remains a moment to receive blessings for the community's and individuals' prosperity. It also continues to be a ludic moment for the locals, which reinforces social relations and place attachment. The tradition of the *Mamuthones* and *Issohadores* procession has kept its vitality and tourism has enabled the Sant'Antonio festival to bring together and protect a traditional cultural expression, while at the same time addressing the need for economic development in a way that has allowed Mamoiada to open itself to the rest of the world after many years of isolation, marginality and poverty.

Acknowledgements

We are very grateful to the *Issohadore* Gesuino Gregu for offering us his valuable knowledge about the *Mamuthones* and *Issohadores*.

References

Adger, W. (2000) 'Social and ecological resilience: Are they related?', *Progress in Human Geography*, 24(3), 347–364.

Arnold, N. (2001) 'Festival tourism: Recognizing the challenges – linking multiple pathways between global villages of the new century', in B. Faulkner, G. Moscardo and E. Laws (eds), *Tourism in the 21st Century: Lessons from experience* (pp. 130–162), London: Continuum.

Associazione Culturale Atzeni-Beccoi (2013) *Mamuthones*. Online: www.mamuthones.it (accessed 20 May 2013).

Associazione Turistica Pro-loco Mamoiada (2013) *Album fotografici*. Online: www.mamuthonesmamoiada.it (accessed 20 May 2013).

Atzori, M., Orrù, L., Piquereddu, P. and Satta, M. (1989) *Il Carnevale in Sardegna*, Cagliari: Editrice Mediterranea.

Boissevan, J. (1992) *Revitalizing European Rituals*, London: Routledge.

Burke, P. (1997) *Varieties of Cultural History*, Ithaca, NY: Cornell University Press.

Dedola, S. (2004) *Toponomastica Sarda*, Dolianova: Grafica del Parteolla.

Derrett, R. (2009) 'How festivals nurture resilience in regional communities', in J. Ali-Knight, M. Robertson, A. Fyall and A. Ladkin (eds), *International Perspectives of Festival and Events* (pp. 107–124), Amsterdam: Elsevier.

Falassi, A. (1987) 'Festival: Definition and morphology', in A. Falassi (ed.) *Time out of Time: Essays on the festival* (pp. 1–10), Albuquerque: University of New Mexico Press.

Gregu, G. (2014) *I fuochi dei Mamuthones e Issohadores*. Online: www.mamuthonesmamoiada.it/images/documenti/i_fuochi.pdf (accessed 3 February 2014).

Iorio, M. and Wall, G. (2011) 'Local museums as catalysts for development', *Journal of Heritage Tourism*, 6(1), 1–15.

Iorio, M. and Wall, G. (2012) 'Behind the mask: Tourism and community in Sardinia', *Tourism Management*, 33(6), 1440–1449.

Le Lannou, M. (1941) *Pâtre et Paysans de la Sardaigne*, Tours: Arrault.

Liori, A. (1992) *Demoni, Iti e Riti Magici della Sardegna*, Rome: Newton and Compton.

Ma, L. and Lew, A. (2011) 'Historical and geographical context in festival tourism development', *Journal of Heritage Tourism*, 7(1), 13–31.

Mamoiada.org (2013) *Archivi*. Online: www.mamoiada.org (accessed 30 May 2013).

Mamuthones (2013) *Video Mamuthones*. Online: www.mamuthonescarrigados.it/mamuthones-video.html (accessed 30 May 2013).

Marchi, R. (1951) 'Le maschere barbaricine', *Il Ponte*, 7(9–10), 1354–1361.

Picard, D. and Robinson, M. (2006) 'Remaking worlds: Festival tourism and change', in D. Picard and M. Robinson (eds), *Festivals, Tourism and Social Changes* (pp. 1–31), Clevedon: Channel View.

Robinson, M., Picard, D. and Long, P. (2004) 'Festival tourism: Producing, translating, and consuming expressions of culture(s)', *Event Management*, 8(4), 187–189.

Sardegna Digital Library (2013) *Mamuthones e Issohadores*. Online: www.sardegnadigitallibrary.it/index.

php?xsl=602ands=17andv=9andc=4459andn=24andc1=mamuthones+e+issohadoresandri c=1 (accessed 25 May 2013).

Sardegna Visuale (2013) *Mamuthones*. Online: www.sardegna-visuale.it/mamuthones. html (accessed 6 June 2013).

Sofield, T. and Li, F.M. (1998) 'Tourism development and cultural policies in China', *Annals of Tourism Research*, 25(2), 362–392.

Turchi, D. (1996) *Maschere, Miti e Feste della Sardegna*, Rome: Newton and Compton.

Turner, V. (1982) *Celebration: Studies in festivity ritual*, Washington, DC: Smithsonian Institution Press.

10 Layers of passage

The ritual performance and liminal bleed of the Beltane Fire Festival, Edinburgh

Ross Tinsley and Catherine Matheson

Introduction

This chapter examines the ritual performance of the Beltane Fire Festival, which occurs annually on 30 April on Calton Hill, Edinburgh. The Beltane Fire Festival is a contemporary reinterpretation of an ancient Celtic festival celebrating the passage of the seasons. It is a spring festival marking the end of winter and the beginning of summer. As such, the underlying symbolism of the Beltane Fire Festival is renewal and rebirth, given the relationship to the passage of the seasons and, furthermore, fertility of people, land and livestock (BFS 2007; Frazer 1922). The contemporary Beltane Fire Festival is an interesting context as, while it is based on a traditional agrarian and calendrical rite of passage celebrating the passage of a season, it also embodies life-crises style rites of passage for many of the performers in its modern reinterpretation as a liminoid experience (Turner 1975). The contemporary Beltane Fire Festival also symbolises a subversion and transgression from social norms as it contains features of Bakhtin's (1965) carnivalesque (see Matheson and Tinsley forthcoming).

Drawing on seminal studies, as well as contemporary work on ritual in festivities as a framework, this chapter investigates the Beltane Fire Festival ritual performance. The research objectives are: first, to investigate the historical developments of this festival; second, delineate the dimensions and performance of ritual; and, finally, to examine performer/organiser experiences of more personal rites of passage. In terms of the latter, a conceptualisation of liminal bleed is offered as a means to frame liminoid experiences that have internally recognised value, even if not formally so by society in the same manner as a traditional liminal rite of passage. Bleed in this instance is borrowed and adapted from the printing term – 'the seeping of a dye or colour into an adjacent colour or area' (Oxford Dictionaries 2010) – to capture the transfer of self-empowering liminoid experiences which bleed into other life settings, whether structured or anti-structured. This conceptualisation is sought to redress the significance of liminoid experience in the context of structured society or experiences in other anti-structured contexts, as there is a tendency to downplay the potentiality of this role not only by Turner himself in his strict segregation of traditional liminality but also in contemporary studies of the liminoid where it may not be explored or only briefly mentioned.

Dimensions and critiques of ritual

Any study involving ritual is indebted to the groundwork laid by van Gennep (1975 [1908]) in establishing the concept of *rites of passage*. In this, he identifies three major phases related to *life crises* and periodic events such as changes of the seasons. In both cases van Gennep referred to these three major phases as separation (pre-liminal), transition (liminal) and incorporation (postliminal). Explaining further the linkage of periodic and life crisis rites, Abrahams (1983: 167) posits: 'because they employ many of the same means of bringing people together in rites of passage, calendared events such as festivals have often been regarded as simply a different kind of rite.' For rituals representing a transitional period in an individual or group's life, sacred status is attained during this time after leaving and before being reincorporated into the profane. However, it was Turner who was ultimately responsible for resurrecting the concept and highlighting its universal relevance to a much wider audience; in particular, his exploration and further development of the liminal phase.

Using structural means, liminal periods of time and space in the cyclical calendar are given to play in terms of thoughts, feelings and will (Turner 1969). In this anti-structural period, which encourages social process reflexivity, 'society becomes at once subject and direct object; it represents also its subjunctive mood, where suppositions, desires, hypotheses, possibilities, and so forth, all become legitimate' (Turner 1969: vii), or what O'Grady (2012: 97) refers to as 'the exploration of potentiality'. Turner (1969: vii) views individual life experiences as consisting of alternating experiences of structure and communitas – between fixed and 'floating worlds'. Communitas can only be revealed when juxtaposed by structure. It is a transformative experience, rich in symbols and metaphors: 'art and religion are their products rather than legal and political structures' (Turner 1969: 128). Turner analyses ritual as processual in itself and not just as a mechanism of redress, emphasising that 'ritual is not just a response to society's needs but involves humanly meaningful action' (Deflem 1991: 22). What we are seeing in Turner's work is an essential dialectic in the pragmatism of structure and the philosophy of communitas. Wisdom lies in the ability to move between the two, while not becoming overly dependent on one.

While his earlier work focused on ritual in technologically primitive societies – 'there are no "simpler" peoples' (Turner 1969: 3) – Turner (1975) later extended his concept of liminality beyond rites of passage to any context that is peripheral to, or outside, daily life. He distinguished these as liminoid or quasi-liminal with attendance in such experiences as voluntary and less official (Turner and Turner 1978). In this, Turner was making a distinction between historical and contemporary society. In the latter, such manifestations seek to challenge the existing social order through social critique or revolutionary re-ordering and not merely inversions within the total social order, as embodied in liminal manifestations (Deflem 1991). However, St John (2001, 2008) makes three criticisms of this latter conceptualisation. He cautions that in comparison with liminality, this notion of the liminoid is under-theorised and, second, there is '[an] absence of sustained ethnographic application' (St John 2001: 226). Regarding the first, Deflem (1991) relatedly stresses criticism of Turner's inability to systematically treat his ideas, resulting in a multitude of labels to characterise his approach. Third, in his critique of Turner and contemporary cultural performance, St John (2008) argues that Turner's determined focus on anti-structure led him to fail to consider liminality in formal and official contexts, for example, state-led formal ceremonies. As argued by St John (2008: 17), these liminal events are controlled and managed centre-stage through economic and political theatre, rather than as marginal and peripheral zones of resistance, and 'a need arises to observe branded subjunctivity, normatized performance, and domesticated virtuality ... How "normative" and "ideological" communitas assists understanding of processes of sociocultural institutionalization'. One such study is Jamieson's (2004) scathing critique of Edinburgh's Fringe Festival as a liminal space that supports and reinforces the status quo (see also Ravenscroft and Matteucci's 2003 study of the San Fermin Fiesta, Pamplona).

Deflem (1991), while largely positive towards Turner's work, also draws attention to Turner's overestimation of both liminal and liminoid phenomena to challenge and subvert social structure while neglecting structural responses to and neutralisation of such endeavours. He also suggests that Turner's conversion and continued devotion to Catholicism renders his understanding of communitas as 'a matter of faith than fact' (Deflem 1991: 19). Deflem posits that Turner 'may have ignored the symbolic dimensions, informalities, and the humanly meaningful within the realm of structured relationships' (1991: 19). Indeed, Turner (1969: 138) did seek to differentiate communitas from 'the pleasurable and effortless comradeship that can arise between friends, coworkers, or professional colleagues any day', arguing that the transformative experience was absent, that this lacked a root experience of 'something profoundly communal and shared'. Such a stance certainly acted as a barrier to investigating the subtler nuances of such structured relations.

Geertz (1980), while appreciative on the whole of the Turner view of ritual theory, not unsurprisingly was critical of its tendency towards homogeneous universalisms that may overlook some of the particularities of locality. One application of the Turnerian paradigm that has come under particular criticism is in the area of pilgrimage where challenges along the lines of Geertz's (1980) remarks have indeed been made (see Eade 1992; Eade and Sallnow 1991; Messerschmidt and Sharma 1981). These studies highlighted distinct interaction and differentiation along structural lines as well as highlighting a contestation of meanings during pilgrimage encounters. Coleman and Eade (2004) argue that Turner and Turner's (1978) classification of pilgrimage as being liminoid, of being extraordinary, has resulted in a lack of research by those seeking to understand everyday life, reducing pilgrimage study to the threshold of academic concern until more recently.

St John's (2001) research on contemporary pilgrimage to alternative lifestyle events also highlights the contested nature of liminoid sites, as well as drawing attention to Turner's downplaying of the sensuous and carnal that can materialise in such spaces. To address these criticisms St John (2001) argues for the concepts 'alternative cultural heterotopia' and 'liminoid embodiment'. Of the former, St John (2001) identifies three spatial qualities: 'otherness', heterogeneity and contestation, which can be applied to the context of the Beltane Fire Festival. His concept of liminoid embodiment also has relevance to the Beltane Fire Festival given its carnivalesque qualities but there is not sufficient space to explore this aspect here (see Matheson and Tinsley forthcoming). While this review has highlighted the main criticisms of Turner's work, it is not intended as an outright dismissal. His paradigm continues to provide insight and be used as a framework for understanding ritual in contemporary society, but the above criticisms act as a reminder for cautionary and adaptive application in (post)modern liminoid manifestations, and the need to be sensitive and reflexive to specificity.

Research methods

Studies investigating ritual and festivity have often adopted a qualitative methodology (e.g. Sherry and Kozinets 2007; Shinde 2010; St John 2001) as it provides an opportunity for a deep understanding (Bryman 2012) of a contextual situation. Eleven interviews were conducted in 2010 with a variety of Beltane Fire Festival stakeholders (each identified as R1, R2 etc.). These included festival founders and performers, contemporary organisers and performers as well as cultural policy and policing stakeholders.

Historical development of the Beltane Fire Festival

The role of festivals and rituals in society is multi-faceted and, as such, they can be a means of celebration (Manning 1983), an expression of identity (Boissevain 1992) and an ephemeral period of *deep play* (Geertz 1973), which provide a commentary about the structures of the social world. More recently, festivals have been utilised for tourism development purposes (Picard and Robinson 2006), particularly as a means to create an *eventful city* that is attractive to tourists (Richards and Palmer 2010). In most respects, the Beltane Fire Festival encapsulates many of these themes, most notably those of celebration and identity; however, this is not a festival developed in response to economic and tourism agendas. Rather, it has evolved on an organic basis to celebrate the passage of the seasons and affirm community identity.

The Beltane Fire Festival has a deep-seated history as illustrated by Frazer (1922), who argued that fire festivals occurred throughout Europe from the Middle Ages. Beltane means 'bright fire' and was a means to mark the changes in the season (BFS 2012). Beltane Fires took place in a variety of forms in different geographical locations within Scotland (Frazer 1922). Key themes in these rituals included: the timing of the fires, which generally occurred in early May; the extinguishing of community fires in preparation for the ritual lighting of the Beltane fire and the actual lighting of the Beltane Fire; festive entertainment in the form of singing and dancing; the creation of a Beltane cake which was distributed among celebrants; and, in some contexts, the symbolic sacrifice of an individual (Frazer 1922). Historically, the Beltane Fire Society (BFS) suggest that the Beltane fires were linked to:

> the growing power of the sun and provide an opportunity to cleanse and renew the conditions of a community – both humans and their animals – that had spent the dark months indoors. In Scotland, the lighting of Beltane fires – round which cattle were drive[n], over which brave souls danced and leapt – would survive into modern times.
>
> (BFS 2012)

In the late 1980s, the Edinburgh Beltane Fire Festival was revived by a group of cultural community stakeholders, which included the involvement of Edinburgh University's School of Scottish Studies. While Beltane is a resurrection of a traditional agrarian festival, reflecting a calendar-based rite of passage, as with many other such festivals, the lifestyle and seasonal dependency associated with it has disappeared (Abrahams 1983). This disconnection was a deliberate factor in the festival's contemporary purpose as it sought to reconnect a perceived loss due to modernisation (R1). While the festival has an urban setting, its location on a parkland hill commands views of nearby Holyrood Park, the Salisbury Crags and the Firth of Forth. The group of performance artists who resurrected it were seeking a release from struggles against the dominant political landscape of Thatcherism (R1). In this search for an outlet of release, there is a clear expression of the subjunctive mood that underpins Turner's (1969) theorising of ritual and communitas, with the Beltane Fire Festival acting as a setting for potentiality to be explored (O'Grady 2012). While the Beltane Fire Festival was intended as a release from the politics of the time, the aforementioned broader political context allows a framing of the ritual performance in the wider counter-cultural landscape of that period. Partridge (2006) traced the sacralisation of British counter-culture free festivals and rave scenes with the transition point from the former to the latter occurring in the late 1980s and early 1990s and the resultant UK government crackdown through the Criminal Justice and Order Act (3 November 1994), the same period in which the Beltane Fire Festival was formed and experienced initial growth. One respondent alludes to that time:

> A lot of road protests were going on, the illegal rave scene was really kicking off … It was like a lot of DIY culture was happening, that was really kind of a different feel then than now. People quite actively engaged, and Beltane was one of those things that people also latched onto.
>
> (R2)

However, by the end of the 1990s another respondent reflects that 'it was no longer needed to make that statement' (R11). While the Beltane Fire Festival is not a dance music festival, the after-party club associated with the night reflected this broader context and overlaps with this movement help further illuminate the context and early days of the contemporary Beltane Fire Festival's growth, including the importance of spirituality and counter-culture (see St John 2004 for more on DIY tribalism and the global protest movement of that time).

In terms of production, the BFS is a community-based organisation reliant predominantly on volunteers, whether that is event management roles or performing. Initially, the festival was non-ticketed and small-scale in terms of audience numbers and performers. As the festival evolved, audience numbers increased significantly: for example, the first Beltane Fire Festival had an audience of approximately 50 to 100 people and by 1999 this had increased to 10,000 (BFS 2013). Event costs also increased as the scale of the festival grew, particularly with additional regulatory interventions in the post-9/11 world, which had financial implications for the management of the event (Matheson and Tinsley forthcoming). These developments had significant ramifications as the festival was cancelled one year. Thereafter, the Beltane Fire Festival moved from being a free to a ticketed event in order to sustain itself financially as well as manage audience numbers (Matheson and Tinsley forthcoming). As the festival has evolved, it has become increasingly professionalised and the BFS now operates under the auspices of charitable status. The Beltane Fire Festival is currently a mature festival contributing to the local cultural landscape in the low tourist season and approximately 300 volunteers participate in the event.

Performance of the BFF ritual

In terms of the performance of the contemporary ritual, there are core and immutable aspects of the Beltane Fire Festival ritual. The central component of the ritual is the procession led by the May Queen who 'represents Mother Earth or the Earth itself as it were' (R9). The May Queen is followed by her attendants, the Whites (Figure 10.1) who are 'a physical representation of her extended spread and reach over the hill, an embodiment of her love and emotions' (BFS 2013). The procession's path round Calton Hill is cleared by the Blues (Figure 10.2) and they play a critical role in the performance of the ritual. While their role has evolved over time, the Blues are, in essence, the elders of the festival. A key aspect of their role relates to the preservation of the ritual and performance because as the festival developed and an ever greater number of volunteers sought to engage with the event, particularly on a performative basis, there was a need to ensure that the central dimensions of the ritual were understood by participants while simultaneously according space to the creative process, as noted by a production stakeholder:

> the Blues became very involved in making sure [and] checking what people were doing and that it was kept to the storyline. But some of us ... felt that you can't do that too much ... There's something about Beltane that the repeat of the ritual is important ... but you have to allow creativity each year otherwise you lose people or you lose energy.

(R2)

Figure 10.1 The May Queen and Whites Procession (source: R. Tinsley).

Figure 10.2 One of the Blues clears the way for the May Queen procession (source: R. Tinsley).

Hence, while there are aspects of the ritual that are protected under the auspices of the elders of the festival, the Blues, the preservation of the ritual is not a static process; rather, there is fluidity and creativity in the protection and development of the ritual. The role of the Blues also highlights elements of hierarchy and structuring both behind the scenes and in the ritual itself. Parallels can be drawn with the ritual elders in Turner's (1969) work on the Ndembu with 'the only remaining structural characteristic in liminality [being] the authority of the ritual instructors' (Deflem 1991: 14). However, the more complex organisation of the Beltane Fire Festival ritual performance and of contemporary Western society means there is further structuring beyond the role of these elders. It is a reminder that even egalitarian and liminal spaces need some element of structuring (van Heerden 2011) because 'a lot of people experience what it's like to work in a different kind of organisation where there's lots of discussions around hierarchy and who makes the rules, and people get very engaged with all of that' (R2). There is hierarchical structuring manifest in the BFS's charity status, with a board of trustees, chairs and committees: 'I think it shocked us all that it's become what it has and it's like its own little world now that sprawls in politics, issues and the governance of it' (R2). Turner's (1969) notion of normative communitas does account for this through the organising of a social system. This can be seen in the transition in the early days from a ritual organised by professional performers to the present conditions. Such experiences of structuring within a liminoid context gives exposure and experience to volunteers in the context of event management – 'half of them have never acted before, half the tech crew have never been in theatre tech' (R9) – suggesting potentiality for liminal bleed. This is similar to Kim and Jamal's findings of spontaneous communitas developing into normative communitas with its own set of social structuring and some hierarchy but crucially 'still maintain close and equal relationships among the members' (Kim and Jamal 2007: 195).

At various points in the procession, there can be a disruption of proceedings by the Reds (Figure 10.3). The Red group is quite different from other groups in that the members can represent disorder and this difference can be most clearly articulated in relation to the White group, as noted by the following: 'the Reds who represent the opposite of the white warriors so they (White Group) are all about purity and order [and] they're (Red group) about chaos and carnality' (R9). Such dualistic tensions are the essence of festival ritual and celebration (Grimes 1983). Additionally, Abrahams (1983: 165) highlights the contradictions of celebration, how the most challenging contrasts are incorporated for fun 'though the play is often deeply serious'. The procession also contains the rebirth of the Green Man. The Green Man plays a significant role in the representation of nature (Grimassi 2001) because he

> represents all the living things on Earth and he tries to become her consort (May Queen) over the course of the festival and is knocked back and knocked back and is eventually killed off because he represents winter and is reborn in spring.
>
> (R9)

The part of the Green Man being stripped of his winter coat, representing his death and rebirth for summer, is the culmination of the Beltane ritual and is classic symbology for the rite of passage in that 'they are being reduced or ground down to a uniform condition to be fashioned anew and endowed with additional powers to enable them to cope with their new station in life' (Turner 1969: 96). In addition to these central characters, there are also other dimensions

Figure 10.3 The Reds (source: R. Tinsley).

to the ritual, such as the Need Fire, which was also documented in Frazer's (1922) depiction of historical Beltane events. Other aspects of the ritual that are more fluid to interpretation include the elemental groups Air, Earth, Water and Fire Point as well as the tongue-in-cheek group No Point. While there is an overt ritual story celebrating the changes of seasons, there are also personal life changes taking place among the performers.

Rites of passage within

As previously illustrated, the Beltane Fire Festival can be a rite of passage for the performer, many of whom are either students studying for a number of years – 'it's a rite of passage for students and other young people, but there's obviously a big student contingent. A few people come back who are aficionados from the old days' (R1) – or other young people on travel experiences, who are temporarily resident in the city – 'a very international scene that was sort of growing up in Edinburgh around the festival and especially in the summer months' (R3). For both of these groups they are already experiencing more traditional rites of passage and are already in a liminal state. As a result of their temporary nature, there is quite a high turnover among volunteers every few years, increasing the importance of experienced participants who commit over a longer period. For the appeal in taking part, 'I think a lot of what Beltane does also taps into that and helps people who are questioning about their place in the world, it does give them something' (R2), with one respondent suggesting they felt very 'disenchanted with western culture' (R3). This corresponds with Turner's (1969: 167) view of liminal time and place 'as potentially a period of scrutinization of the central values and axioms of the culture in which it occurs'. The Beltane Fire

Festival can have appeal as part of a broader spiritual exploration at a personal level:

> The whole of my time in Edinburgh was very much characterised by a sort of deepening exploration of the great mystery and spirituality, and also a deepening awareness of ecology and the natural world, and the cycles of the natural world and also of pagan heritage ... a sort of approach to being human which isn't particularly part of the dominant culture nowadays.
>
> (R4)

The wider liminal space in which many of the volunteers are immersed, as well as the specific liminoid space of the Beltane Fire Festival (see below), allows for an exploration of such concerns that if positive can bleed back into feeling more complete in everyday life. This individual quest is a common theme in research on spirituality in contemporary Western culture (see, for example, Fredrickson and Anderson 1999; Kale 2004; Timothy and Conover 2011; Willson 2011; Zinnbauer *et al.* 1997). It is also encapsulated in Turner's (1969) identification of liminoid experiences in secular (post)modernised nations.

For performers, the experience of participating in the ritual can be profoundly transformational. In the case of the Green Man, the role itself is often used as a pre-determined catalyst: 'it was like people laying themselves bare. It is usually some-body who's going through [something] – using it as something to change, as a personal change' (R2). For others, it is more spontaneous to the evening itself when adopting the character's role: 'Beltane allows you to become one with everybody else, and it also allows for a personal transformation because you're turning your-self into somebody else for the night' (R2) and 'when I was Red there were times when I forgot who I was and it was the character' (R3). This transformation into character is done in two main approaches. One is through a physical threshold and is part of the overall performance – the Fire Arch – which in the Beltane ritual sym-bolises the May Queen and her procession entering the Underworld, resulting in a symbolic cleansing and the beginning of their journey in reuniting the elements (BFS 2012). In terms of territorial passage, van Gennep (1975 [1908]) refers to portals with rites of spatial passage becoming rites of spiritual passage. The fire arch in Beltane represents one such ritual within the broader Beltane ritual. Additionally, the process of costuming-up represents another symbolic threshold within the Beltane ritual. For the performers this is a threshold within a threshold, as in their costumes and body paint they have transitioned over to the ritual performer:

> Before we go onto the hill, you go through a change, you know, you paint yourself up but there was also the introduction of little rituals within groups, so they laid their old selves at the door and they were then ... all together ... you are one with this group ... That whole thing of painting yourself and there are also rules about not speaking on the hill and all of those things are designed to deepen the experience for people.
>
> (R2)

It represents the passing of a mental as well as physical threshold from off-stage to on-stage (Calton Hill), with deeper meaning and experiences beyond the broader Beltane festival (Figure 10.4). It is this deeper transcendental experience that makes Beltane truly ritualistic rather than the mere performance of a ritual story, as one respondent illustrates:

> As a performer, one of the highlights for me was being a blue man ... and that was an extraordinary sort of personal rite of passage being almost naked, painted blue on Calton Hill going through the intense cold of being out there ... Feeling I was totally immersed in an almost like a different world view and it was almost approaching a sort of tribal, primal kind of experience, as much as a twenty first century westerner could have.
>
> (R4)

This is what Grimes (1983) refers to as symbolic stripping, a deconstruction as a means of negation. It is experienced as a reconnection to something that has been lost, denied or excluded from the (post)modern secular world. This links back to one of the primary purposes of the resurrected festival, as a vehicle for reconnecting to a time lost to modernity.

For some of the people involved, such ritual experiences and feelings of communitas can have profound and long-lasting effects beyond the ritual performance on Calton Hill: 'it was just this incredibly rich part of my life and had a huge kind of bearing on, you know, who I am and what I've gone on to do creatively' (R4). Another respondent speaks of how this has affected quite a broad range of volunteers:

> The alumni is striking ... a key player in the Woodford festival in Australia which is a massive arts event out there. And there's other people who have

Figure 10.4 Being in the ritual state; silence and non-eye contact with the audience (source: R. Tinsley).

gone on to do Burning Man and things like that so the Beltane community worldwide and the skills people have learned are significant. It really does do what it should do in the sense it creates a group of people that can do this anywhere in the world which is wonderful. I really don't know how many folk have passed through our doors in total and what they have gone on to do but I think you'd be astounded to be honest.

(R9)

This exemplifies liminal bleed as experiences gained in taking part in the Beltane Fire Festival – 'being in this incredible cauldron of creativity as [a] social and cultural milieu' (R3) – have influenced future directions. This is in line with Hollands' (2010) findings of alternative festivals fostering social bonding and cultural networks for young workers and performers. Based on his own sustained research into psytrance festivals, St John (2001) argues that the reincorporation aspect loses its importance as experiences gained only retain significance within future festivals and not in everyday society. However, a narrative analysis approach may reveal greater significance as part of an individual's life story.

Considering further the liminoid space of the BFS that also encapsulates the Beltane Fire Festival, encountering other like-minded people taking part can encourage feelings of communitas: 'there's a big social aspect to it and people who … come to the city then feel really connected into like-minded people, people who care about something or they find soulmates and people to talk to' (R2). This confirms O'Rourke *et al.*'s (2011) notion of a *community within* that engenders belonging and shared lived experiences. In particular, the months of preparation beforehand and the bonding with the particular group the performer is a part of results in heightened moments of communitas that occur before as well as during the actual performance: 'that strength of community going away, spending long periods of time together and developing a comradeship, ritual focus, developing their skills and the integrity of what they're going to do – that's so authentic and sincere' (R1). These periods draw parallels with Turner's (1969) notion of ritual subjects being separated from everyday society; however, as these are liminoid examples these periods away are not sustained but instead interspersed with everyday life and routine. The BFS also celebrates other key periods in the Celtic calendar, whether through public or private rituals, including a fairly large-scale production for Samhain (a procession along Edinburgh's Royal Mile, celebrating the Celtic New Year and the coming of winter, held annually on 31 October). Additionally, there are many opportunities for social gatherings directly or indirectly related to the BFS, which altogether can result in what St John (2001) refers to as liminal culture. This also confirms Kim and Jamal's (2007) findings of those who experienced a more permanent change (see below) having sustained continuity *off-site* within the subculture. Turner (1969) identifies three stages of communitas development: spontaneous, normative and ideological with the BFS being normative in nature, reflecting its organisation as a social system. Similarly to Turner's (1969) caution on communes that attempt to make the liminal state permanent which can lead to institutionalisation (ideological communitas) and the dualistic importance of structure vs. anti-structure, one respondent cautions:

> You can kind of get hooked on it in a way. At a certain point you need to get out there and make your own friends and try and lead your own life and not let it constrict you because it takes up a lot of time and can prevent you from getting on with your life.
>
> (R3)

Such extended immersion in liminoid space can become entrapping rather than liberating and can become an inhibitor to re-entering structured life. However, as will be seen below, that the liminoid space of the Beltane Fire Festival is actually a contested space, as well as having a significant turnover, helps to avoid a more ideological formation of communitas, even if there can be individual appeal in sustained immersion.

While the BFS has unifying elements in a social context and in the ritual performance of the night in question as noted above, there is nevertheless marked heterogeneity and contestation. In line with criticisms within the literature of communitas in liminoid settings, the Beltane Fire Festival culture demonstrates a semblance to St John's (2001) *alternative cultural heterotopia* with conforming qualities of spatial *otherness* in its celebration of nature and carnivalesque hedonism (see Matheson and Tinsley forthcoming), and, as will be seen, in its spatially marked heterogeneity and contested spaces. These atypical Turnerian characteristics of the liminoid space are present to varying degrees both in its current formation and in its evolution since its contemporary beginnings. Of the heterogeneous nature of the volunteers, one respondent comments:

> You'd be astounded the cross-section of performers that take part. It's not dissimilar to the cross-section of the audience but it's far from a bunch of ragged hippies. You'd be amazed how many investment bankers and lawyers, fairly clean cut professions but when you think about it it's not entirely surprising, it's exactly the same escapism the audience is trying to reach.
>
> (R9)

On matters of belief, there is not 'one core set of beliefs amongst those involved in Beltane' (R2), with another adding, 'we've had people who just like to wear paint, people who just want to walk around naked, and people who deeply believe they are celebrating a change in seasons and are practising pagans' (R3). Regarding the last group, Manson's (2006) study highlights the significance of Beltane and Samhain rituals to contemporary neo-pagans and it is another emergent theme in respondent discussions. It also raises contested perceptions of BFS:

> The organisation is perceived to be pagan. We are not pagan but people perceive it to be pagan, I think we should recall ourselves the Beltane Not

Pagan Society [laughter] ... We celebrate traditional Celtic festivals, a modern reinterpretation of traditional Celtic festivals, some of our members are pagan but we as a society aren't.

(R10)

Another respondent suggests the actual number of practising pagans is 'quite low' (R11). While the discourse does not reveal precise details it paints a general picture of the overall make-up. The following reflection on past times from a more recent volunteer tends to suggest generalisations and simplifications similar to the aforementioned external perception of the BFS: 'the olden days it all used to be hippies and it all used to be pagans so there wasn't such a diversity of people who got involved' (R10). Another respondent who was there at the time describes a different terminology of these contesting groupings:

They put together a group called the Sativa Drummers who were these radical drummers from a club, with the Samba Drummers ... You can't put somebody who's really kind of flaky and very hippyish and wanting to wave bits of cloth and dress in multi colours with someone who's basically got piercings.

(R2)

It alludes to a particularly contested time in the festival's evolution when the event had to move to a more regulated, ticketed and curfew-driven model: 'This is a festival of the people for the people. It should be a free festival', and then other people who were saying 'With all the rising costs associated with health and safety, we need it to be ticketed' (R2). While the statement is a simplification of the context, it does highlight divisional groups and contested narratives rather than unifying communitas.

These divisional aspects can also be seen in the variety of different performance groups and the manifestation of competitiveness – 'currently the society has this one-upmanship thing again where the torches are more important than the stewards' (R11) – and of desirability – 'there's something very interesting round that dynamic and the whole aspiration to be Blue and also the difficulties of being Blue' (R2). The Blues, in particular, while coveted, are also highly contested in their leading role and position, 'watching the development of that as a powerhouse within the organisation and where it's come into criticism, where it's stepped outside its original remit' (R2). As well as inter-group there can also be intra-group tensions, as one respondent reflects on being in Earth Group:

it was such a wide diverse range of different ideas and different ways of thinking and I really liked that but the side-effect of that is when you have in one group people who are pagan, are spiritualist, are Christian, are atheist then you can't have a common ground ... Every group has a different equilibrium and every group has a different feel to it.

(R10)

Drawing upon performance studies, Alexander (2004) argues that the affirmation of metaphysics and consensual belief of traditional ritual has seen the addition of negotiation and reflexivity in contemporary society, resulting in moments that are just as likely to lead to discord as to integration. In the context of the Beltane Fire Festival, this dualistic tension is clearly apparent and a necessary feature of its social structuring as will become further apparent:

> It's interesting this notion of tension. There are clearly tensions arise because all the different groups and I always hear talk of the tensions and arguments, and they always seem to wash out ... Sometimes you'll get people who are more riding on their ego and they're driving themselves from their ego and when that manifests itself in something like Beltane that can be quite in a bad way.
>
> (R1)

In the context of the Beltane Fire Festival, more dramatic discord occurs in punctuated events in the festival's evolution (Matheson and Tinsley forthcoming), which, given the festival's long-running nature, displays a tendency of 'it should be a lot more fraught than it is but actually the fact that people share their passion for the festival actually carries through an awful lot' (R9). According to Alexander (2004: 529), in such segmented and differentiated society, the successful actor needs to be able to 're-fuse' such disparate elements in a convincing and effective manner – 'more ritual-like' (Alexander 2004: 529) – to the intended audience. In this case the overall narrative of passion and commitment to the festival succeeding takes precedence.

Conclusion

In Duffy's (2008: 102) examination of the role of music and emotion in festival dynamics, she notes that the connections and sense of belonging that take place in the festival space 'often spills out into our everyday spaces'. One of the key aspects of this research on the Beltane Fire Festival has been to emphasise the significance of liminal bleed. In these liminoid as opposed to liminal experiences, it can be argued that the emphasis is less externally recognised in terms of their traditional purpose of marking a new and elevated status in structured life. However, such a stance then serves to downplay what can still be significant – at the very least as simple rejuvenation – and sometimes life-changing experiences. As a research tool narrative analysis is best served as a technique for uncovering these stories, for revealing implications for moments beyond liminoid junctures of potentiality. There may also be more loosely tied narratives of individual life journeys punctuated by different types of liminoid experiences. The study also revealed confirmatory findings with contemporary critiques of the liminoid suggesting a contested space with division and differentiation being just as likely to be present as the unifying features of communitas. While this may be at odds with Turner's work, this research suggests these features contained in liminoid settings may help to avoid the negative effects of sustained communitas which can end in militancy and fanaticism. The key is maintaining an equilibrial tension. The Beltane Fire Festival's membership turnover, while challenging from a management and training perspective, was seen as healthy in terms of avoiding sustained communitas, retaining freshness in the festival and as a result has played a significant role in its long-running nature.

Kimball (1975), in his introduction to van Gennep's seminal work, argues that there is no evidence suggesting that the secular modernised world has less need for ritualised transitions but that these have become more private, less openly acknowledged, often alone and with *private symbols* resulting in greater mental strains for the individual during difficult transition periods – individual crisis. The BFS and its rite of passage for volunteers is one such outlet, which can as a more public and traditionally supportive rite of passage. This chapter concludes by emphasising the potentiality of liminoid space to be harnessed in a way that encourages the ideals of liminality and, in so doing, questioning the solidity of Turner's segregation of the two related concepts both in future research and for practitioners of liminoid space.

References

Abrahams, R. (1983) 'The language of festivals celebrating the economy', in V. Turner (ed.), *Celebration: Studies in festivity and ritual* (pp. 161–177), Washington, DC: Smithsonian Institution Press.

Alexander, J. (2004) 'Cultural pragmatics: Social performance between ritual and strategy', *Sociological Theory*, 22(4), 527–573.

Bakhtin, M. (1965) *Rabelais and His World*, Bloomington: Indiana University Press, 1984 edn.

BFS (Beltane Fire Society) (2007) *Beltane*. Online: http://staging.beltane.org/festivals/beltane (accessed 12 December 2012).

BFS (2012) *The Reds*. Online: http://beltane.org/about/reds (accessed 24 November 2012).

BFS (2013) *A Detailed History of Beltane*. Online: http://beltanefiresociety.wordpress.com/a-detailed-history-of-beltane (accessed 14 November 2013).

Boissevain, J. (1992) 'Play and identity: Ritual change in a Maltese village', in J. Boissevain (ed.), *Revitalising European Rituals* (pp. 137–154), London: Routledge.

Bryman, A. (2012) *Social Research Methods*, Oxford: Oxford University Press.

Coleman, S. and Eade, J. (2004) *Reframing Pilgrimage: Cultures in motion*, London; New York: Routledge.

Deflem, M. (1991) 'Ritual, anti-structure, and religion: A discussion of Victor Turner's processual symbolic analysis', *Journal for the Scientific Study of Religion*, 30(1), 1–25.

Duffy, M. (2008) 'Possibilities: The role of music and emotion in the social dynamics of a music festival', in *WSEAS International Conference: Proceedings, Mathematics and Computers in Science and Engineering*. Online: www.wseas.us/e-library/conferences/2008/crete/cuht/cuht17.pdf.

Eade, J. (1992) 'Pilgrimage and tourism at Lourdes, France', *Annals of Tourism Research*, 19(1), 18–32.

Eade, J. and Sallnow, M. (1991) *Contesting the Sacred: The anthropology of Christian pilgrimage*, London: Routledge.

Frazer, J.G. (1922) *The Golden Bough: A study in magic and religion*, abridged edn, London: Macmillan.

Fredrickson, L. and Anderson, D. (1999) 'A qualitative exploration of the wilderness experience as a source of spiritual inspiration', *Journal of Environmental Psychology*, 19(1), 21–39.

Geertz, C. (1973) *The Interpretation of Cultures: Selected essays*, New York: Basic Books.

Geertz, C. (1980) 'Blurred genres: The refiguration of social thought', *American Scholar*, 49(2), 165–179.

Grimassi, R. (2001) *Beltane: Springtime rituals, lore & celebration*, Woodbury, MN: Llewellyn Publications.

Grimes, R.L. (1983) 'The lifeblood of public ritual: Fiestas and public exploration projects', in V. Turner (ed.), *Celebration: Studies in festivity and ritual* (pp. 272–283), Washington, DC: Smithsonian Institution Press.

Hollands, R. (2010) 'Engaging and alternative cultural tourism?' *Journal of Cultural Economy*, 3(3), 379–394.

Jamieson, K. (2004) 'Edinburgh: The Festival gaze and its boundaries', *Space and Culture*, 7(1), 64–75.

Kale, S. (2004) 'Spirituality, religion, and globalization', *Journal of Macromarketing*, 24(2), 92–107.

Kim, H. and Jamal, T. (2007) 'Touristic quest for existential authenticity', *Annals of Tourism Research*, 34(1), 181–201.

Kimball, S.T. (1975) 'Introduction to the English Edition', in A. van Gennep, *The Rites of Passage* (1908), Chicago: University of Chicago Press.

Manning, F. (1983) 'Cosmos and chaos: Celebration in the modern world', in F. Manning (ed.), *The Celebration of Society: Perspectives on contemporary cultural performances* (pp. 3–30), Bowling Green, OH: Bowling Green University Popular Press.

Manson, B. (2006) *An Examination of Samhain and Beltane Rituals in Contemporary Pagan Practice*, Unpublished Masters thesis, Concordia University.

Matheson, C.M. and Tinsley, R. (forthcoming) 'The carnivalesque and event evolution: A Study of the Beltane Fire Festival', *Leisure Studies*.

Messerschmidt, D. and Sharma, J. (1981) 'Hindu pilgrimage in the Nepal Himalayas', *Current Anthropology*, 22(5), 571–572.

O'Grady, A. (2012) 'Spaces of play: The spatial dimensions of underground club culture and locating the subjunctive', *Dancecult: Journal of Electronic Dance Music Culture*, 4(1), 86–106.

O'Rourke, S., Irwin, D. and Straker, J. (2011) 'Dancing to sustainable tunes: An exploration of music festivals and sustainable practices in Aotearoa', *Annals of Leisure Research*, 14(4), 341–354.

Oxford Dictionaries (2010) *Oxford Dictionary of English*, Oxford: Oxford University Press.

Partridge, C. (2006) 'The spiritual and the revolutionary: Alternative spirituality, British free festivals, and the emergence of rave culture', *Culture and Religion*, 7(1), 41–60.

Picard, D. and Robinson, M. (2006) 'Remaking worlds: Festivals, tourism and change', in D. Picard and M. Robinson (eds), *Festivals, Tourism and Social Change: Remaking worlds* (pp. 1–31), Clevedon: Channel View.

Ravenscroft, N. and Matteucci, X. (2003) 'The festival as carnivalesque: Social governance and control at Pamplona's San Fermin Fiesta', *Tourism Culture and Communication*, 4(1), 1–15.

Richards, G. and Palmer, R. (2010) *Eventful Cities: Cultural management and urban revitalisation*, Amsterdam: Butterworth-Heinemann.

Sherry, J.F. and Kozinets, R. (2007) 'Comedy of the commons: Nomadic spirituality and the Burning Man Festival', *Research in Consumer Behavior*, 11, 119–147.

Shinde, K.A. (2010). 'Managing Hindu festivals in pilgrimage sites: Emerging trends, opportunities and challenges', *Event Management*, 14(1), 53–69.

St John, G. (2001) 'Alternative cultural heterotopia and the liminoid body: Beyond Turner at ConFest', *The Australian Journal of Anthropology*, 12(1), 47–66.

St John, G. (2004) 'Counter-tribes, global protest and carnivals of reclamation', *Peace Review*, 16(4), 421–428.

St John, G. (2008) *Victor Turner and Contemporary Cultural Performance*, Oxford: Berghahn.

Timothy, D.J. and Conover, P. (2011) 'Nature religion, self-spirituality and New Age tourism', in D.J. Timothy and D.H. Olsen (eds), *Tourism, Religion and Spiritual Journeys* (pp. 139–155), London; New York: Routledge.

Turner, V.W. (1969) *The Ritual Process: Structure and anti-structure*, New York: Aldine de Gruyter.

Turner, V.W. (1975) *Dramas, Fields, and Metaphors: Symbolic action in human society*, Ithaca, NY: Cornell University Press.

Turner, V.W. and Turner, E. (1978) *Image and Pilgrimage in Christian Culture*, New York: Columbia University Press.

Van Gennep, A. (1975 [1908]) *The Rites of Passage*, Chicago: University of Chicago Press.

Van Heerden, E. (2011) 'The social and spatial construction of two South African arts festivals as liminal events', *South African Theatre Journal*, 25(1), 54–71.

Willson, G.B. (2011) 'The search for inner peace: Considering the spiritual movement in tourism', *The Journal of Tourism and Peace Research*, 1(3), 16–26.

Zinnbauer, B.J., Pargament, K.I., Cole, B., Rye, M.S., Butter, E.M., Belavich, T.G., Hipp, K.M., Scott, A.B. and Kadar, J.L. (1997) 'Religion and spirituality: Unfuzzying the fuzz', *Journal for the Scientific Study of Religion*, 36(4), 549–564.

11 Hogmanay rituals

Scotland's New Year's Eve celebrations

Elspeth Frew and Judith Mair

Introduction

New Year's Eve (or Hogmanay as it is known in Scotland) is celebrated in many countries around the world, and often takes the form of a public celebration with fireworks, music and a carnival atmosphere. However, Hogmanay itself is a long-standing festival in Scotland with roots going far back into pagan times. Some of the rites and rituals associated with Hogmanay are centuries old, and the tradition of celebrating New Year's Eve (as Hogmanay) on a grander scale than Christmas has been a part of Scottish life for many hundreds of years.

While academic research has examined the public celebrations of New Year (e.g. Derrett 2003; Foley and McPherson 2004), less attention has been paid to the original Scottish traditions of Hogmanay. This may be because these are often private events, held for individuals, families and social groups (Getz 2013), with deep traditions and historical resonance. In smaller, regional centres in Scotland there are many examples of grass-roots, celebratory gatherings reflecting a sense of community. However, the nature of the events has changed and developed as Scotland has become a modern nation. Hogmanay is now also a time for public themed celebrations. For example, the Edinburgh New Year's Eve Party attracts 80,000 people each year to the city. These events do not reflect pagan or indeed Scottish traditions but rather reflect generic New Year's Eve celebrations found anywhere around the world. While some New Year's Eve festivals are large celebrations (for example, in New York and Sydney), many other festivals are under pressure to commercialise to ensure their survival. The concern is that in rushing to bow to the commercial imperative, such festivals are losing their traditions and their heritage, becoming almost generic public celebrations, devoid of the original rites. However, it may also be the case that although the history and pagan nature of the rites and rituals are no longer commonly understood, the actual rituals themselves are still affectionately carried out – perhaps through sheer force of custom (Taft 1994). Recent research into cultural events festivals has also considered their increased commercialisation (see, for example, Anderton 2008; Caves, 2000; Finkel 2009; Frew and Ali-Knight, 2010; Richards and Wilson 2006). Thus, this chapter examines the extent to which Scotland is at risk of losing an important part of its heritage if the traditional rituals become diminished in the face of the increasing commercialism of festivals.

Scottish Hogmanay

Hogmanay is the Scottish word used to describe 31 December, the last day of the year and the associated New Year's Eve celebrations in Scotland (Robinson 1985). Hogmanay retains many of its rites and rituals in Scotland, yet is celebrated (as New Year's Eve) in many countries around the world as nothing more than a huge party. Of course, we acknowledge that there are rituals associated with New Year in other countries, such as setting New Year's resolutions, but there appears to be little evidence that these were ever part of the traditional Scottish Hogmanay. Further, while it is common around the world to sing 'Auld Lang Syne' at midnight on New Year's Eve, in Scotland this tradition is generally associated only with public organised events, rather than any private celebrations.

The celebration of Hogmanay undoubtedly has pagan origins and can be traced back to pre-Christian times, and according to Douglas (1999) is a celebration of the passing of the darkest days of winter. Although Hogmanay is the best-known name for this celebration, it used to be known as Cake Day (in the north of England), Singing E'en (evening) and Yule (in the Shetland Isles). These names all indicate different parts of the tradition: namely, giving and receiving of food, singing and celebration and close ties with the winter solstice and later Christmas traditions (Douglas 1999). The derivation of the word 'Hogmanay' itself is far from clear, but it may originate from the old French expression *'auguillaneuf'* or *'Au gui l'an neuf'*, referring both to mistletoe (*gui*) and New Year (*l'an neuf*) (Kirkpatrick 2005).

The original celebrations of Hogmanay took place at the winter solstice – 21 December – a hugely important marker of the passage of time in Europe, as the day with the least amount of daylight (McNeill 1956). This turning point was celebrated with feasting, drinking and special rites to bring good fortune and ensure the return of the sun (Douglas 1999), and even after Christianity became the most prevalent religion in Scotland, this celebration of the sun remained an important part of the calendar. Ancient superstitions involving mistletoe and evergreens were constantly re-enacted and fires were lit across the land (Douglas 1999). Despite protestations from the Scottish Kirk (Church of Scotland), these pagan celebrations continued down the ages, but in time the date of the Hogmanay celebration was moved from the solstice to 31 December each year (McNeill 1956).

The main rituals associated with Hogmanay in Scotland remain commonplace in homes across the country today. It has always been considered bad luck to 'see in' the New Year with a dirty or untidy house, and so traditionally houses were scrubbed, pantries emptied of anything old and the fireplace completely emptied of ashes ready for the first open fire of the New Year. A further and perhaps better-known tradition is that of 'first footing' – the first person to cross the threshold after the stroke of midnight brings luck with them for the year ahead, good or bad. In order to ensure good luck for the house, tradition dictates that the 'first foot' should be a tall, dark, handsome man and that he must not arrive empty-handed.

While many of the traditional rites take place at home, it became the custom over the years to gather at a convenient central point such as a town square or mercat cross, in order to bring in the New Year as a community. In times past, people then returned home from the community celebration either to act as hosts for the first foot, or to be a first foot themselves. However, the modern interpretation of Hogmanay appears to be losing the tradition of returning home for the first footing, with many celebrations in towns and cities being in public spaces in the open air, without the trappings of the traditional celebrations. The most famous New Year's Eve celebrations in the United Kingdom are in Edinburgh but even this event has become less popular over the years with the event possibly being a victim of its own success (Ross 2007). When Edinburgh's New Year's Eve party became a formal part of the city calendar in 1992–1993, over 25,000 revellers attended. By 1996 the event had grown to 350,000 people in the city celebrating at midnight. In 1997 the event became a ticketed event due to crowd safety and congestion concerns (Hughes 1999), but even in 2000, 180,000 celebrated the Millennium in Princes Street (Ross 2007). Recently, the number of revellers has dropped further to just 80,000 in 2012 (Smith 2012).

Methods

This study used a duoethnographic approach to gather the data. Duoethnography involves two peers collaborating to exchange reflections about a mutually agreed upon cultural topic. Storytelling is used to simultaneously generate, interpret and articulate data. The stories are then reported and interrogated in a collegial conversation. During the conversation the two individuals compare their experiences with each other. In effect, the authors are both the researcher and the researched (Norris 2008; Spencer and Paisley 2013). As such, duoethnography examines how different individuals give both similar and different meanings to a shared phenomenon and looks to the margins to create a range of meanings (Norris and Sawyer 2012).

This duoethnographic approach allowed us to examine the rites and rituals associated with Hogmanay from personal perspectives. We considered the traditions of Hogmanay experienced throughout our lives and reflected on our similar and different approaches to Hogmanay, how we acquired these beliefs and how this may have influenced our actions and the meanings they gave to these New Year's Eve related activities. We met formally and laid out the parameters of the discussion. We agreed to discuss our memories of Hogmanay and our individual involvement in related activities during key periods of our lives. The conversation lasted just over an hour. We found similarities and differences in our experiences of Hogmanay. Some of the similarities reflected our common semi-rural upbringing in small country towns in Scotland. Both of us were children in the

1970s and 1980s and therefore our recollections refer to the traditions and rituals carried out at that time. Both of us spent our school years living in towns with populations of between 5,000 and 8,000 people (namely Kirriemuir in the county of Angus and Dunoon in the county of Argyll), each town having particularly strong traditions associated with Hogmanay. As we discussed our experiences, it became apparent that the similar Hogmanay traditions that we experienced were related to engaging with family and friends and with shared hospitality via particular food and drink.

We found that the recollection of Hogmanays past and present was an emotional experience, recalling good times and good memories as well as reflecting on family and friends who had formed part of these memories but who had since passed away. These recollections support Norris (2008), who suggests that the purpose of duoethnography is to explore how the life histories of different individuals affect the meanings they give to experiences.

Findings and discussion

The findings of the study will initially be discussed in relation to both the rites and ritual elements that were present during Hogmanay as remembered from childhood. The findings will then move on to consider how Hogmanay and its related celebrations have changed during our lifetimes, and will conclude with reflections on the place of Hogmanay as a festival in the twenty-first century.

Rites of purification

> One of the things I remember my Gran saying, was cleaning the house on New Year's Eve ... you weren't supposed to bring in the New Year with a dirty house. Her mother, we're talking my great grandmother here, actually stripped the house, chucking stuff out of the cupboards, scrubbing the decks, you couldn't see the New Year in with a dirty house.

There appeared to be a strong element of cleaning or purification associated with Hogmanay in Scotland. This tradition goes back a long way, and McNeill (1956) makes reference to the idea that even the fire was extinguished in the hearth on Hogmanay, so that the ills of the previous year would leave the house, and the New Year would start afresh and bring good luck. However, the fact that neither of us spends much time on this ritual in our own homes, nor do we know anyone who does, suggests that this part of the Hogmanay tradition may have been consigned to history.

Rites of passage

The movement of one state to another during a festival (as per Falassi 1987) is reflected in the memories of family members becoming very emotional on New Year's Eve and crying about the fact that another year was over:

My dad's parents were from Shetland and ... they would cry on New Year's Eve.

Yeah ... my sister-in-law's mother used to bawl the place down on New Year's Eve. It was awful. I hated it.

Well why?

She spent the time thinking of all the things that had happened in the year. Thinking of how another year has passed, and I don't know if it was another year closer to the grave, or whether it was just that things had happened ... your daughter will never be four again. I don't know. But I found that quite distressing ... My sister-in-law, she used to find it a bit of a strain as well. She would say 'Oh, I'm just going down to see my Mum. She'll be crying again.'

We also reflected on the images we associated with Hogmanay as representing a crucial time in a person's life and the passage of time:

'Cause my Mum used to go on about the image of New Year's Eve ... as an old man, do you remember this? It's an image of an old man, like death.

It's like Old Father Time.

Rites of conspicuous display

Falassi (1987) explains the rites of conspicuous display as being of important symbolic value – even being almost a space of pilgrimage. Hogmanay does reflect this notion of place (Douglas 1999) and for many Scots, these associations are very strong: 'I think that if you speak to someone from Scotland, wherever they are now, they'd still be able to tell you where you went at the bells [at midnight] in their home town.' We could both clearly recall the place for Hogmanay in our own towns – 'In Kirriemuir we go to The Square, that's where you would be at midnight when the bell rang on the town hall clock'; and 'In Dunoon we all gathered round the Jubilee Lamp – a town landmark'; and 'Forfar had its own place for the bells – in Edinburgh, obviously, it's the Tron, you go to the Tron and it's fantastic'. This led us to reflect that places were strongly recognised by all locals as being important community spaces at that particular time: 'That's where you go for the bells.'

Rites of conspicuous consumption

Most people who have heard of Hogmanay (in its traditional Scottish form) probably associate it with eating and drinking to excess. Indeed, for some it is a stereotype of Scotland. We both recall quite clearly that food and drink were important parts of the celebration of Hogmanay: 'So Mum would have this fantastic spread ... and those parties were amazing', but our recollections were mostly about food and drink as generosity, rather than food and drink to excess.

Indeed, there were even rituals about when you could eat the food: 'You had to sit and look at all the sweets and things sitting out and you weren't allowed to touch them until midnight!'

In terms of drinking, Hogmanay was recognised as an opportunity to enjoy yourself and perhaps have 'one too many'. Interestingly, we both recall that although alcohol was extremely prevalent, the aim was to share a drink with friends and neighbours:

> My Dad reckons that you didn't really have that much alcohol in the house – you'd have a bottle of sherry and a bottle of whisky and that was it, and you'd have a nip of each bottle that people brought … that was it;

and

> You bought a bottle of whisky and you took it from door to door and gave people a drink out of your bottle … it's your bottle, you're giving a drink of it to people … it's not that you get plastered by drinking in everybody's house.

However, it must be acknowledged that there was, and still is, a strong association between Hogmanay and drinking to excess: 'alcohol and Hogmanay are indistinguishable'.

Rites of exchange

The rite of exchange (of ritual gifts and visits) identified by Falassi (1987) appears to have relevance to Hogmanay traditions. We each recalled slightly different versions of the tradition, but the key features were the same – at midnight, people went from house to house (usually family, friends and neighbours), taking gifts of food, drink and something for the fire (usually coal), in a symbolic gesture of sharing and communitas. The key message that came out of the discussions was: 'You would never go empty handed.' This is such a strong social norm that even today, most Scots will take a present the first time they visit someone after Hogmanay, even if it is days afterwards. The traditional gifts were shortbread and black bun (fruit cake), but with considerable regional variations based on what was available and would make a good gift:

> Black Bun … it's an expensive thing to make with all the dry fruit and sugar that goes in it, so these are things that people didn't make every day. I think what people did was take what they had that would represent generosity … you weren't first footing with the back end of a loaf or anything … you went with something nice.

The first person over your threshold after midnight on Hogmanay was known as the 'first foot': 'The first person over the threshold after midnight – they had to be tall, dark and handsome'. For one of us,

First footing was so important, that my boyfriend at the time had to leave our house just before midnight and wait outside during the bells so that he could first foot us – he stood outside and brought the New Year in on his own so that he could come in straight after the bells with the pre-arranged food, drink and coal.

Another reminiscence further recounted the strength of this social norm:

My Dad told me this story, this guy came to the door and he didn't have anything to bring and so ... he went to the front gate and took it off the hinges and brought the front gate to the house because he didn't want to come empty handed.

It is interesting to consider the burden that these norms and rites placed on people (particularly women) to have a clean house, with lots of food and plenty to drink, and to be awake and available for visitors practically all night after midnight on Hogmanay. Little wonder, then, that sometimes this became a bit too much: 'I think that they had big parties in that house. I think ... it just got too much for my Mum. That's probably why she kept it low key.'

Rites of devalorisation

The marking of the end of the festival time and the return to normal time and space regarding socialising (Falassi 1987) is blurred, with Hogmanay having no formal ending and people continuing to celebrate well after midnight, into the wee hours of the morning and for a couple of days later:

I always remember ... visiting Glasgow on say the 2nd and 3rd of January, and there were down and outs, real drunks, but still saying Happy New Year to people because they'd obviously ...

They hadn't quite realised that a few days had elapsed.

But I always remember thinking that people would say Happy New Year to you for ages into New Year. The first time after, on the 2nd, the 3rd, the 4th, the 5th of January, people would go 'Happy New Year, oh I haven't seen you since before New Year'.

Liminality

The notion of liminality suggests a space for people to behave in ways that they do not normally behave (Turner 1982; Wang 2000). We both remembered that there was an expectation that people may drink more than they normally would during other times of the year, and indeed behave in a way that they might not normally, as reflected in the following:

And I remember quite clearly about how we were trying to get drunk – 'cause that's what you do on New Year's Eve – you get drunk. And you have to plan your drinking quite ahead. You've actually got to, if you want to get drunk – you have to plan it.

You have to drink before you go out for a start, 'cause it's too expensive.

But I remember going to someone's house … to first foot them … and we get there, and what she gave us was a steak pie. And I remember I was given this piece of steak pie and I remember saying [to my friend], 'Doesn't she know how much money we've spent to get drunk this evening. I'm not eating this steak pie 'cause it's going to sober me up!'

Changes over time

While we were both able to reminisce about the rites and rituals of Hogmanay that we associated with childhood and early teens, it became clear that many things had changed since then, both in terms of our personal circumstances, but also with regard to the way that Hogmanay is celebrated. In the first place, there is considerably more emphasis on Christmas as a holiday and a celebration than there used to be in Scotland: 'It's changing now, Christmas, with the amount of presents the kids get, no wonder they think Christmas is better than New Year.' Also, New Year's Eve is becoming a much bigger celebration internationally; Edinburgh's Hogmanay attracts over 80,000 visitors.

Tourism has changed things. In Edinburgh, Hogmanay is an event now. I'm sure there are Edinburgh locals that go to the Hogmanay [celebrations], but I'm sure there are locals that run away to another corner of the country, because it's just grim [unappealing].

In the face of increasing commercialisation, changes in the way Hogmanay is celebrated became clear:

Now it's ticketed and organised. It's just too full on. So we decided that we would hire a cottage somewhere in Scotland and go and have a week away with friends, we had this massive party in the house and it was amazing, but it was all about escaping from Edinburgh, from the crowds.

We both now live in Australia, and despite some of our early efforts in Australia to maintain some of the rituals from the traditional Scottish Hogmanay, it seems that these traditions are fading away:

When we came to Australia, we started a New Year's tradition of holding a party in the house. And we would invite every single person we had ever met … I'm talking like the people from the kinder group, all the neighbours, young and old. I made a point of having someone tall, dark and handsome and he had to go out round the house, and then come back in after the bells – I gave him a bowl of sweets or something to bring in with him.

Once we stopped doing the parties, we go down to the Mornington Peninsula camping, and basically it's more like a family thing. It was just getting too much.

Yeah, the thing that we do here is go to the city to see the fireworks. My boys love them – they get to stay in the city until midnight!

One of us reflected on her father's regular visits from Scotland to Australia each year around the time of Hogmanay. If a Hogmanay party was being held, there was an expectation that he would say something as he represented 'Scottishness':

He'll wear ... a Scottish rugby top or something, and he'll go ... OK, here's the bells, we're going to have to do a big count down. And then we'd go five, four, and then ... he becomes the guru of Scottish...

...The Custodian of the ancient traditions.

Correct. He's the custodian of ancient traditions ... everyone is like 'Oh what he's going to say, this is a Scottish person, really Scottish'...

A real Scottish person.

...You can hardly understand him, and he's about to say something poignant on New Year's Eve [and he would say] 'Well thanks very much for coming'.

However, we felt a sense of loss, and a wish for the traditions and rituals of our childhood, and our heritage, to remain:

But there is nothing Scottish about it [New Year in Australia] whatsoever – no first footing, no shortbread or black bun, any of that, it was just that we got to stay up late and go into the city and that was the exciting thing. And it's fine, but it doesn't feel like New Year to me. New Year should be dark, it should have a fire, it should have lots of food and drink, it should have lots of family and friends.

Have you ever tried the first footing thing in Australia?

No ... people wouldn't understand.

Conclusion

The traditional Hogmanay celebration has many rites that reflect aspects of hospitality and socialising. Some of the traditions in rural Scotland have survived to the present day, such as meeting in a public place to celebrate the change from one year to another at midnight. Other traditions, such as the cleansing of houses are now less obvious and further, such aspects seem to have been less transferable to other countries compared to other Scottish traditions such as Scottish pipe bands and Highland gatherings which have been established in numerous countries around the world (particularly in English-speaking nations such as Canada and New Zealand). It is likely that the Scottish diaspora around the world has taken aspects of Hogmanay with them and has cemented only those aspects that revolve around public celebrations into the psyche of their new environment. This may help to explain why only some parts of the Hogmanay traditions and rituals have persisted outside Scotland. However, further research in this area is needed to investigate this proposition.

Greater commercialisation has been identified at New Year's Eve celebrations around the world where such events attract thousands of people to public places, with associated entertainment such as fireworks. However, further research is needed to establish the extent of the preservation of deep-rooted traditions of first footing, particularly in rural and semi-rural parts of Scotland. Research in these areas would reveal very strong traditions in these remote areas but recognise the reduction in such traditions elsewhere in Scotland and overseas.

References

Anderton, C. (2008) 'Commercializing the carnivalesque: The V Festival and image/risk management', *Event Management*, 12(1), 39–51.

Caves, R. (2000) *Creative Industries: Contracts between art and commerce*, Cambridge, MA: Harvard University Press.

Derrett, R. (2003) 'Making sense of how festivals demonstrate a community's sense of place', *Event Management*, 8(1), 49–58.

Douglas, H. (1999) *The Hogmanay Companion: Everything you wanted to know about New Year's Eve*, Glasgow: Neil Wilson.

Falassi, A. (1987) *Time out of Time: Essays on the Festival*, Albuquerque: University of New Mexico Press.

Finkel, R. (2009) 'A picture of the contemporary combined arts festival landscape', *Cultural Trends*, 18(1), 3–21.

Foley, M. and McPherson, G. (2004) 'Edinburgh's Hogmanay: In the society of the spectacle', *Journal of Hospitality and Tourism*, 2(2), 29–42.

Frew, E.A. and Ali-Knight, J. (2010) 'Creating high and low art: Experimentation and commercialisation at Fringe Festivals', *Tourism, Culture & Communication*, 10(3), 231–245.

Getz, D. (2013) *Event Tourism*, New York: Cognizant.

Hughes, G. (1999) 'Urban revitalization: The use of festive time strategies', *Leisure Studies*, 18(2), 119–135.

Kirkpatrick, B. (2005) *Haggis, Hogmanay and Halloween*, Edinburgh: Crombie Jardine.

McNeill, I. (1956) *The Silver Bough, Volume 1: Scottish folk lore and folk belief*, Edinburgh: William McLellan.

Norris, J. (2008) 'Duoethnography', in L.M. Given (ed.), *The Sage Encyclopedia of Qualitative Research Methods* (Vol. 1, pp. 233–236), Thousand Oaks, CA: Sage.

Norris, J. and Sawyer, R.D. (2012) 'Towards a dialogic methodology', in J. Norris, R.D. Sawyer and D. Lund (eds), *Duoethnography: Dialogic methods for social, health, and educational research* (pp. 9–40), Walnut Creek, CA: West Coast Press.

Richards, G. and Wilson, J. (2006) 'Developing creativity in tourist experiences: A solution to the serial reproduction of culture?' *Tourism Management*, 27(6), 1209–1223.

Robinson, M. (1985) *The Concise Scots Dictionary*, Aberdeen: Aberdeen University Press.

Ross, S. (2007) 'Call to scrap Hogmanay party tickets', *The Scotsman*, 31 December, p. 3.

Smith, S. (2012) 'The glorious twelve', *The Sunday Mail*, 1 January, pp. 4–5.

Spencer, C. and Paisley, K. (2013) 'Two women, a bottle of wine, and *The Bachelor*: Duoethnography as a means to explore experiences of femininity in a leisure setting', *Journal of Leisure Research*, 45(5), 695–716.

Taft, M. (1994) 'Adult Halloween celebrations on the Canadian prairie', in J. Santino (ed.), *Halloween and Other Festivals of Life and Death*, Knoxville: University of Tennessee Press.

Turner, V. (1982) *From Ritual to Theater: The human seriousness of play*, New York: Performing Arts Journal Publications.

Wang, N. (2000) *Tourism and Modernity: A sociological analysis*, Oxford: Pergamon.

Part III
The Americas

12 Punishment and the rite of purification at the Angola Prison Rodeo, Louisiana, USA

Mary Rachel Gould

We are now far away from the country of tortures, dotted with wheels, gibbets, gallows, pillories; we are far, too, from the dream of the reformers, less than fifty years before: the city of punishments in which a thousand small theatres would have provided an endless multicoloured representation of justice in which the punishments, meticulously produced on decorative scaffolds, would have constituted the permanent festival of the penal code.

(Foucault 1977: 306)

From the gallows to the rodeo ring

Michel Foucault ends *Discipline and Punish* with a solemn outlook on the future of the prison system and the illusion of humane treatment resulting from the privatisation of punishment. No longer subject to the brutal acts of punishment that Foucault (1977) details with precision in the chapters, 'The Body of the Condemned' and 'The Spectacle of the Scaffold', the soul of the condemned now suffer the consequences of a re-envisioned form of disciplinary power. That the mechanisms of discipline have only become more institutionalised, scrupulous and inhumane in the decades since the first publication of Foucault's work would likely come as no surprise to the theorist who was profoundly critical of the subtlety of state power. The death of the spectacle, and an end to what Conquergood (2002: 340) termed a 'theatre of violence', and shift to techniques of coercion, surveillance and normalisation enacted upon the incarcerated, become much more difficult to flesh out. Yet, there are still occasions when Foucault's bold pronouncement of the end of the theatrics of punishment are challenged; where the power of the state to enact physical discipline is boldly put on display for an audience. As Conquergood (2002: 341) observed, after witnessing the executions of Timothy McVeigh (11 June 2001), and Juan Raul Garza (19 June 2001), 'modern judicial punishment' has not 'advanced well beyond the deployment of raw, physical force'. Though the enactment of capital punishment in the presence of a viewing audience is the example par excellence of spectacular discipline, at the end of Louisiana State Highway 66, another such theatre of violence can be found.

For three years (2006–2008) I travelled to the Louisiana State Penitentiary at Angola to sit among crowds of spectators and witness a raucous display of state power. The Angola Prison Rodeo, staged by incarcerated men at the largest maximum-security prison in the country, is more commonly known as 'The Wildest Show in the South'. Once described as 'America's worst prison' and the 'bloodiest and most infamous prison in the South' (Stagg and Lear 1952: 13), Angola opens its gates to visitors five times a year – every Sunday in October and one weekend in April – for a rodeo and day-long crafts fair (Figure 12.1). Upon entering the Louisiana State Penitentiary the contradiction is palpable at the functioning prison and frequent pop-up tourist attraction. As a prison, the former plantation has served as a warehouse for Louisiana's condemned since 1901. As a tourist attraction, more than 70,000 visitors each year are lured by write-ups in local papers promising 'untrained convicts thrown every which way' (Bergner 1998: 4).

More than 1,000 men (one-fifth of the prison population) sell hobby crafts at the fair or suit up in black and white striped snap-button Western shirts to stage an amateur rodeo for a stadium full of curious onlookers. The rodeo involves many traditional events such as bareback horse riding, calf roping and barrel racing. There are also events specifically designed for the prison rodeo, the names of which imply a certain connection to the public fantasy of incarceration. 'Bust Out', 'Down and Dirty' and 'Buddy Pick Up' each conjure the image of animalistic, hypersexual and desperate inmates. Central to the efficacy of the

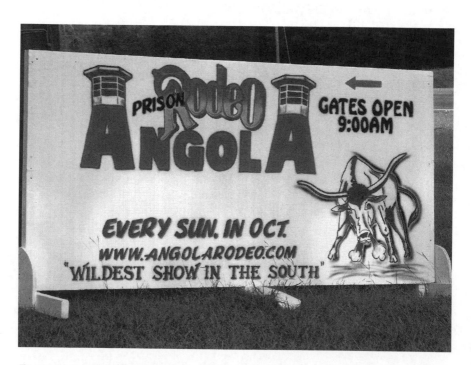

Figure 12.1 Angola Prison Rodeo roadside advertisement on Louisiana State Highway 66. Taken 22 October 2006 (source: M. Gould).

rodeo event is the ritual purification of the community that comes as a result of witnessing public punishment. Deeply rooted in a political and religious framework that functions to create a scapegoat out of the condemned, this event is the newly envisioned spectacle of discipline that Foucault suggests had ended with the removal of the scaffold from the town square. I argue that the Angola Prison Rodeo is simply a variation of the gallows and a repackaging of state-sanctioned public discipline.

Through the lens of the ritual of purification and the theory of the scapegoat this chapter reveals the ways in which the incarcerated play the role of the dangerous *other*, and the spectator, the role of the community member whose presence is needed to ensure that the public punishment occurs and order is returned to the community. What emerges during this ritual of purification is the dominant theme of otherness that Roy (2004: 329) suggests is 'used over and over again in the construction of a violent, seditious ... predator', such as the individual convicted of transgression against the community. The performance of punishment at the rodeo serves to inoculate the community from the impurities of crime and transgression and upholds the mythologies that 'sustain American identity ... [as] an innocent nation' (Butterworth 2008: 5). As a result, in the collective consciousness of the nation, the man (or woman) convicted of a crime functions as a scapegoat, publicly punished to purify the community. The emergence of the prison rodeo as a popular form of entertainment and the spectator's participation in the public punishment enacted at the event reinforces a carceral history of brutality and dehumanisation couched in a rhetoric of redemption and rehabilitation.

Angola and the crisis of mass incarceration

This is the end of the road. This is where all the lifers, all the long timers and all the people other institutions don't want, wind up ... Angola is different and has to be operated differently from other prisons because you've got a different type of convict.

(Former Angola Warden, Hilton Butler, quoted in Rideau and Wikberg 1989: 21)

The United States incarcerates its own citizens at alarming and unprecedented rates. According to the National Council on Crime and Delinquency (Hartney 2006) the incarceration rate in the United States (738/100,000) is more than four times that of the world average (166/100,000). The Pew Charitable Trust (2009) reports that 1 in 100 adult citizens is in prison or jail (2.3 million men and women) and 1 in 31 adult citizens is under some form of state supervision (prison, jail, parole or probation), accounting for approximately 7.3 million men and women. The crisis of incarceration in the United States is also a crisis in representation, as the currently incarcerated rarely engage in shared experiences or dialogue with non-incarcerated citizens and non-incarcerated citizens rarely engage with the prison system beyond representations on television and in film. Because few prisons throughout the United States are open to public participation, a culture of silence and fear defines most non-incarcerated citizens' relationship with the prison system. Situated within the context of the current crisis of mass incarceration in the United States, the Louisiana State Penitentiary is unique in the access provided to non-incarcerated citizens and the glimpse it offers of the complex history of the US prison system.

Upon entering the gates of the former Angola Plantation, the aesthetic of pre-Civil War America is not lost. In the antebellum period, every inmate in Louisiana was turned over to Major Samuel Lawrence James, who created his own penal colony on the former plantation of Angola, Louisiana. The community was named for the region of Africa that served as the point of origin for most of the slaves who worked the land (Schrift 2008). Today the self-sustaining prison is a fully functioning farm with inmates working fields of soybeans and cotton, the South's most notorious crops, for very low daily wages. Salaries at Angola range between 4 and 20 cents an hour (Schenwar 2008). Like those before them, many of the men currently working the field at Angola have little chance of freedom. Louisiana is known for handing down some of the most severe sentences. The average sentence at Angola is 93 years (Robertson 2012: A18), and it is estimated that '86% of Angola's 5,100 inmates will die in prison' (Kennedy 2013: 313). The state prison system in Louisiana is also one of the most underfunded in the nation. According to a study conducted by the Vera Institute's Center on Sentencing (2012), Louisiana spends an annual average of $17,486 per inmate. Three states – Alabama ($17, 285), Kentucky ($14,603) and Indiana ($14,823) – spend less than Louisiana; New York ($60,076) spends the most on corrections per inmate. The history of Angola, as a plantation and site of convict leasing, reflects a legacy of inhumane treatment that is still evident in the practices of the plantation-turned-prison-turned-tourist attraction.

The rodeo and crafts fair has been part of the annual function of the prison since 1965, and remains the longest-running event of its kind in the United States. Originally established to bring 'recreation for the inmate population as well as to provide a source of entertainment for employees', the public was first allowed entry in 1967 (Angola Prison Rodeo Charter 2006: n.p.). The event quickly became a financial success for the prison and the community. In 1969, to accommodate growing interest in the rodeo, the inmates built a 4,500-seat public arena. Three decades later they constructed the 7,500-seat rodeo stadium that remains the home for the event (Angola Museum 2013). Opening the rodeo (and day-long crafts fair) to the public certainly permits access to a space of secrecy and silence, but the success of the event is in restoring the audience to their traditional place in the performance of discipline, as spectators are put in the position to collude in the ritual punishment of the condemned and cleansing of the community (Figures 12.2 and 12.3).

Public punishment and the ritual of purification

For anthropologists and sociologists, most notably Victor Turner (1977), Mary Douglas (1966) and Erving Goffman (1959), it is generally agreed that 'ritual

Figure 12.2 Angola Prison Rodeo contestants and audience anticipate the start of the Bull Riding event. Taken 22 April 2007 (source: M. Gould).

Figure 12.3 A few hours before the Angola Prison Rodeo begins the incarcerated participants relax in the arena. Taken 22 April 2007 (source: M. Gould).

performance proliferates along social faultiness, pressure points, cracks in the system, the jagged edge of belief' (Conquergood 2002: 342). The Angola Prison Rodeo does what Turner (1988: 75) contends is one of the most liberating aspects of performance, it makes the unknown present to the audience, where 'individuals leave their normal, profane worlds to enter extraordinary, or sacred, realms of experience'. The rodeo event reveals the secret world of privatised punishment by allowing spectators to access what is most often closed off or, as Turner (1977: 13) writes, is 'sealed up'. During the Angola Prison Rodeo the audience watches a few of the inmates succeed, but most often watches them fail and suffer painful punishment. The public punishment happens to the cheers of an approving crowd, and in return the spectator is absolved of any identification or association with the incarcerated. Spectators are absolved of feeling sympathy for the inmates not only because they have committed crimes, but also because the punishment is presented as sport and entertainment.

Turner's (1977) work further aids in providing a framework to understand the symbolic use of the body of the inmate in the performance of the ritual of purification. For Turner ritual symbols have three levels of meaning: exegetical, operational and positional. At the exegetical level the symbol is named, is given physical attributes and a manner of production (e.g. the rodeo announcer introduces the audience to the inmate-participant before each event). At the second level, as the name implies, the symbol has a functional meaning and serves a specific, pragmatic purpose (e.g. the inmate-participant enters the ring to engage in the rodeo event). At the third level the symbol has a positional relationship with other symbols in the ritual process (e.g. the inmate-participant not only is perceived as part of the rodeo and engaged in an event but is seen in relationship with the bull or other rodeo animal). Though it is not the case that the battle between inmate-participant and bull is a fight to the death as was the expectation of ancient gladiator contests, in both cases the beast (bull or lion) is also a ritual symbol, representative of the brute power of the state to inflict bodily harm (punishment) on the person deemed to have transgressed.

For Douglas (1966: 3), rituals of purification offer 'public displays of patterned symbolic elements involving powers and truths that cannot be attained by mere conscious effort'. Such events transfix the audience into participating in vivid sequences of events that transcend contemporary notions of morality, purity or righteousness (Patterson 2011). Beyond the ritual's 'mystical and emotive aspects', they also serve a significant social function, including 'enhancing group solidarity, defusing social contradictions, channeling and resolving social conflict, and, as Michel Foucault has argued, exercising power' (SpearIt 2013: 6). Masked as an event serving as 'rehabilitation' through entertainment, the prison rodeo depicts a classic representation of punishment, where the offender is publicly subdued under the supervision of a representative of the state. In this case, Angola's warden serves as the institutional surrogate.

Rites of purification, like the Angola Prison Rodeo, are not only an entry into the increasingly privatised world of punishment, they are often steeped in religious practices that were historically enacted in order for the community member (spectator) to achieve righteousness. The connection between crime, punishment and religion is not unique to the rodeo event as the prison itself is deeply rooted in a tradition of piety. The first penitentiary in the United Sates appeared in 1790 with the opening of the Walnut Street Jail in Philadelphia. The jail, modelled under the Quaker influence, relied on a strict regimen of prayer, silence and work for redemption. The religious undercurrent guiding the rodeo event reflects the historical linking of religion, redemption and punishment, specifically enacted through the creation of a scapegoat.

Religious purity and the creation of a scapegoat

> And Aaron shall lay both his hands upon the head of the live goat, and confess over him all the iniquities of the children of Israel, and all their transgressions in all their sins, putting them upon the head of the goat, and shall send him away by the hand of a fit man into the wilderness.
>
> (Leviticus 16: 21)

As a theoretical frame, the scapegoat serves to demonstrate how the body of the inmate is a potent symbol of immoral and illegal behaviour and convenient symbolic representative of the worst of the imagination of the community. The scapegoat mechanism, revealed through Girard's (1977: 82) influential mimetic analysis of ritual violence, suggests that it is a contest over resources that leads to violence and because of the mimetic inclinations of human nature the community needs a way to end such 'forms of violence that beguile imagination and provoke emulation'. For Girard (1977), whether it is capitalism, the nuclear arms race or the story of Cain and Abel, competition eventually leads to violence. Further, Girard (1986) suggests that society needs the ritual sacrifice of a scapegoat as a means to maintain stability and order, and keep violence outside the community. Scapegoating is one way for a community to deal with the guilt associated with creating and supporting a system of haves and have-nots, where the blame for the violence resulting from the desire to acquire goods and resources can be placed directly back onto the transgressor. Burke (1969: 406) is quick to remind us that it is always the scapegoat that 'performs the role of vicarious atonement'. What is most problematic about the scapegoat mechanism is that it is steeped in practices of violence and has little space for healing the breach that precipitated the punishment.

The rhetorical function at play in the creation of a scapegoat is closely tied to the communicative conditions necessary to the process of identity formation and the discursive and operational marking of *us* and *them*. Hall (1996: 3) writes of this process: 'since ... it [identity] operates across difference, it entails discursive work, the binding and marking of symbolic boundaries, the production of "frontier-effects"'. Hall continues, 'It [identity] requires what is left outside, its constitutive outside, to consolidate the process'. When non-incarcerated citizens construct their identity as 'law abiding' they are immediately defining themselves and 'the groups to which we belong' against 'the groups around us'

(Carter 1996: 6). Various discursive elements of the rodeo performance aid in the process of us-versus-them identity formation. For example, at the rodeo a sub-plot of ridicule underwrites the event's script. Throughout the rodeo inmate participants are presented as inept objects deserving of punishment. According to the Angola Prison Rodeo Program (2006: 32), the unskilled inmate makes for 'hilarious entertainment' where the animals are even able to 'mock the frustrated riders'. Scapegoating is, in effect, part of this process of othering where the abject, what is *not us*, is constructed as a repository for our fears and aggressions about crime and violence and those who are accused of committing such acts.

Not only is the practice of scapegoating deeply rooted in political traditions there is also a significant linking of the scapegoat as a religious practice. Ritual sacrifice plays a major role in most religious systems where the process of selecting and acting out violence against an other leads to the cleansing (purification) of a larger group. Acts of ritualised violence also helps to displace collective feelings of aggression and anger towards a perceived perpetrator of a crime. As Burke (1970: 223) observes, the cathartic effect that results in the sacrifice of the other generally is a result of 'the slaying of scapegoats'. The scapegoat is symbolically sacrificed as a representation of chaos and discord. The elimination of the scapegoat is a means to return harmony to the community.

The tradition of the scapegoat traces its origins to the Hebrew Bible and the story of Leviticus, in which Aaron is commanded to bring an offering to the temple (two goats and a bull), to atone for his sins and those of his family. During the ceremony, the priest, laying his hands on the head of a goat, confesses over it all of the sins of the community; literally putting the transgressions 'upon the head of the live goat' (Leviticus 16: 21). The goat, driven into the wilderness, takes with it the transgression of Aaron, his family and the community. The commandment to 'drive him [goat] out into the wilderness' is not unlike what state and federal governments have done to prison populations as prisons are increasingly built in the rural outskirts of communities. No longer is it the case that a prison is in the town centre, where the community must, on a daily basis, face their other; now it is more likely that a prison is built in a remote community where land is cheap, neighbours are infrequent and low-wage jobs are welcome. The story of Leviticus, the precursor to our contemporary notion of the scapegoat, demonstrates how the collective transgressions of the community were symbolically displaced onto the head of a goat and literally driven out of the community. The prison rodeo, like other ritual events involving a scapegoat, institutionalises violence as the only means for dealing with conflict or guilt, and the sacrifice of the scapegoat as the only means to return order and purity to the community.

Performing purity at the Angola Prison Rodeo

The ritual of purification at the Angola Prison Rodeo begins with a performance by the *Glory Riders*, the only horseback-mounted Christian Ministry in the country. According to their website (Glory Riders 2013), the *Glory Riders* 'ride under the banner of Jesus Christ' with the mission to 'promote God and America' in the 'western tradition' (Figure 12.4). The *Glory Riders* add to a performance steeped in patriotism and religion, and enhance the appearance of an event designed upon the premise of morality, rehabilitation and redemption. After a few of the introductions standard to a sporting event – the presentation of flags, acknowledgement of sponsors and the singing of the national anthem – a procession of rodeo participants ends with the warden entering the stadium in a chariot, like a latter-day Caesar entering the Coliseum. The start of the rodeo is not unlike the early American Puritan executions that Conquergood (2002: 345) describes as 'elaborately staged and exquisitely paced ritual dramas seething with suspense, tension, ambivalence, crisis, reversals, revelations, and breathtaking spectacle'. Throughout the day spectators cheer the successes and failures of the inmates and jeer the participants who demonstrate any reticence in facing their competition.

Spectators bear witness to the punishment suffered by untrained and unskilled rodeo participants, most of whom are pitted against much more seasoned and skilled opponents (trained rodeo animals). The violence of the rodeo itself serves as a key element in the production of the ritual and its purifying function. The actual spilling of blood, which is not uncommon at the rodeo, is often a key ingredient in the process of 'sacred cleansing' and the 'renewal of spirituality' (Roy 2004: 330). The rodeo ring and its layers of dirt is also symbolic in the cleansing ritual as dirt and the process of making a dirty experience tidy involves the 'reflection of order to disorder, being to non-being, form to formlessness, life

Figure 12.4 The Christian ministry team, *The Glory Riders*, ride as part of the opening to the April 2006 event. Taken 21 April 2007 (source: M. Gould).

to death' (Douglas, as cited in Benatar 2004: 2). It is in the last event of the day that the potential for the spilling of blood onto the dirt of the rodeo ring, and as a result the purification of the community, is most likely.

Simply known as 'Guts and Glory', the rodeo finale pits the will of the contestants against the sheer force of a bull. In 'Guts and Glory' inmates can check any potential 'rodeo skill' at the ring's gate, as the event only requires a high tolerance for pain. As the name implies, it takes guts to win, and the man who is victorious walks away with the glory (including a $500 cash prize). The winner is the contestant who can tear away a red poker chip that has been tied to the horns of a bull (Figure 12.5) and rests between its eyes. The event is given a 15-minute time limit; many participants spend the entire time hugging the edges of the ring. There are only a few men in the ring who even approach the bull and many are discarded with little effort from the powerful beast. Regardless of the winner – an inmate or the bull – the crowd cheers this last event, especially if blood is spilled.

The limits of entertaining the masses

The adoration of the crowd fades quickly and spectators do not return to their seats and instead make their way to the exits. Dusk is the curtain that signals the

Figure 12.5 The Angola Museum displays a taxidermy bull head with attached poker chip used in the rodeo event 'Guts and Glory'. Taken 22 October 2006 (source: M. Gould).

end of the performance. As the unruly procession of spectators leaves the arena, the inmates are shuttled back to their housing units with much more organisation. The reality of life at Angola can only be suspended for so long. The 'inmate cowboys' have succeeded in entertaining the non-incarcerated spectators by participating in a performance that mocks the political nature of incarceration and in the process stages an age-old ritual of public punishment and purification. In exchange, the spectator leaves the event with an exaggerated sense of the divide between us and them and the unfounded confirmation of their own morality.

Incarcerated men and women in the United States are ideologically and geographically removed from the daily experiences of non-incarcerated citizens. In the terms Friere (1993: 61) used to describe the experience of individuals existing on the margins, incarcerated men and women are 'beings for others', used by the media, politicians and everyday citizens to distinguish between moral, law-abiding behaviour and immoral behaviour and/or criminal activity. The incarcerated in the United States not only lose many freedoms during the time of their confinement they are also prevented from being or becoming 'beings for themselves'. Robert Perkinson (2010: 17), after conducting an extensive history of American prisons in *Texas Tough*, concludes that the only way to 'imagine a way out of our current criminal justice imbroglio' is to humanise the experience of the millions of men and women in US prisons. Dehumanising the incarcerated men at Angola, by using them as props for a staged performance, does none of the work Perkinson outlines.

The Angola Prison Rodeo provides the material and symbolic arena for the construction of a scapegoat, providing the spectator a moral high ground where they can identify as not being 'wrong or morally degenerate or irredeemably malicious' (Carter 1996: 7). In contemporary culture the incarcerated individual has great utility as a social scapegoat, particularly during times of social turmoil, such as the current crisis of mass incarceration and a time when the infrastructure that holds together the system of discipline and power in the United States is coming into question. Changes to mandatory sentencing laws, deincarceration mandates in California and concerns over the drastic cost of incarceration in federal and state budgets are but a few examples of the ways that politicians and citizens are being forced to reconsider judicial policy and practices. In the midst of shifting attitudes about extreme sentences and over-incarceration a backlash is also occurring, contributing to an even greater need for a scapegoat. Increasingly, non-incarcerated citizens require a distraction to absolve them of the need to consider the thin line that exists between legal/illegal or moral/immoral actions or the reality that a currently incarcerated person might one day leave prison and become a member of their community.

Opening up the prison to non-incarcerated men and women provides an unusual level of access and does permit interaction between the public and the currently incarcerated. But at Angola these interactions happen at a great and unacceptable social cost. Visitors are treated as pleasure-seeking spectators colluding in the state's display of disciplinary power. As Foucault (1977) demonstrates in *Discipline and Punish*, the spectator's participation in punishment (public and private) is an integral component of the process of discipline. In the move from public performances of capital punishment to the creation of private prisons, the non-incarcerated citizen is no less a part of practice discipline. In democratising discipline, the community member became the *judge*, legitimising and authorising the power of the state to punish (Foucault 1977).

At the Angola Prison Rodeo non-incarcerated spectators are given the opportunity to reaffirm their position in the social hierarchy, to project any of their own fear of crime onto the head of the scapegoat, and to purge themselves of any guilt associated with living in the nation that incarcerates more of its own citizens than any other country in the world. As a public spectacle and under the guise of rehabilitation, the Angola Prison Rodeo deepens the crisis of mass incarceration in the United States. The ritual of purification enacted at the rodeo further illustrates that although models of punishment have been privatised, and in theory become more humane, spectacle and the brutality of bodily punishment, to the cheers of an audience, continues to prevail as a dominant form of social control.

References

Angola Museum (2013) *40 Years of Guts and Glory*. Online: www.angolamuseum. org/?q=RodeoHistory (accessed 25 September 2013).

Angola Prison Rodeo Charter (2006) *Angola Prison Rodeo Program Guide*, n.p.

Benatar, M. (2004) 'Purification and the self-system of the therapist', *Journal of Trauma & Dissociation*, 5(4), 1–15.

Bergner, D. (1998) *God of the Rodeo: The quest for redemption in Louisiana's Angola Prison*, New York: Ballantine.

Burke, K. (1969) *The Grammar of Motives*, Berkeley: University of California Press.

Burke, K. (1970) *The Rhetoric of Religion: Studies in logology*, Berkeley: University of California Press.

Butterworth, M. (2008) 'Purifying the body politic: Steroids, Rafael Palmeiro, and the rhetorical cleansing of Major League Baseball', *Western Journal of Communication*, 72, 145–161.

Carter, C.A. (1996) *Kenneth Burke and the Scapegoat Process*, Norman: University of Oklahoma Press.

Collins, R. (1992) *Sociological Insight: An introduction to non-obvious sociology*, Oxford: Oxford University Press.

Conquergood, D. (2002) 'Lethal theatre: Performance, punishment, and the death penalty', *Theatre Journal*, 54(3), 339–367.

Douglas, M. (1966) *Purity and Danger: An analysis of the concepts of pollution and taboo*. London: Routledge & Kegan Paul.

Foucault, M. (1977) *Discipline and Punish: The birth of the prison*, New York: Vintage.

Friere, P. (1993) *Pedagogy of the Oppressed*, New York: Continuum.

Girard, R. (1977) *Violence and the Sacred*, Baltimore: Johns Hopkins University Press.

Girard, R. (1986) *The Scapegoat*, Baltimore: Johns Hopkins University Press.

Glory Riders (2013) Online: www.gloryriders.org (accessed 12 August 2013).

Goffman, E. (1959) *The Presentation of Self in Everyday Life*, Gloucester, MA: Smith.

Hall, S. (1996) 'Who needs "identity"?', in S. Hall and P. Du Gay (eds), *Questions of Cultural Identity*, Thousand Oaks, CA: Sage.

Hartney, C. (2006) 'US rates of incarceration: A global perspective', *National Council on Crime and Delinquency*. Online: www.nccdglobal.org/sites/default/files/publication_pdf/factsheet-us-incarceration.pdf (accessed 10 October 2013).

Kennedy, L. (2013) '"Longtermer blues": Penal politics, reform, and carceral experiences at Angola', *Punishment & Society*, 15(3), 304–322.

Patterson, P. (2011) 'And we shall purify: On truth-seeking after cruelty and repression', *Administrative Theory & Praxis*, 33(1), 80–104.

Perkinson, R. (2010) *Texas Tough*, New York: Metropolitan Books.

Pew Charitable Trust (2009) 'One in 31: The long reach of American corrections', *State and Consumer Initiatives*. Online: www.pewstates.org/research/reports/one-in-31-85899371887 (accessed 3 August 2013).

Rideau, W. and Wikberg, R. (1989) 'The omen', *The Angolite*, 14(3), 19–23.

Robertson, C. (2012) 'In prison, play with trial at its heart resonates', *New York Times*, 6 May, p. A18.

Roy, A. (2004) 'The construction and scapegoating of Muslims and the "other" in Hindu nationalist rhetoric', *Southern Communication Journal*, 69(4), 320–332.

Schenwar, M. (2008) 'Slavery haunts American's plantation prisons', *Black Agenda Report*, 3 September. Online: http://blackagendareport.com/content/slavery-haunts-america%E2%80%99s-plantation-prisons (accessed 1 August 2013).

Schrift, M. (2008) 'The wildest show in the South: The politics and poetics of the Angola Prison Rodeo and inmate arts festival', *Southern Cultures*, 14(1), 22–41.

SpearIt (2013) 'Legal punishment as civil ritual: Making cultural sense of harsh punishment', *Mississippi Law Journal*, 82(1), 1–44.

Stagg, E.W. and Lear, J. (1952) 'America's worst prison', *Collier's Magazine*, 22 November, p. 13.

Turner, V. (1977) *The Ritual Process: Structure and anti-structure*, Ithaca, NY: Cornell University Press.

Turner, V. (1988) *The Anthropology of Performance*, New York: PAJ Publications.

Vera Institute of Justice (2012) 'The price of prisons: What incarceration costs taxpayers', *Fact Sheet*. Online: www.vera.org/sites/default/files/resources/downloads/the-price-of-prisons-40-fact-sheets-updated-072012.pdf (accessed 11 October 2013).

13 Mardi Gras Indians

Rituals of resistance and resilience in changing times

Sue Beeton

Mardi Gras is a carnival based around the Christian calendar, lasting from one day to many months. In certain cultures it commences on Twelfth Night (or Epiphany) and culminates on Shrove Tuesday (or Fat Tuesday, which is the direct English translation of the French *Mardi Gras*), being the day before the commencement of the 40-day penitential season of Lent. Mardi Gras, or Carnival, is celebrated in many parts of the world from Europe (where it has its origins) to the United States and South America, including the renowned Venice Carnevale and the largest celebration in the world in Rio de Janeiro in Brazil. The culturally diverse New Orleans Mardi Gras was initially celebrated by French colonial settlers in Louisiana in the early eighteenth century. Popular Mardi Gras practices include wearing masks and costumes to balls and in parades, involving at times complex rituals that invert and overturn social conventions. However, there are other, far more intricate meanings and rituals that have been developed under the aegis of Mardi Gras, especially in New Orleans.

An important aspect of Mardi Gras is the ritual of *masking* – covering one's face in order to retain anonymity and generalised *right to be other*, enabling the role inversion and escapism central to so many such carnivals (Gotham 2005). In New Orleans, along with the formal *Mardi Gras Krewes* that host lavish masked balls and extensive street parades, another group arose away from the dominant culture, that of the Mardi Gras Indians comprising a series of African-American tribes or gangs. Forged in a highly racist time of black persecution, the black Indians have been intentionally secretive for many years, and remain a relatively closed society that is rarely shown on telecasts of New Orleans Mardi Gras parades and parties. Today, they still do not rate a mention in the official Mardi Gras Museum in New Orleans in Jackson Square.

While the first Mardi Gras parade in New Orleans was in 1827, the black community did not mask as Indians until the early 1880s, but were not allowed to cover their faces. Hence, the term *masking* refers to the wearing of costumes themselves, not simply the masks. Dressed in spectacularly beaded and feathered suits, the Indians present a formidable sight as they parade through the backstreets of New Orleans and ritualistically battle with other tribes for the 'prettiest suit', proudly separate from the official Mardi Gras parade schedule, with no defined route or permit.

This chapter begins by tracing the tumultuous history and antecedents of the Mardi Gras Indians and tries to unravel what is at times a confusing folklore surrounding the tribes, coming from an oral tradition. What is of particular interest is the evidence that the tribes were formed in the late nineteenth century, not as a copy of the more accepted and formalised Krewes, but as a statement of resistance and identity at a time of emancipation, coupled with intense racism, in what is arguably one of the most racially polarised regions in the United States (Lipsitz 2006). The tribes themselves are highly stylised, and ritualised, creating a space for community connection, while providing a secret place only available to insiders. The Mardi Gras Indians also present a model of resilience, as profiled in the HBO TV series, *Treme* (2011–2013), with the character of the Big Chief in that series being based on real-life Chief, Donald Harrison, Big Chief of the Guardians of the Flame.

In order to combat a violent past and negative reputation even within their own community, as well as to provide a sense of stability and strength in the period post Hurricane Katrina, the Indians are working to improve understanding and to be seen as a positive force in their communities while becoming a little more open to outsiders by allowing us to participate in some of their more public rituals, such as the street parades. Consequently, this chapter moves on to take a more (auto)ethnographic approach, describing my own interest in the Indians and experiences with this culture before, during and after Mardi Gras, presenting primarily an outsider's perspective, one that can be considered as a *lived experience* as developed by Dilthey (1985). He describes *lived experience* as embodying values that are relevant to our purposes, rather than simply a theoretical representation. Further discussion of the lived experience as a research approach can be found in van Manen (1990), among others. Van Manen explains that such experiences are subjective, natural and un-edited until one applies self-reflection and analysis, which sits very well with my autoethnographic approach, as outlined in the next section. Carnival is described by Bakhtin (1984) as a participatory, lived experience where there is no distinction between the viewers and participants – everyone is involved.

The Mardi Gras Indian experience is a far cry from the formalised and controlled Mardi Gras parades with their large floats and officially sanctioned krewes parading along pre-determined routes where the spectators are separated from the procession, begging for throws (such as beads, plastic doubloons or cups) from the floats. These are examples of *spectacle*, where the audience simply watches, as opposed to the more participatory carnival as described by Bakhtin (1984). While these official parades remain family oriented, other celebrations have, at times, fallen to the depths of women (usually tourists) baring their breasts for beads – an act not occurring until the mediatisation of the culture and tourism of the late twentieth century (Gotham 2002). Referred to as a form of 'playful deviance', such public nudity activities, while localised to the area of the French Quarter, 'are increasingly assuming a commodified character and marketed to a global audience' (Gotham 2005: 313). Lipsitz (2006) interpreted the comments by George Bush, President of the United States, on his post

Katrina visit reminiscing about his own pleasurable visits to New Orleans in his youth, to be referring to the highly limited and mediatised version of the city found in Bourbon Street – a site of excessive drinking, lurid sex shows and public behaviour.

In this chapter, we leave the French Quarter far behind and venture into the local black communities to look at the role and meaning of the Mardi Gras Indians' rituals in relation to these communities and their wider influence. This is done through personal, lived experiences and reflection, taking an autoethnographic approach.

Autoethnography

The application of autoethnography for this study is crucial due to the very personal and highly emic nature of the experience. The rituals surrounding the Mardi Gras Indians present an immersive, emotional experience, even to an outsider. While also wishing to gain a more insider-based perspective, the only way to address this for now is to examine my own experience.

Autoethnography, while remaining controversial in some research fields, presents us with a powerful research approach, where the researcher is the subject (or data), and is closely related to the aforementioned process of studying one's lived experience. To be successful and provide some meaningful results, this approach requires intense and honest introspection and reflection; however, this is what we (as professional researchers) do to others, so it should not be impossible to do this to ourselves. Naturally, issues of bias and subjectivity are present; however, they exist in all research – the beauty of autoethnography is that such biases and subjectivity are acknowledged and transparent.

When discussing the potential of self-observation in consumer research, Rodriguez and Ryave (2002) explain that the topics best suited to this type of analysis are 'single, hidden or elusive phenomena that are concrete, specific, intermittently occurring, bounded or short duration, presented in the vernacular, and without extended definitions or limiting examples' (Rodriguez and Ryave 2002: 14). This suggests that where topics are complex, socially sensitive and often fleeting, rendering them unsuitable for other research methods such as surveys, interviews and experiments, reflexive approaches such as autoethnography come into their own (Mick 2005).

Mick (2005) lists some examples in consumer behaviour that are suited to autoethnographic study, including those where one experiences goals, desires or intense emotions, supporting my argument for taking this approach here, while Noy articulates the synergy between the autoethnographic approach and the tourism experience, noting that 'exploring tourists' experiences autoethnographically … illuminates the fuzzy and liminal space that lies between tourism experiences and everyday experiences' (Noy 2007: 352).

Taking an autoethnographic approach allows us to examine an intimate, lived experience based around a powerful ritual performed by others. In February 2013 I participated in the *Fi Yi Yi* Mardi Gras Indian tribe's ritualised celebration of

Mardi Gras. A few months later, I returned to New Orleans and was able to meet two community leaders from the *Guardians of the Flame* tribe, Big Queen Cherice Harrison-Nelson and her mother Herreast, which has gone some way to bringing this discussion into an even more faithful, insiders' realm, providing further depth and insight into my experience. After our meeting, I was humbled when Cherice invited me to contribute to *The Spy Boy Annual*, a publication outlining the stories of many of the Mardi Gras Indian Spy Boys (Beeton forthcoming).

How and why the Mardi Gras Indian?

Their own history is little known beyond its oral tradition, which for the oldest organised gang surviving today begins about 1885 (Smith 1994a: 55)

It has been argued that the roots of the Mardi Gras Indian tradition are embedded in the early-nineteenth-century Maroon culture of the colonial Americas (Smith 1994a). The Maroons have been described as 'enslaved Americans who had managed to escape plantations and form new societies in the wilderness' (Bilby and N'Diaye 1992: 54). Bilby and N'Diaye (1992) also note that these cultures have combined African and non-African elements in unique ways, reflected not only in the Seminoles of Florida to which they refer, but, as Smith (1994a) argues, also to the Mardi Gras Indians (also known as black Indians) of New Orleans. While such connections are difficult to quantify, Smith (1994a), a long-time chronicler of the Mardi Gras Indians, notes the many conversations he had with black Indians who contend that they are directly descended from the Maroons of the colonial period. Hall (1992) supports this, arguing that the swamps surrounding New Orleans became the organising centres for many of the Maroons. Certainly, those fleeing into these swamps and marshes were often aided by Native Americans (Kennedy 2010).

In New Orleans, *The Place des Negres* (known today as Congo Square) was a place where slaves, Maroons and Indians gathered during their free time on Sundays to trade, socialise and reaffirm their spiritual beliefs. After the Louisiana Purchase in 1804, the incoming Anglo-American society feared such freedom of expression, working to suppress and even replace it. However, a distinctive African-American parade, dance and music culture, similar to that practised today by the Mardi Gras Indians and their related Social Aid and Pleasure Clubs as well as the Baby Dolls, continued underground (Johnson 1991; Smith 1994a).

The Social Aid and Pleasure Clubs are a series of mutual aid, benevolent societies that were established in the nineteenth century to support their communities with health care and burial insurance, and soon were providing other community support to their communities, both educational and social. Along with their community work, they host an annual parade that has become known as a *second line*. Spectators are welcome to walk or dance with them through their neighbourhoods, which bring others 'through the cracks and crevices of your neighbourhood to allow everybody an opportunity to be part of it' (Breunlin and Lewis 2009: 184). The Baby Dolls began around 1912 as a small group of black Creole women, primarily from the dance halls and brothels of New Orleans, who also used Mardi Gras as a means to break from traditional social and gender segregation of their society (Vaz 2013). They dressed as *innocents*, imitating little girls with short skirts and bonnets and participated in the Social and Pleasure Club parades as well as during Mardi Gras.

In what some may consider an obfuscation of the linear historical narrative, there was another more prosaic influence that seems to have affected at least some of the black Indians. In 1884, Buffalo Bill Cody's Wild West Show toured the region and at the very least one influential black Indian, Brother Tillman, the Big Chief of the Yellow Pocahontas tribe, having some Indian heritage, was heavily influenced by the theatricality of the show and the Indian costumes (Backstreet Cultural Museum interpretive material).

While the Social Aid and Pleasure clubs that also developed during this time became more mainstream, ultimately accepting Anglo-American regulations such as incorporation and parade permit registration, the Mardi Gras Indians remained tribal and autonomous, performing their music in the backstreets of New Orleans. This distinction is important, as the black Indians 'refuse to subject themselves to the humiliation of being monitored and controlled by hostile authorities, [as] to do so would betray the function and historical meaning of their independent spirit' (Smith 1994a: 48). Smith (1994b) also sees gangs (or tribes) such as the Mardi Gras Indians as a reflection of a culture that retains its pride in the black working class community against all the effects of racism and urbanisation, which is also seen in the famous saying, 'won't kneel, won't bow, don't know how' (Blank 1978).

While Smith's comments were made some years ago in 1994, the friction between the City of New Orleans and the Mardi Gras Indian tribes continues today, sadly reflected in the dramatic death of Big Chief Allison 'Tootie' Montana (known today as the Chief of Chiefs) in 2005 while representing the right of the Indians to traverse and occupy urban space without a permit. The moment of Tootie Montana's death is recorded in the documentary, *Bury the Hatchet* (Walker 2011), where we see him utter his last words, 'This must stop' before collapsing in the City Court. The attending Mardi Gras Indians begin to quietly sing the eponymous song, *Indian Red* (the song traditionally performed at the beginning and end of the black Indian Mardi Gras) while the court mourns. A symbol of peace as well as resistance, an enormous statue of him (Figure 13.1) has subsequently been erected in Armstrong Park. As Lipsitz explains, 'the Mardi Gras Indians balance the completing claims of commercial culture and folk culture, of America and Africa, of *resistance and accommodation*, and of spontaneity and calculation' (1988: 103; my emphasis).

Furthermore, Lipsitz notes that, while on the surface the Mardi Gras Indians' behaviour appears similar to other groups related to carnival, particularly in relation to what Bakhtin (1984: 159) refers to as a general 'right to be other', they are distinguished by 'their use of conventional forms for unconventional purposes' (Lipsitz 1988: 102). The black Indians use ritual not only to invert and subvert but also to provide 'coded expression to values and beliefs that operate

Figure 13.1 Statue of the Chief of Chiefs, Allison 'Tootie' Montana, in Armstrong Park (source: S. Beeton).

every day in the lives of black workers in New Orleans' (Lipsitz 1988: 102). While the Mardi Gras Indians parade to a European Christian carnival traditional agenda, the cultural meaning and spectacle is not European, while the references to native American Indians are not purely Indian and the modes of expression from Africa are also removed from African ritual. This results in a highly complex, individualised identity that is pure working class, black New Orleans. Also, 'the Indian tribes' disguise brings out into the open dimensions of repression that the dominant culture generally tries to render invisible' (Lipsitz 1988: 104).

Being more than simply frivolous sites of celebration, the tribes, along with the Social and Pleasure Clubs, function as mutual aid societies, helping community members in many aspects of their lives, such as to meet the cost of emergencies, home repairs, lost wages and so on. As Lipsitz (2006: 462–463) explains, such organisations are necessary as 'systematic segregation and discrimination prevent black people from acquiring assets that appreciate in value, from moving to desirable neighbourhoods ... and from reaping the rewards of home ownership'.

The use of ritual is central to the Mardi Gras Indians in that it provides a place for community spirit and identity in a culturally complex city that remains divided along racial and socio-economic lines.

Community importance and cultural expansion

> Every Mardi Gras day, 'tribes' of anywhere from fifteen to thirty working-class black males dress as Plains Indians and take to the streets of New Orleans. They parade through black neighbourhoods, displaying their costumes and flags, singing and chanting in a specialized argot, while treating themselves to the hospitality offered in neighbourhood bars and private homes ... Organised into a rigid status hierarchy of official positions (spy boy, flag boy, wild man, third chief, second chief, big chief and council chief), the tribes celebrate their own worthiness in chants and songs, while remaining vigilant for competing tribes who might challenge them with aggressive word play to compare costumes, dances, or singing and rhyming ability ... They practice all year in bars, and they bring a group of neighbourhood residents into the streets behind them as a 'second line' of supportive singers and dancers.
>
> (Lipsitz 1988: 101–102)

The black Indian community is beginning to cautiously open up to outsiders, including tourists. The reasons for this are multi-faceted, but certainly leaders such as Cherice Harrison-Nelson, co-founder of the Mardi Gras Indian Hall of Fame and Big Queen of the Guardians of the Flame, and Sylvester Francis, founder of the Backstreet Cultural Museum, believe that it is central to creating a prosperous future for their communities. Also, by engaging with outsiders, misconceptions and falsehoods regarding the Black Indians can be rectified – a simple example of this is that many people believe this group to be American Indians rather than African Americans.

The annual Jazz and Heritage Festival has been where many people began to have the opportunity to experience a small taste of the vibrancy and power of this tradition, through the Mardi Gras Indian musical performances on the Heritage Stage. However, few manage to see past the spectacle of feathers, beads and music to catch even a glimpse at their meaning.

From the outside in …

Why do I, a privileged white Australian, have such an interest in a black subculture such as this? I am still not sure, but I do know that I am drawn to groups who have searched (or still are searching) for an identity, a place in the world … I believe, however, that the intense responses I experience towards such people and their plight comes from my own sense of not quite belonging that has dogged me throughout most of my life. I know I am not alone in this, and continue to examine how others have dealt with this and what that can mean to me. Consequently, I feel that much of the travel we do, and rituals in which we participate (or create), is in response to a deep-seated need to truly belong, to be grounded in a place and meaning, and to be remembered.

On my first visit to New Orleans in 1998, I became aware of the Mardi Gras Indians, but knew little beyond the fact that they had something to do with Mardi Gras, were black and wore fantastic costumes (or suits). Yet, even then I felt there was something more than the Mardi Gras partying that we were hearing about from other visitors to the city. Yes, it is a party town, but I sensed a strong culture seeping up from the very streets I walked along – the music, the food, the art and the mixed history all merged to become something else.

I first began to get this when I came across a group known as *Bamboula 2000*, which was established in 1994 to preserve, develop and perpetuate the multicultural roots that reach deep into the soil of Congo Square. On a visit in 2000, I attended a gathering presented by them in Armstrong Park where, apart from one journalist, I was the only white person, and definitely the only tourist. I found this surprising as I had heard of this event from an interview on the local community radio station WWOZ. This event related the story of the development of black culture in New Orleans from the early days of slavery, voodoo and the dances of the bamboula, calinda and congo through to Mardi Gras, finishing with us all participating in a Second Line parade (which dances behind the musicians) to Congo Square (where the tourists eventually found us). While there were no masked Mardi Gras Indians, they did have a member of the Northside Skull and Bone Gang (a skeleton), who heralds the beginning of Mardi Gras day (Fat Tuesday) throughout the community, and is closely connected with certain tribes – in this instance, the Fi Yi Yi tribe.

The audience were nearly all school children, and the organiser and Bamboula 2000 band leader, Luther Gray, explained to me how important it was to keep the knowledge and stories going as they were becoming lost. It was here that I really started to see and feel the complexity of the cultural heritage that has made this city so fascinating to me and many others. While the Mardi Gras Indians only mask twice a year (on Fat Tuesday and St Joseph's Day), I began to see that their influence went far deeper, and that the ritual surrounding these outings was central to their lives and an expression of much more.

In subsequent visits, I spent time at the Backstreet Cultural Museum in the district of Treme, where the owner, Sylvester Francis, would provide visitors with information on the role of the Mardi Gras Indians, the Social and Pleasure Clubs, various musicians and jazz funerals. Viewing the collection of suits and other memorabilia is in itself a powerful experience; however, I also felt that I was only being told what he wanted me to know and that there was more to this culture. Quite possibly he assumed I did not want to know any more – it was hard to ascertain, as at times he (or his wife) would seem to misunderstand my questions and continue with what had become a more stock standard response to tourists.

Then, as a supporter of the museum, I received an email that talked about Mardi Gras Day and stated that everyone was welcome to share this local, family day with the Fi Yi Yi tribe. I revisited the museum in 2012 and confirmed that I would be welcome, as I had no desire to misunderstand the invitation from what I know had been a very closed community.

Lived experiences with the Fi Yi Yi Tribe

So, on Fat Tuesday 2013, my travelling companion and I rose comparatively early and headed over to the Backstreet Cultural Museum in Treme. However, we were not early enough to witness the departure from Mr Sylvester's home of the Northside Skull and Bones Gang (Figure 13.2), who left before dawn to

Figure 13.2 Northside Skull and Bone Gang at St Augustine Church (source: S. Beeton).

awaken the neighbourhood, reminding people of their ancestry and significance of this day and the place of the black Indian tribes in their lives. We did see them later in the morning as they returned from their travels, seemingly exhausted as they created a tableau at the St Augustine Catholic Church around the corner from the museum. Following the sound of the drums, I rounded the corner to witness a scene that could have been a few hundred years old – the gang lying around the churchyard, surrounded by trees covered in Spanish moss, accompanied by the incessant rhythm of drums. Along with sporting skeleton outfits and masks, they carried with them large bones covered in scraps of meat and blood, with one member walking on stilts, presenting an impressive sight.

Already the chant and responses and rhythmic percussion was having its effect, with us dancing and performing in the street, much to the bemusement of some passers-by, on their way to the more mainstream events. One woman in particular (Figure 13.3) seemed to have joined into the spirit of the event, rattling

Figure 13.3 Mardi Gras 2013 (source: S. Beeton).

a *skekere* (a gourd percussion instrument from West Africa), chanting and wailing. This spectacle was everything I had hoped for, and just as I was wondering whether she was play-acting, she moved towards the Skull and Bones Gang coming from the church. As she did so, she fell to her knees, shaking and was surrounded by the gang, to an ever-increasing crescendo of drumming. As they moved on, she remained, transfixed by her trance, and I realised that this was no show – whatever was happening to her was genuine. She was protected by two other women who shielded her from our curiosity and cameras (most of us had stopped taking photos by this stage) while she crouched exhausted in the street. She recovered and continued with us to Claiborne Street after the Fi Yi Yi Tribe emerged. I found out later that she was a visitor to New Orleans and had not expected, or looked for, such an experience.

As we returned to the street outside the museum, another Indian, Albert Mercadel, passed by on his way to meet up with his tribe, the Washataw Nation. He was dressed resplendently in a black feathered suit with a bird headdress incorporating a bird with a jewel in its mouth. He posed for photos with the waiting crowd and then moved on, telling us that he was the tribe's Witchdoctor (taking a role similar to the Wild Man), a further reflection of the African connection.

So, after much priming and anticipation, around 1.30 p.m. Sylvester Francis announced that the Fi Yi Yi tribe were about to emerge. Eager to experience this as intimately as possible, I had positioned myself next to the house from which they would emerge. Then, accompanied by a heady blast of smoke and fine talcum powder, Big Chief Victor Harris emerged in a yellow suit with the extensive, intricate beading for which he is known (Figure 13.4). He was preceded by his Spy Boy and accompanied by his Wild Man, Flag Boy, Big Queen and others.

The tribe and followers, including us, came together in the street, with many taking photos, dancing and singing. We then headed down the street to parade through the neighbourhood, meet other tribes and finally end up at Clayborne Road under the I-10 overpass, known as The Bridge, which became infamous during the post-Katrina days as a graveyard for thousands of vehicles.

We were now heading through the local neighbourhoods that would normally be off limits to a white tourist such as myself, and while I did not feel at all threatened, we stayed close to the Wild Man, whose role it is to protect the Big Chief, my theory being that this was the safest place to be. Tourists who think they are automatically safe in New Orleans can find they turn the wrong corner and it all can go to pieces. It also meant we were very close to the tribe and musicians, being more a part of the 'first' line than the more usual second line that follows. As opposed to the parades of the Mardi Gras Krewes that separate the revellers from the paraders, I was able to be more than a spectator – the barriers were down and we were all part of the parade. Also, this was more than simply walking along – it was impossible not to dance and chant the refrains and respond to the *call and response* songs and be part of the Second Line. The Indians preened, strutted, sang and posed for the appreciation of all they passed. It was also impossible not to be moved by some sort of primal emotion and deep,

Figure 13.4 Victor Harris emerging from Sylvester Francis's house (source: S. Beeton).

deep joy. As we moved along, people joined in and dropped out, but the core 40 or so people from the Backstreet Museum remained.

When the Spy Boy, whose role it is to go ahead and spot potential danger and/or other tribes (Beeton forthcoming), spots another tribe, he signals back to the Flag Boy and then Big Chief, and the most important element of this ritual begins.

In the past, when tribes met, it was often violent, where grudges were settled and territorial disputes acted out, but over the years such encounters have become more ritualised, particularly under the influence of leaders such as Tootie Montana. Today, after the Wild Man clears a path through the throng, who all begin to press close in anticipation, the Big Chiefs meet and touch their heads together. While in such close proximity, they chant and sing about their own achievements, dance moves and their *pretty* suits. This is impromptu and made up on the spot, and the chiefs are very proud of their creative prowess (Kennedy 2010). Eventually, one will concede that the other chief is the prettiest and turn his back and bow slightly.

When Fi Yi Yi met the Yellow Pocahontas Hunters Black Indian Tribe I was close to the chiefs and was pushed even closer by the throng, able to hear a scrap of the rhyming poetry or rap exchange between them, until they moved even closer and blocked us all out. There was much chanting and drumming going on, and eventually our chief conceded that Big Chief Darryl Montana's suit was prettier (Figure 13.5). These suits can weigh over 150 pounds, are new each year, hand-sewed by the wearer and tell a significant story, particularly through the intricately beaded panels.

In a show of great community spirit, continuance of tradition and education, we also saw some of the tribe acting out such rituals with young chiefs in their costumes, while some of the small queens also preened and acted out the roles they hoped to have in the future.

After resting and eating at a local home, the tribe then moved on to The Bridge (Claiborne Avenue), stopping outside the home Big Chief Tootie Montana, who has now *become an ancestor*, paying respect to him and his family. On the way, a young man shared a beer with me and advised us not to be there after dark – we had no intention of doing so, but it was kind advice. Before the I-10 highway was constructed, this area comprised a wide boulevard, where the community would set up their cars and picnic all day. Today, the environment is not quite so conducive to family gatherings, but remains popular. Once we arrived under the I-10 (Figure 13.6), the noise exploded – the drummers were louder, joining with many other tribes, and the noise bounced around and off all of the concrete surfaces above, below and between us. This was getting delightfully scary as big men approached in their pretty outfits. One elder, Big Chief Percy Picton of the Yong Brave Hunters tribe, was granted special respect by our tribe, which again reaffirmed the role of this ritual in community cohesion and respect.

I noticed that there was no police presence here or throughout our parade, unlike all the other Mardi Gras parade routes and crowded party sites in New Orleans which all had a very high police attendance and used mobile security cameras. I wondered if this was due, in part, to the influence of pleas from leaders such as Tootie Montana for the Indians to be free to gather and move around their neighbourhood. Or had the police simply given up? After about 30 minutes, we noticed that we were the only white people remaining, so decided to

Figure 13.5 Big Chief Darryl Montana and Victor Harris (source: S. Beeton).

take our leave and head back to the more mainstream French Quarter. It was close to 4:00 p.m., and we had been with the gang since around 9:00 a.m.

So, what did this mean to me? For a start, to even be allowed to participate in such a close community ritual was very special, and I felt humbled and privileged.

Figure 13.6 Under the I-10 on Claiborne Avenue (source: S. Beeton).

I also felt that, through the music, the chanting and the parading, I had experienced some of the very primal emotions that others around me also had, in a small way giving me an emotional insight into this complex and important ritual and culture. Certainly at times I had tears in my eyes and joy in my heart, as well as excitement and a little fear. Feelings of resilience and resistance were also evident in them as well as me. As Big Chief Gerald Jake Millman of the White Eagles Tribe explained, in a 1976 documentary on the Black Indians, in order to understand the Mardi Gras Indians, 'You've gotta be *part of the feeling* of what it's all about' (Martinez 1976; my emphasis). It is clear that the Mardi Gras Indians are an integral element of the black communities in New Orleans, and a repository of pride and retainer of a living heritage, yet somehow I also experienced a (very small) sense of belonging.

As Bakhtin noted when studying representations of carnival in the Middle Ages:

> Carnival is not a spectacle seen by the people; *they live in it*, and everyone participates because its very idea embraces all the people ... [I]t is a special condition of the entire world, of the world's revival and renewal, in which all take part. Such is the essence of carnival, vividly felt by all its participants.
>
> (1984: 7–8: my emphasis)

Some concluding thoughts

While I have participated in and, by my presence and the publication of this chapter, contributed to the opening up of the Black or Mardi Gras Indians to a wider community, there are those expressing concerns about such activities. Criticism includes the possibility of the Black Indians altering and commodifying their rituals for an external audience. But, on the other hand, exposing their culture to a wider audience on their own terms may well contribute to their cultural survival and well-being. When discussing the move for the Indians to connect with a more mainstream environment, of which tourism is a part, Becker (2013) ponders:

> When Indians move from the backstreets to Main Street [figuratively speaking], the danger exists that they will not retain control over their artistic creations and what was once a symbol of racial identity and empowerment may be reduced to an ethnic commodity that symbolizes black New Orleans. At the same time they cannot survive without commodification. As the suits become more elaborate, the cost increases and Indians struggle to find money for next year's suit. So the question is, how can Indians move this culture into the mainstream and still maintain ownership of it?
>
> (Becker 2013: 49)

This is reminiscent of many of the criticisms of tourism as a neo-colonial activity that dilutes, changes and overtakes the cultures it seeks to experience (de Kadt 1978; Hall and Tucker 2004; Timothy and Nyaupane 2009). However, being able to participate in a Second Line with the Black Indians is an experience I will long remember, and one that has given me great respect for this culture and its antecedents. I would not like to see these practices changed to suit tourists, but also, they are a fluid representation of a culture and community that is in flux and change.

As with many cultures, the opening up of the local cultural practices of New Orleans cannot be easily pigeon-holed into 'good' or 'bad' especially in relation to tourism, which is so important to this city. When I asked Cherice Harrison-Nelson how she felt about Mardi Gras Indians posing for photos (Figure 13.7) in the tourism epicentre of Jackson Square for cash, she said that it was better they did that rather than not work at all. At the time, I did not ask her about the suits I saw for sale in a second-hand shop (Figure 13.8), but again it is the individual right of the owners of such suits to do as they see fit, and it is not for an outsider such as myself to judge. My own opinions remain divided on these issues. In subsequent communications, Cherice explained that:

> It is each person's personal right to do as they wish with their personal suit. It is freedom of expression and free will. Personally, I would not engage in that type of activity. However, it is impossible to know what brings a person to make certain decisions. So I judge not. Just never know, unemployment

Figure 13.7 Mardi Gras Indian posing for tourists (source: S. Beeton).

is high and maybe some feel it is an honest way they can make money. Again, not my personal choice for myself, but who knows why the choice to be photographed by [a] tourist was made.

Nevertheless, I am amazed as to how this powerful culture and its rituals remains so unknown by mainstream America, in spite of the Mardi Gras Indians performing at the first New Orleans Jazz and Heritage Festival in 1970 and ever since (Smith 1994b). I have found that even visitors to New Orleans (during as well as after Mardi Gras) have no knowledge of the Mardi Gras Indians, and presume they are American Indians. I can only postulate that this is in part due to the intense cultural and touristic segregation of New Orleans and continued localisation of the black culture, yet even some local residents I spoke to were wary of the Mardi Gras Indians and presented an extremely limited understanding and a perspective often tainted by their violent past. However, nothing is simple in New Orleans, and I look forward to returning to study and internalise this city through more lived experiences, simultaneously exploring my own emotional response and attraction to this sub-culture.

Figure 13.8 Mardi Gras Indian suit for sale (source: S. Beeton).

Acknowledgements

I would like to acknowledge and thank Big Queens Cherice Harrison-Nelson and Sabrina Mays-Montana for their guidance with this chapter.

References

Bakhtin, M. (1984) *Rabelais and His World*, Bloomington: Indiana University Press.

Becker, C. (2013) 'New Orleans Mardi Gras Indians: Mediating racial politics from the backstreets to Main Street', *African Arts* (4692), 36–49.

Beeton, S. (forthcoming) 'Spy Boy Roger Hulbert', in C. Harrison-Nelson (ed.), *The Spy Boy Annual*, New Orleans: Mardi Gras Indian Hall of Fame.

Bilby, K. and N'Diaye, D.B. (1992) 'Creativity and resistance: Maroon culture in the Americas', *1992 Festival of American Folklife*, Washington, DC: Smithsonian Institute.

Breunlin, R. and Lewis, R.W. (2009) *The House of Dance and Feathers: A museum by Ronald W. Lewis*, New Orleans: Neighbourhood Story Project.

de Kadt, E. (ed.) (1978) *Tourism: Passport to Development? Perspectives on the social and cultural effects of tourism in developing countries*, New York: Oxford University Press.

Dilthey, W. (1985) *Poetry and Experience: Selected works, vol. 5*, Princeton, NJ: Princeton University Press.

Gotham, K.F. (2002) 'Marketing Mardi Gras: Commodification, spectacle and the political economy of tourism in New Orleans', *Urban Studies*, 39(10), 1735–1756.

Gotham, K.F. (2005) 'Tourism from above and below: Globalization, localization and New Orleans's Mardi Gras', *International Journal of Urban and Regional Research*, 29(2), 309–326.

Hall, G.M. (1992) *Africans in Colonial Louisiana*, Baton Rouge: Louisiana State University Press.

Hall, C.M. and Tucker, H. (eds) (2004) *Tourism and Postcolonialism: Contested discourses, identities, and representations*, London: Routledge.

Holt, N.L. (2003) 'Representation, legitimation and autoethnography: An autoethnographic writing story', *International Journal of Qualitative Methods*, 2(1).

Johnson, J. (1991) 'New Orleans's Congo Square: An urban setting for early Afro-American Culture Formation', *Louisiana History*, 32(2), 117–157.

Kennedy, A. (2010) *Big Chief Harrison and the Mardi Gras Indians*, Gretna: Pelican.

Lipsitz, G. (1988) 'Mardi Gras Indians: Carnival and counter-narrative in black New Orleans', *Culture Critique: Popular Narrative, Popular Images*, 10, 99–121.

Lipsitz, G. (2006) 'Learning from New Orleans: The social warrant of hostile privatism and competitive consumer citizenship', *Cultural Anthropology*, 21(3), 451–468.

Mick, D.G. (2005) 'I like to watch', *ACR News*. Online: www.acrwebsite.org (accessed December 2009).

Noy, C. (2007) 'The language(s) of the tourist experience: An autoethnography of the poetic tourist', in I. Ateljevic, A. Pritchard and N. Morgan (eds), *The Critical Turn in Tourism Studies: Innovative research methodologies* (pp. 349–370), Oxford: Elsevier.

Rodriguez, N. and Ryave, A.L. (2002) *Systematic Self-Observation: A method for researching the hidden and elusive features of everyday life*, Thousand Oaks, CA: Sage.

Smith, M.P. (1994a) 'Behind the lines: The Black Mardi Gras Indians and the New Orleans second line', *Black Music Research Journal*, 14(1), 43–73.

Smith, M.P. (1994b) *Mardi Gras Indians*, Gretna: Pelican.

Sublette, N. (2008) *The World That Made New Orleans: From Spanish silver to Congo Square*, Chicago: Lawrence Hill.

Timothy, D.J. and Nyaupane, G.P. (eds) (2009) *Cultural Heritage and Tourism in the Developing World: A regional perspective*, New York: Routledge.

Van Manen, M. (1990) *Researching Lived Experience: Human science for an action sensitive pedagogy*, London, ON: Aithouse.

Vaz, K.M. (2013) *The 'Baby Dolls': Breaking the race and gender barriers of the New Orleans Mardi Gras tradition*, Baton Rouge: Louisiana State University Press.

DVD documentaries

Blank, L. (1978) *Always for Pleasure*, Flower Films.

Harrison-Nelson, C. (n.d.) *Guardians of the Flame: A View from Within*, Guardians of the Flame.

Martinez, M. (1976) *Black Indians of New Orleans*, Doorknob Films.

Walker, A. (2011) *Bury the Hatchet*, Cinemarais/Aaron Walker.

14 Gender, subversion and ritual

Helldorado Days, Tombstone, Arizona

Warwick Frost and Jennifer Laing

Introduction

Many traditional events are primarily masculine, with male participation mirroring the gender dominance of these cultures. Festivals celebrating the American West are typically male-oriented. This is the land of Billy the Kid, Buffalo Bill, Wild Bill Hickok and Wyatt Earp. Western cinema, which has shaped so much of how we imagine the West, is dominated by John Wayne, James Stewart, Clint Eastwood and Kevin Costner (Frost and Laing forthcoming). The language of the West reflects this masculinity – it is populated by *cowboys*, *lawmen*, *badmen* and *hombres*. Not only are females usually subordinate, it has been argued that the popularity of the western myth starting in the late nineteenth century was a reaction to the perceived feminisation of urban civilisation leading to a degeneration of manly qualities among American youth (Hausladen 2003; Slotkin 1992; Watts 2003).

This masculinity is apparent in studies of Western festivals – though it is so all-pervading that it is rarely discussed in detail. Many of these festivals are distinguished by re-enactment of historical events and the donning of western costume. In line with how the West is imagined, there is often a strong emphasis on what may be seen as exclusively male activities, particularly gun-play, robberies and displays of horsemanship. In contrast, women are relegated to subordinate roles, such as food preparation and serving and rarely given prominence in performances. Examples of events that fit this masculine model are the Mountain Men Rendezvous, recreations of the trading meetings of fur-trappers during the early nineteenth century (Belk and Costa 1998); annual re-enactments of the Battle of Little Bighorn (Elliott 2007); the Lone Pine Western Film Festival (Frost 2008); and the Calgary Stampede (Kelm 2009).

However, such a gender imbalance is not universal. In this chapter, we aim to explore one traditional Western festival in which women do have highly active and visible roles in the rituals and performances. This is the instance of Helldorado Days, staged annually at Tombstone, Arizona since 1929. Not only are women active players in this festival, they take full advantage of the opportunity to – like males – construct and live out fantasy roles. As with many events, the appeal for them is in leaving the everyday behind and temporarily entering and expressing themselves in another world.

Representing women in the West

The experiences of women in the West are the subject of much debate. Was venturing into the frontier a liberating or restricting experience? Recent new directions in western historiography have only confounded the issue. The *New Western History* – coming to prominence in the 1990s – argued for a shift away from seeing the West in terms of conquest and towards a focus on race, class, gender and environment. Even then, there was uncertainty as to whether to view these as triumphs or tragedies (Limerick *et al.* 1991; White 1991). *Environmental History* – another growing field – also grappled with contradictions as to how women should be viewed. On the one hand, there was an idea that women were intimidated and marginalised by the harsh physical environment and dangers of pioneering. On the other hand, there was evidence that many women were captivated by the wilderness landscape and sought out the freedom of travelling and living in such a frontier (Riley 1999).

Such unresolved arguments spill over into *Cinema Studies*. It is often contended that film privileges a male vision of the West, usually ignoring or downplaying female perspectives. According to Loy, 'Westerns are action films about men ... women ... are almost always subordinate to the hero and lead villain' (2004: 274), while Horrocks contends that 'the patriarchal framing of the western is not in doubt: men have come to the untamed west to create homes and build empires' (1995: 60). Women are merely their 'helpers' (p. 60) or in some cases 'the spoils of battle' (p. 61). Indeed, there are some Westerns in which females are completely absent, for example *The Good, the Bad and the Ugly* (1966). However, Hausladen (2003) contests this interpretation, arguing that many Western films had strong female leads. This accords with our view. Though obviously masculine, many films built dramatic stories and tensions around female characters. Just as there is a common motif of pitting the *good* man against the *bad*, there are many films that juxtapose the *good* Western female (settler, schoolmistress) against the *bad* (prostitute, dance hall singer). After the Second World War, changes in taste and the rise of television led to the rise of the *Adult Western*, exploring themes that could not be shown on television (Frost and Laing forthcoming; Laing and Frost 2012; Loy 2004). As with the *Film Noir* genre, the greater emphasis in Westerns on sex, power, greed and morally ambiguous heroes required that female characters be given prominence in plotlines.

A few examples are worth noting. John Ford's *Stagecoach* (1939), the ground-breaking first Western, brings together a group of Western archetypes. The two women juxtaposed are a prostitute and a cavalry officer's wife. In *My Darling Clementine* (1946), Ford contrasts a nurse with a dance hall singer. In *Shane* (1953) and *3:10 to Yuma* (1957), the lives of a struggling farmer and his wife are upset by the arrival of a gunslinger. The wife is attracted to the exotic and dangerous stranger (torn between good and bad) and the farmer strives to uphold his masculinity. In turn, the gunman reveals his vulnerability (arguably his feminine side) in that he really would like to settle down, but cannot. *How the West Was Won* (1962) follows two sisters West; one marries a farmer, the other becomes a dance hall singer. The fluidity of Western marriages underlies *Will Penny* (1968), which dwells on the vulnerability of those alone on the frontier.

In the 1960s, the growth of Women's Liberation led to females who were the equal of men, as in *Cat Ballou* (1965) and Wrangler Jane in *F Troop* (1965–1967). Later films were also more open about prostitution, such as in *Once Upon a Time in the West* (1968), *Heaven's Gate* (1980) and *Unforgiven* (1992). The contrasting good versus bad roles remained a feature. In both *Two Mules for Sister Sara* (1970) and *The Train Robbers* (1973), helpless women – a nun and widow respectively – appeal to a reluctant hero for assistance. It is only in the final reel that it is revealed that they are worldly tricksters who have put on this act to gain help. The idea of strong female characters is best played out in the cult favourite *Johnny Guitar* (1954). This utilises the classic Western plot of a saloon owner and rancher ruthlessly fighting it out for control of a town. Except in this case, both are females. Furthermore, all the male characters are weak, narcissistic and easily manipulated (Frost and Laing forthcoming).

Tombstone

The town gained its evocative name in 1877 through prospector Ed Schieffelin. Heading out into unsettled southern Arizona, some soldiers warned him that all he would find would be his own tombstone. When he found payable silver, he registered the location of his claim as 'Tombstone and Graveyard' (Eppinga 2010; Tefertiller 1997). The resulting rush led to a boom town. Like many Western mining towns, it drew in gamblers and prostitutes as well as miners. Frontier justice was complex and confused:

> Law enforcement had three tiers: the county sheriff … the city marshal, an elected official … and the U.S. marshal … jurisdictions often overlapped, officers disagreed over their responsibilities; the situation was primed for chaos. This structure helped make Tombstone one of the most intriguingly complicated stories in frontier history. At different times, the lawbreakers were the lawmen, and the lines between good and evil blurred in the eyes of the community.
>
> (Tefertiller 1997: 36)

A multi-sided struggle developed over control of the town, particularly over the elected position of town sheriff and the opportunities offered by saloons and gambling. The Earp brothers (Wyatt, Virgil, Morgan and James), with John 'Doc' Holliday, formed one faction. Increasing tensions with a loose gang of rustlers and stagecoach robbers known as the 'Cowboys' escalated into a full-blown vendetta. The most well-known incident in the feud was the 'Gunfight at the OK Corral', at Tombstone on 26 October 1881, in which the Earps and Holliday shot and killed 'Cowboys' Billy Clanton, Frank McLaury and Tom McLaury. However, this was not the end. After the controversial acquittal of the

Earps for murder, reprisals came when Morgan was shot in the back while playing pool in a saloon and Virgil ambushed in the street. The final reckoning came when the remaining Earps and Holliday rode out to confront the 'Cowboys'. In the resultant *man-on-man* showdown Wyatt gunned down 'Cowboy' leader 'Curly Bill' Brocious. The other notorious 'Cowboy' leader, Johnny Ringo, was shot dead by an unknown assailant (in films, this is often Doc Holliday, though the evidence places him elsewhere).

The massive newspaper coverage of the ongoing feud and gunplay extended Tombstone's reputation as the last of the Wild West towns across the United States. With the advent of cinema, the already infamous action at Tombstone was readily utilised, especially as Wyatt Earp had moved to Los Angeles and often hung around with actors and directors (Blake 2007). Given the Hollywood treatment, the Gunfight at the OK Corral was simplified as a classic showdown between good and evil. Television continued the trend, with series such as *The Life and Legend of Wyatt Earp* (1955–1961). Even *Doctor Who* materialised in Tombstone, with the Doctor mistaken for Doc Holliday. This wide variety of productions constructed a mediated reality, reinterpreting the story and its features and privileging visual representations of how the West supposedly looked. It is particularly noticeable that the film *Tombstone* (1993) sets the scene for Helldorado Days. Conceived as an accurate telling of the story, this successful film was notable for the great attention to detail in costumes and weaponry (Blake 2007; Frost and Laing forthcoming; Hughes 2008). At Helldorado Days in 2012, the film poster from *Tombstone* was everywhere (even used as the logo for the Chamber of Commerce), many participants dressed as characters from the film and people discussed their favourite actors and scenes.

Helldorado Days

This annual festival commenced in 1929, inaugurated for the fiftieth anniversary of the town being established (Helldorado Inc. 2012). Delyser (2003) notes that quite a number of western towns were established around the 1870s and 1880s and accordingly there were a cluster of commemorative events 50 years on. She also argues that the increase in automobiles encouraged a rise in western motoring holidays and that these tourists could still meet and yarn with *old-timers*, so that festivals were a way to harness this interest and encourage economic development through tourism. The ageing of the pioneer generation stimulated concerns that their experiences had to be recorded while there was still time. Laura Ingalls Wilder, for example, was encouraged to publish her reminisces in what became known as *The Little House on the Prairie* series (Laing and Frost 2012).

The establishment of Helldorado Days certainly fits these patterns. In 1929, the *Tombstone Epitath* newspaper provided a clear justification of the commemoration:

A half century has passed since these events transpired and Tombstone is entering a new era in the history of its development. Climate, scenery and the attraction of the great outdoors will take the place of silver and gold. Thousands of Americans seeking these things will find them at their best in Tombstone ... What could be more fitting than to introduce the new period in the history of Tombstone with a celebration commemorating its establishment. The thousands of people who have read ... books and magazines have promised themselves a trip here.

(quoted in Helldorado Inc. 2012: 6)

Emphasising its elegiac quality, the promoters of the 1929 festival recruited surviving pioneers in John Clum (the first mayor of Tombstone) and former deputy sheriff William Breakenridge. Such connections with the Old West were fast disappearing. Tombstone lost its most famous son just before the first Helldorado Days, with the death of Wyatt Earp in early 1929.

Many societies construct a heritage based around a *Golden Age* in the not too distant past, often eulogised with the passing of those who remember it. Imagining it as better than the present, many people try to recapture this through living history re-enactments and events (Frost and Laing 2013).

Such is the case with Helldorado Days and the festival in 2012 was a lively and multi-faceted affair. The main street, with traffic diverted and gravel laid down, was the central venue for a wide variety of performances. Of particular interest for this study were a number of *skits*. These are historical re-enactments. Ranging between five to ten minutes, they are staged by amateur groups, many of whom perform at a number of different festivals throughout the West. Props are minimal, barrels and planks suggest a saloon bar and a rough timber frame serves as a doorway. In contrast, a great deal of attention is paid to the authenticity of firearms and costumes, as is common with many historical re-enactment events (Frost and Laing 2013). Those taking part are good examples of *serious leisure*, the 'systematic pursuit of an amateur, hobbyist, or volunteer activity that is sufficiently substantial and interesting for the participant to find a career there in the acquisition and expression of its special skills and knowledge' (Stebbins 1992: 3).

Many of the skits are conventionally masculine and macho. These fall into two categories. The first consists of gunfights between the Earps and various miscreants. These are played dead straight. The Earps are upright heroes bringing justice to the town. Great attention is placed on both looking the part – especially in terms of the film *Tombstone* – and living the role of a frontier lawkeeper. The second grouping is deliberately humorous, though, if anything, these skits result in a much higher body count. There is no concept of re-enacting a real event, part of the fun is in the imagination of absurdly over-the-top shootouts. Nonetheless, authenticity of performance and outfit are paramount. An example of a semi-humorous skit was the elaborate *The Mexican*. In this a Mexican walks into a saloon. He is thrown out by locals proclaiming 'we don't like Mexicans around here' (which provokes some nervous laughter from the audience). From the street, the Mexican calls on these toughs to come out and fight. One by one they take up the challenge, but all fall to the Mexican's deadly

Figure 14.1 Over-acted shootouts, the aftermath of 'The Mexican' (source: W. Frost).

accuracy. Each dies with a great flourish reminiscent of childhood games (Figure 14.1). The only female in this performance is a bargirl, who encourages the increasingly frightened patrons to be manly and go outside and finish him off.

While much of Helldorado Days is masculine in this manner, there are also a significant number that contrastingly focus on women. These are worth considering in some detail as they present a different, possibly subversive, re-creation of the traditions and rituals of the Wild West.

The widows

Two middle-aged widows arrive in Tombstone (Figure 14.2). Dressed in black, they are on their way to California, but lose all their money. The women from a saloon suggest that they can earn some money as dancehall girls. At first the widows are hesitant. They are, after all, respectable. With seemingly no other choices, they agree and change into colourful and revealing costumes. Some miners come in for a good time. The experienced women coach the widows in their new roles. They need to encourage the miners to spend up big. The widows are successful. In highly comic scenes, the miners drink too much (Figure 14.3) and lapse into semi-consciousness (thereby avoiding any possibility of sex). The widows warm to their job and decide they will stay in Tombstone.

Figure 14.2 The widows come to town (source: W. Frost).

Figure 14.3 The widow is transformed, the happy miner is drunk (source: W. Frost).

This is a transformative parable. At first the widows are meek and passive – *invisible* in their sombre black clothing. Once changed into more revealing clothes, they are sexualised and desirable. Their age is now unimportant. In their new roles they are in charge. It is the miners, willing to pay for company and drink, who are passive, powerless and objects of our derisory laughter.

Saloon girls with guns

A number of humorous skits concern the loot from a stagecoach robbery. In the saloon, greed and mistrust begins to grow and the outlaws kill each other off. In this variation, it is the saloon girls who take the lead. First, they get the outlaws liquored up and encourage the squabbling. Eventually all are dead and the females look to divide up the money. However, the arrival of the sheriff and a posse means the prize looks likely to slip from the grasp. Undaunted, the saloon girls pull out their rifles and shotguns (Figure 14.4) and proceed to kill off the lawmen with great gusto. These are doubly subversive performances, not only are the women more competent with their weapons than the men, but these are the only skits where the law is defeated.

Little Egypt

In the main street two women perform belly-dancing. At first glance, it seems incongruous. A modern fashion at odds with the careful attention to period detail

Figure 14.4 Saloon girls with guns (source: W. Frost).

that characterises most other participants. However, the master of ceremonies announces that this is part of Tombstone's heritage.

The noted exotic dancer Little Egypt (also known as Fatima) (Figure 14.5) appeared at the Birdcage Theatre in the 1880s. It is a reminder, he states, that Tombstone was so wealthy that it did pull in all manner of theatrical acts.

What the announcer does not state is that the story is not so black and white. The Birdcage Theatre contains a painting of a bare-breasted Middle-Eastern dancer, named as Little Egypt. That performer's real name was Farida Mazar Spyropoulos. Of Syrian background, she was a sensation at the 1893 Columbian World Exposition in Chicago, dancing in the Egyptian Theatre. At the time, her dance style was termed *Hootchee-Kootchee* (memorialised in the song 'Meet Me in St Louis, Louis', written in 1904 for that city's world's fair). She continued to perform until well into the twentieth century, as did a number of imitators who often used her stage name. However, apart from the painting, there is no documentary evidence that she ever visited Tombstone (Eppinga 2010).

An 1890s Fashion Show

One performance is an 1890s Fashion Show (Figure 14.6). Of course, Tombstone in that period did not have fashion shows. Rather this is a creative imagining of what that sort of modern event would look like if it was transposed from

Figure 14.5 Fatima dances (source: W. Frost).

Figure 14.6 1890s fashion show (source: W. Frost).

today into the nineteenth century. The result is half-a-dozen women parade in their finest outfits, while a commentator points out the nuances in period costuming. In contrast to much of what happens at Helldorado, the byword here is respectability. The suggestion is of middle-class women and the mail-order purchases of the finest fashion from back East.

La Passeggiata

In addition to formal proceedings, Helldorado features an ongoing informal performance. Hundreds of costumed participants promenade around the town and along the wooden sidewalks in their finest (Figures 14.7 and 14.8). It is a parade that echoes the spirit of the past, where there was entertainment and status in seeing and being seen. A key component of this modern iteration is that many are pleased to be stopped and photographed. For these serious amateurs, there is a strong focus on staying in character and showing off their practised Old West drawl and mannerisms. Such a phenomena is suggestive of the division between *performers* and *dressers-up* observed by Wallace (2007) at Second World War re-enactments in England. Performers, Wallace argues, follow scripts and live their characters. Dressers-up, in contrast, are unscripted, happy to be photographed and motivated by the attractions of socialising.

Figure 14.7 La Passeggiata (source: W. Frost).

Figure 14.8 La Passeggiata (source: W. Frost).

For men the most common look is the Earps, but this is mediated through the film *Tombstone* (1993), which on the evidence of the number of posters on display is the most popular of the films set in the town. Participants aim to channel Kurt Russell (and intriguingly *not* Henry Fonda, Burt Lancaster or Kevin Costner, who have also played Wyatt Earp in successful films). Others influenced by films go for the John Wayne look. Two aberrations provocatively challenge notions of Western masculinity. A cavalry officer in a very neat uniform with much brass and braid flourishes a small dog on a lead. Another jokester is convincingly dressed as Deputy Sheriff Barney Fife (Don Knotts) from the *Andy Griffiths Show* (1960–1968). He is neither Western nor nineteenth-century, but perfectly fits the carnivalesque atmosphere.

However, there are just as many women and men in this passeggiata. Many of these women are influenced by the fashions in the film *Tombstone*. Just as men want to look like Kurt Russell or Sam Elliott playing the Earp men, women aspire to represent the Earp women (played by Dana Delaney and Joanna Pacula). The Earps were complex moral characters. Though often represented as soberly dressed lawmen, they were also involved in saloons, gambling and prostitution. Their common law wives were also involved in prostitution. Such shades of grey are well-known and seemingly embraced by participants at Helldorado Days. A further subversive element comes with the popularity of Kate Elder, Doc Holliday's companion. Nicknamed as 'Big Nose Kate' for her inquisitiveness, she was a prostitute who was also romantically involved with Johnny Ringo. Furthermore, she was a Hungarian whose real name was Mary Harony (Tefertiller 1997). Foreign, duplicitous and permissive, she has evolved to become the iconic Tombstone woman. Accordingly, many participants want to dress like the *bad* woman and lean towards corsets, feather boas and fishnet stockings.

Discussion and conclusion

Tombstone is an instructive example of a *place of imagination* as conceptualised by Reijnders (2011). While real, visitors are attracted by how they imagine it to be based on media sources. Through the performances, ceremonies and rituals at Helldorado Days an ambivalent image of Western heritage is constructed. The result is an elegiac vision of a Golden Age of the 1880s. Though situated beyond the memory of anyone currently living, it is imagined as a better time. For participants, it is mediatised through film, particularly the popular *Tombstone*. The influence of this cinematic representation of history is twofold. First, it disseminates an interpretation of what happened in Tombstone; a story presented as authentic and that becomes a shared heritage as the real narrative. Second, the visual imagery of the film, particularly costumes and weapons, provides a template for participants. In imitating the film, those in costume receive validation that they too are honouring history and are authentic.

However, such playful imaginings throw up some serious contradictions. Normally, Golden Ages are valorised for being better than the modern world.

Whereas contemporary society is criticised for rising crime rates, disrespect for authority and abandonment of civilised institutions, the past is celebrated for being more ordered and stable (Laing and Frost 2012). Such an idyllic fantasy hardly describes Tombstone in the 1880s. It had no stable rural base, no entrenched aristocracy nor meritocracy. Its features were violence, theft, prostitution and gambling. Curiously, Helldorado Days valorises gunplay and immorality.

How then can such a hellhole now be looked upon so fondly? Tombstone and other tourist towns in the Wild West provide a completely different model of the heritage yearnings for a better past. Their success in attracting visitors is in playing up the lawlessness of the frontier, of appealing to a deep fascination with outlaws and crime (Frost 2006; Kooistra 1989; Wheeler *et al.* 2011). This is a phenomenon that requires further research; it suggests something akin to Dark Tourism, though is clearly different. There is a sense of play and fantasy, yet the heritage it is built on seems at odds with good order and respectability in modern society.

One way to interpret the contradictions of Tombstone is to draw on the argument of Falassi (1987) that most events follow a *Ritual Structure*. Underpinned by the notion of the universality of human experience, Falassi reasoned that many events followed a common ritual structure that provided meaning and satisfaction to their participants. He noted that this structure was rarely deliberately planned by organisers, but rather grew organically or subconsciously as a response to our basic human needs and beliefs. At Helldorado Days, three of Falassi's rites are strongly apparent and help to explain the appeal of the event.

The first is that this event allows for a society's most treasured stories to be performed and retold, ensuring through repetition that they are passed on to later generations. In traditional societies these might be foundation myths or of a religious nature. At Tombstone, they similarly relate to identity, telling how and why the town has a special place in history. In essence, this is no different to Coventry (UK) staging a festival about Lady Godiva or Belfast (UK) commemorating the anniversary of the *Titanic*.

The second is the rite of conspicuous display. Festivals and events often allow people to dress up in their finest costumes or show off their most treasured artefacts. Paradoxically, this functions as both an opportunity to blow off steam and a way that certain groups – whether based on wealth, ethnicity or lineage – are able to demonstrate their special status. At Helldorado Days the emphasis is on displaying nineteenth-century outfits and weaponry. Most importantly, notions of authenticity are valued highly.

Finally, Falassi's rites of reversal are on display. Helldorado Days allows society a limited time and space to reject normal notions of law and order. It provides the chance for people to dress and act like gunfighters, to parade in the scanty costumes of prostitutes and dancehall girls. To be outfitted this way normally would attract derision and criticism, but within the confines of this festival, people can act out their fantasies in a socially approved manner. Furthermore, such boudoir chic seems to be provocatively juxtaposed to the embroidered cowgirl look generally promoted through popular culture (George-Warren and Freedman 2001).

The use of such outfits, for both men and women, may be compared to masks and costumes in more traditional festivals and rituals. Wearing such clothes, talking and behaving a certain way are all means to disguise one's everyday image and adopt a completely different persona. The mask or costume gives the participant a licence to be a completely different person – perhaps who they want to be in their dreams. The festival is a liminal space and time and the costume and the pretence that goes with it are the means for a temporary transformation.

References

Belk, R. and Costa, J.A. (1998) 'The Mountain Man myth: A contemporary consuming fantasy', *The Journal of Consumer Research*, 25(3), 218–240.

Blake, M.F. (2007) *Hollywood and the O.K. Corral*, Jefferson, NC: McFarland.

Delyser, D. (2003) '"Good, by God, We're Going to Bodie!" Ghost towns and the American West', in G.J. Hausladen (ed.), *Western Places, American Myths: How we think about the West* (pp. 273–295), Reno and Las Vegas: University of Nevada Press.

Elliott, M. (2007) *Custerology: The enduring legacy of the Indian wars and George Armstrong Custer*, Chicago and London: Chicago University Press.

Eppinga, J. (2010) *Tombstone*, Charleston, SC: Arcadia.

Falassi, A. (1987) 'Festival: Definition and morphology', in A. Falassi (ed.), *Time out of Time: Essays on the Festival* (pp. 1–10), Albuquerque: University of New Mexico Press.

Frost, W. (2006) '*Braveheart*-ed *Ned Kelly*: Historic films, heritage tourism and destination image', *Tourism Management*, 27(2), 247–254.

Frost, W. (2008) 'Projecting an image: Film-induced festivals in the American West', *Event Management*, 12(2), 95–104.

Frost, W. and Laing, J. (2013) *Commemorative Events: Memory, identities, conflict*, London and New York: Routledge.

Frost, W. and Laing, J. (forthcoming) *Imagining the American West through Film and Tourism*, London and New York: Routledge.

George-Warren, H. and Freedman, M. (2001) *How the West Was Worn*, New York: Harry N. Abrams.

Hausladen, G.J. (2003) 'Where the cowboy rides away: Mythic places for Western film', in G.J. Hausladen (ed.), *Western Places, American Myths: How we think about the West* (pp. 296–318), Reno and Las Vegas: University of Nevada Press.

Helldorado Inc. (2012) *Official Publication: Helldorado 83rd Anniversary Celebration*, Tombstone: Helldorado Inc.

Horrocks, R. (1995) *Male Myths and Icons: Masculinity in popular culture*, London: Macmillan.

Hughes, H. (2008) *Stagecoach to Tombstone: The filmgoers' guide to the great Westerns*, London and New York: I.B. Tauris.

Kelm, M.-E. (2009) 'Manly contests: Rodeo masculinities at the Calgary Stampede', *Canadian Historical Review*, 90(4), 711–751.

Kooistra, P. (1989) *Criminals as Heroes: Structure, power & identity*, Bowling Green, OH: Bowling Green State University Press.

Laing, J. and Frost, W. (2012) *Books and Travel: Inspiration, quests and transformation*, Bristol: Channel View.

Limerick, P.N., Milner, C. and Rankin, C.E. (eds) (1991) *Trails: Toward a new Western history*, Lawrence: University of Kansas Press.

Loy, R.P. (2004) *Westerns in a Changing America 1955–2000*, Jefferson, NC: McFarland.

Reijnders, S. (2011) 'Stalking the Count: Dracula, fandom and tourism', *Annals of Tourism Research*, 38(1), 231–248.

Riley, G. (1999) *Women and Nature: Saving the 'Wild' West*, Lincoln and London: University of Nebraska Press.

Slotkin, R. (1992) *Gunfighter Nation: The myth of the frontier in twentieth century America*, New York: Athenaeum.

Stebbins, R.A. (1992) *Amateurs, Professionals, and Serious Leisure*, Montreal and Kingston: McGill-Queen's University Press.

Tefertiller, C. (1997) *Wyatt Earp: The life behind the legend*, New York: Wiley.

Wallace, T. (2007) 'Went the day well: Scripts, glamour and performance in war-weekends', *International Journal of Heritage Studies*, 13(3), 200–223.

Watts, S. (2003) *Rough Rider in the White House: Theodore Roosevelt and the politics of desire*, Chicago: University of Chicago Press.

Wheeler, F., Laing, J., Frost, L., Reeves, K. and Frost, W. (2011) 'Outlaw nations: Tourism, the frontier and national identities', in E. Frew and L. White (Eds), *Tourism and National Identities: An international perspective* (pp. 151–163), London and New York: Routledge.

White, R. (1991) *'It's Your Misfortune and None of My Own': A new history of the American West*, Norman: University of Oklahoma Press.

15 Voodoo in Haiti

A religious ceremony at the service of the 'Houngan' called 'Tourism'

Hugues Séraphin and Emma Nolan

Introduction

Voodoo is intimately linked to the culture and history of the Caribbean island of Haiti, yet paradoxically Haitians are predominantly Christians. It is said that Haitians are 80 per cent Catholic and 100 per cent Voodooist and religion is the mainstay of Haitian society. It is perhaps all that remains for the poor of a country that has been ravaged by centuries of political and economic unrest. And at a time when many of the Caribbean islands are prospering from a buoyant tourism industry, Haiti is still very much seen as an insecure destination (Higate and Henry 2009) and a place where the worst is always likely to happen (Bonnet 2010). Our objective is to establish a clear link between Voodoo events and tourism and identify if the two are compatible. Developing tourism offerings to include Voodoo events that are based on staged ceremonies could provide Haiti with a unique selling proposition that will enable the country to redevelop its tourism industry and stabilise its fragile economy. What must also be considered is that Voodoo emerged as the result of the introduction of slavery to the island. While the religion contributes significantly to the Haitian cultural identity, it is also linked to servility. The development of service industries like tourism is also reinforcing the notion of Haitians as servile and the introduction of Voodoo events, where visitors will pay to attend a service, may reinforce this.

The Caribbean is very diverse and only some of the islands are 'vested in the branding and marketing of paradise' (Sheller 2004: 23). For example, the Dominican Republic, Haiti's neighbour, is one of the most visited islands of the Caribbean, yet Haiti is very much the poor relation. Our key questions therefore are as follows: if tourism is to play a major role in stabilising Haiti's economy, can Voodoo events form part of tourism? If yes, what are the likely impacts of this on Haitians and on Voodoo as a religion? To answer these key questions we have selected a qualitative analysis supporting an inductive approach. As there is very little relevant literature, an analysis of Ian Thomson's 2004 travel journal *Bonjour Blanc: A Journey through Haiti*, will form a valuable and substantive part of this chapter, particularly as Thomson notes there are no written theories or explanations of the history of Voodoo practices. This book is the tale of a life experience in Haiti and as such it has witness value and may be considered trustworthy (De Ascaniis and Grecco-Marasso 2011). It also functions as a microcosm of life in Haiti and provides detailed information on the tourism, events and hospitality sectors.

Academic literature on tourism very often highlights the benefits of the industry without providing substantiated evidence of those benefits (Holden 2013). There is a dearth of academic research associated with the tourism or events sectors in Haiti, therefore this chapter will contribute to the meta-literature by focusing on how event tourism might have an impact on the cultural aspects of a destination, namely its religious practices and in our case on Voodoo ceremonies. Two elements are of interest in this chapter: first, the choice that some territories have to make between culture and money and the long-term risk of losing their originality, either partially or wholly; second, establishing a link between slavery, Voodoo and tourism.

Haiti and voodoo

A history in brief

Haiti lies between the North Atlantic and the Caribbean Sea in the Greater Antillean archipelago. It occupies the western, smaller portion of the island of Hispaniola, which it shares with the Dominican Republic. Haiti is a former French colony, and in the eighteenth century it was one of the empire's richest overseas territories, fondly referred to as the 'Pearl of the Antilles'. The island's wealth was generated by a thriving exportation industry and to sustain growth, thousands of African slaves were transported to Haiti to bolster the workforce. The atrocious trade in humans was, at the time, considered to be a legitimate form of commerce. A total of approximately 18 million Africans were exported into slavery between 1500 and the late 1800s (Reader 1998). The large Haitian slave community, commanded by a comparatively small group of white masters, staged an uprising in 1791. This led to a 13-year war of liberation, with General Toussaint L'Ouverture leading the Haitian slave army to freedom. Consequently, while retaining its links with France, Haiti became the first black republic. Since this declaration of independence, the country has endured more than two centuries of oppression, occupation, unrest and rebellion. Sustained political and social turmoil has deeply scarred the nation and today Haiti is one of the poorest countries in the world.

The Haitian economy

Between 1800 and 2009, Haiti's service sector rose in value from less than 5 per cent to approximately 60 per cent of GDP, replacing the dwindling exportation trade. The development was led by a change of activity on the part of the majority of the population (Paul et al. 2010) and featured a developing tourism industry.

Tourism is often described as one of the world's largest industries (Cooper and Hall 2004: 252) and the Caribbean has long been a popular destination due to the images of sunny, white beach paradise islands, colourful cocktails and lively music that the name invokes. Capitalising on this image, Haiti became the most popular tourist destination in the Caribbean in the period between the 1940s and the 1960s (Séraphin 2010) and as such attracted an international jet set. Mick Jagger, Charles Addams and Jackie Kennedy were among those who popularised Haiti (Thomson 2004), and by 1956 visitor numbers had risen to nearly 70,000.

Such popularity was to be short-lived, as in 1957 François Duvalier became dictator. His 14-year reign of terror crippled the tourism industry and visitor numbers steeply declined. In 1990, the country instated a democratic government and for a short time the country stabilised. Further economic and socio-political crises have continued to take their toll and by 2004, the number of tourists had dropped again to around 240,000, a reduction of 54 per cent in 17 years. The earthquake in 2010 further damaged the tourism industry and the Haitian resolve. Today, Haiti is one of the least visited nations in what is one of the world's most popular regions.

Voodoo

Voodoo derives from the West African religion Vodun and was developed in Haiti by African slaves. The religion was used as a means to cope with the degradations of slavery including being forced to convert to Christianity and speak Creole. Voodoo became a way for the slaves to retain a connection with their African roots and also to retain some of their humanity (Damoison and Dalembert 2003). It also helped slaves to resist their master's cultural oppression (Saint-Louis 2000) and to adapt to their new environment.

As a religion, Voodoo is based on the belief in a *Grand Maître*, a Great Master or Creator, as well as several *loa* or spirits. The practice of Voodoo involves ritual celebrations at a temple led by a *Houngan* or priest. Metraux (1958) explains that a good Houngan will perform many roles: priest, healer, fortune teller, exorciser and entertainer. Voodoo rituals involve recognisable religious practices such as prayers, music and dance alongside the more mystical rituals of witchcraft and dark magic including the use of poisons and the creation of zombies.

Modern-day Haitians are mostly practising Catholics and since the Pope's visit in 1983 the ten dioceses on the island have flourished. Yet Voodoo is and will always remain an intrinsic part of Haitian culture and beliefs. Haitians can maintain both a Catholic and Voodooist following as, for example, Voodoo ceremonies are not allowed to take place during key Christian festivals including Easter and Christmas. Although some of the rituals involved in the two religions are radically different, both Catholic and Voodoo ceremonies involve reading from the Bible and reciting the same prayers, plus candles and flowers are some of the symbols common to both religions.

Ogude (1981) confirms that a shared memory of slavery has defined and continues to shape black people today. And as Voodoo played a key role in the

Haitian survival of the slave trade it continues to provide the islanders with a common identity and connection with their past. According to Andrews and Leopold (2013), participating in religious ritual, whatever that ritual may be, is a public expression of a shared understanding and acceptance of a common identity. Therefore it is understandable that on this small Caribbean island that has endured a tumultuous history, two such divergent religions jointly provide a Haitian identity.

Key concepts

Tourism in developing countries

Haiti is by current standards a developing country. It suffers from a very poor level of human development with average life expectancy of 62 years. Some 50 per cent of the adult population are illiterate, 60 per cent are unemployed and 65 per cent of Haitians are living below the poverty threshold (Roc 2008). Despite once having a thriving tourism industry, Haiti is now one of the least visited of the Caribbean islands for three main reasons: the political instability, the climate of insecurity and, last but not least, the lack of facilities for tourists (Séraphin 2011). Furthermore Haiti is unable to attract foreign direct investment (FDI) and therefore economic recovery must be delivered from within the country, thus the performance of the destination is utterly dependent on the Haitian community.

In their *Action Plan for National Recovery and Development of Haiti* (2010), the Haitian government has identified tourism as a critical economic activity that can contribute to recovery. The newly appointed Minister for Tourism, Stéphanie Balmir-Villedrouin, has already obtained support for the plan from the World Travel Organisation, airlines such as *Air Caraïbes*, tour operators such as Nomade and tour guides including *Lonely Planet*. These encouraging developments have confirmed the long-term commitment of the government to the development of Haiti and although the plan for regeneration is ambitious, the Haitians have a history of determination and resilience to realise these plans. The majority of government funding is allocated to marketing and the development of visitor accommodation. Naturally these are key elements of a successful tourism campaign but a programme of events is also vital to the long-term success of a tourism strategy. Bowdin *et al.* (2010) and Bladen *et al.* (2012) agree that cultural events in particular should form part of a public-sector strategy. These types of events have the potential to strengthen community cohesion and contribute to social capital. Furthermore, as Getz (2012) confirms, tourists are particularly interested in having an authentic cultural experience in the destination and such events can be comparatively low cost to organise.

Tourism, cultural identity and social representation

Despite the plan for the rejuvenation of the tourism industry in Haiti, some organisations are voicing their concerns about the proposals. Tourism Concern (Barnett

2010) are particularly apprehensive about the country's ability to foster a sustainable economy based on tourism. Principally they warn that it could have a negative impact on the destination's culture (Holden 2013). Furthermore, Nunn (2008) asserts that a culture of mistrust has evolved in Haiti, emerging from the survival of slavery, and it can be argued that despite the abolition of this practice, the spirit of slavery remains in the form of a systematic pillaging of public funds by those in office that has kept the people in poverty for centuries (Thomson 2004). However, in an effort to support the hospitality sector, the government has invested in the conversion of residents' homes into guest houses. This initiative is a low-cost investment that results in an increase in the amount of visitor accommodation, provides some of the poorest of the Haitian population with employment and involves them in the country's economic development. Moreover, staying in a guest house is another way of providing the tourist with the authentic experience they are seeking. Thomson (2004) and Metraux (1958) also indicate that hospitality providers are best placed to be intermediaries between Houngan and tourist. Local hoteliers and guest house owners are able to facilitate arrangements for visitors to attend staged Voodoo ceremonies. However, critics may argue that employment within the tourism, hospitality and events sectors is once again putting Haitians into submissive roles and thus it may represent a re-enactment of slavery.

Ogude (1981) contends that the common shared racial memory of slavery has defined and continues to shape black people today; slavery is the fate of an entire race, and is unfinished business. As it is widely accepted that tourism in Third World countries is strongly associated with servility, should the government's plans for developing tourism and ergo hospitality and events be approached with caution? Given that Haiti cannot attract FDI, tourism offers the country a realistic (and possibly the only) chance of economic prosperity. The tourism offering is utterly dependent on the performance of the destination, and thus the community. As Voodoo is almost unique to Haiti it may provide the island with a unique selling proposition. Thus a tourism offering that includes authentic guest house accommodation and attendance at a Voodoo ceremony may enable the country to enter into a vastly competitive global industry.

Should such a visitor experience be established, it will be important for the government to monitor the cultural development of the people of Haiti alongside this. This may be achieved via the use of a social representation framework that relates directly to the development of tourism (Meliou and Maroudas 2010). Social representation is a collective system of meanings that may be expressed, or whose effects may be observed, in values, ideas and practices. Such a model can be used to understand how different groups think about tourism (Pearce *et al.* 1991). In other words, social representations are products of interconnectedness between people and processes of references through which we conceive the world (Deaux and Philogene 2001). They are built on a shared knowledge and understanding of a common reality (Moscovici 1961). Thus tourism and events in Haiti that are built around Voodoo rituals and practices have the potential to become a social framework by which Haitians can recognise and celebrate their cultural history and identity.

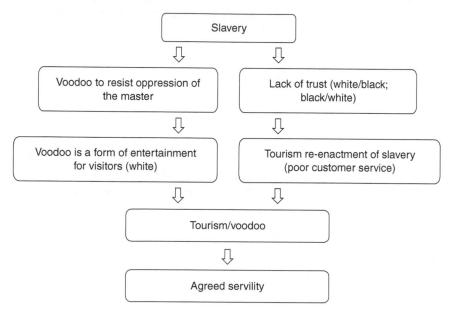

Figure 15.1 The link between Voodoo and tourism in Haiti.

To explain this idea further, Figure 15.1 illustrates the development of the relationship between slavery, Voodoo and tourism. Voodoo emerges as a means to endure oppression and today it is evolving as a form of entertainment for visitors. In parallel to this development we see how Voodoo was established as a result of a lack of trust between the black slaves and the white masters and how today tourism replicates this relationship between customer and tourist (Séraphin and Butler 2013). Today both tourism practices and Voodoo events are examples of agreed servility.

Analysis, results and discussion

Voodoo ceremonies as a commercial product

Thomson's work *Bonjour Blanc: A Journey through Haiti* provides detailed information about the destination and his journey illustrates the concept of adventure tourism. Although he travelled all over Haiti, he rarely visited popular local tourist sites or areas. Instead he chose to spend time with the locals and as an unconventional travel writer he took advantage of several opportunities to attend authentic Voodoo ceremonies.

Thomson presents a very detailed description of the rituals inherent in the Voodoo ceremonies: one must be over 25 in order to attend; one must bring specific gifts to the ceremonies to give to the Houngan (tallow candles and bottles of rum); a particular dress code should be observed (black trousers or skirt and red shirt); attendees bear torches and proceed to the temple at the pace of a funeral cortège; there follows a procedure of handshaking and exchanging passwords with the Houngan at the entrance of the temple; once inside, a drum roll signifies the start of the seance and cabbalistic signs are traced in front of the altar with maize flour. Finally, there are prayers and singing.

Thomson was invited to attend events that were not purely for his entertainment but that were authentic religious ceremonies. Despite admitting that they left him feeling terrified, he continued to attend them and usually paid for this privilege, noting that 'a Voodoo priest is usually an astute businessman' (2004: 202). He also explains that tourists could make similar arrangements to attend a modified Voodoo event at their hotel: 'Friday night in the Oloffson [hotel] was traditionally the night for a voodoo extravaganza carefully choreographed by ... the showgirls' (2004: 46). These events consisted of mostly dancing and drumming and clearly they are designed to entertain and not terrify the audience. Their authenticity is questionable, especially given the hotel environment; nonetheless Thomson infers that the Houngan were content with the arrangements and their performances were well received.

Tourism, events and colonisation

Indigenous tourism is identifiable when indigenous people are directly involved in a form of tourism either through control of the operation and/or when their culture is the attraction. It is embedded in an industry that is dominated by non-indigenous individuals and organisations (Hinch and Butler 1996). Lovelock and Lovelock (2013) highlight that the history of tourism is closely linked to the history of imperialism; hence tourism has been labelled the 'new colonialism' (Figure 15.2) where indigenous populations are re-colonialised by an industry that relies on their presence for its consumption. The academic viewpoint is that the tourism industry is a double-edged sword for indigenous populations. On the one hand it offers the potential for indigenous people to market themselves and take advantage of economic gain from the commodification of culture. On the other hand, there are a number of factors that militate against the tourism industry serving as a panacea for the challenges faced by indigenous populations.

This raises the following questions:

How much control do Houngans have over the type of performance they deliver?
How much control do locals in Haiti have over their tourism product?
What are the impacts of tourism on the evolution of Voodoo and, overall, on local culture?

Thomson's (2004) insight into Voodoo events combined with Metraux's (1958) description of the Houngan as priest, healer, fortune teller, exorciser and entertainer suggests several answers. In all descriptions of Voodoo ceremonies, it is

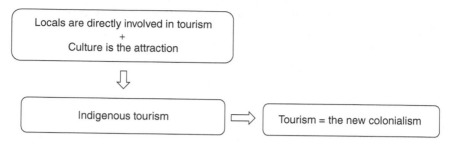

Figure 15.2 Tourism: the new colonialism.

clear that the Houngan is in control of the performance. This is evident when the performance is part of an authentic event at a temple and the attendees take an active role in the ritual, and when the performance is staged in a hotel where visitors have a passive role. Andrews and Leopold (2013) suggest that whether or not the audience are passive or active, within a staged event such as a Voodoo demonstration, the performer directs the event. This places the performer in control of the event and this is the key to the successful embedding of Voodoo events within Haiti's tourism offer as Haitians are no longer in servile roles. Furthermore, it is of great importance to involve the locals in the tourism sector so that they contribute to the visitor experience (Séraphin 2013). As Voodoo is an integral part of the island's culture, sharing this with visitors can also contribute to Haitians developing a better self-awareness, understanding and acceptance of this heritage.

Additionally, history has shown that both the Houngan and the Voodoo religion (which was developed as a means to survive difficult conditions) are flexible and perfectly able to adapt to their environment in order to survive. Thus we can conclude that Voodoo events can adapt into tourism products to meet the needs of different visitors without necessarily losing authenticity. The tourism product is often viewed as synonymous with the destination, because there is an amalgam of destination elements including attractions and supporting services such as accommodation, food, beverage and transportation (Cooper and Hall 2004). Hotel-based Voodoo events still have the potential to offer a culturally rich experience to visitors. However, this needs further investigation and it could be of value to reconsider the role of the tourist in a Voodoo event as much more than that of a consumer but equally a producer (Hirschman and Holbrook 1982: 132–140) or a co-creator (Chronis 2005).

It must, however, also be noted that there is little data that informs us of the beneficiary impacts of tourism development on the poor. Existing data tends to be at the micro-level focusing on a single enterprise or a community (Holden 2013). Because of this newness of the information it is legitimate to wonder if Voodoo as a tourism product is worth being exploited in Haiti as it may be damaging for this ancestral religion in the long term. Of course the danger of the commodification of religious events is that they may lose authenticity. Interestingly, both Andrews and

Leopold (2013) and Getz (2012) assert that the commodification of religious events created by an indigenous population, in particular, can have a particular cultural value and power that can negate the effects of colonisation. Furthermore they suggest that should a community feel that there was an over-commodification of a tradition-based event, they would not abandon it but seek to change it. Thus, this notion gives hope to our suggestion that Voodoo events are a realistic proposition for the future prosperity of Haiti.

Conclusion

Since the election of Stéphanie Balmir-Villedrouin as the Tourism Minister, the Haitian government has designated the tourism sector as the vehicle for the economic development of the country. As Haiti lacks visitor attractions the development of an authentic events programme is going to be an essential part of the ongoing tourism strategy. Culturally rich events are part of the appeal of a destination and can be cost-efficient to organise. Furthermore it is well documented that planned events have the ability to improve communities, as 'They provide the means to achieve a diverse range of social outcomes, including community cohesion, educational development, support for families and regional development' (Bladen *et al.* 2012: 379). If the development of events can provide positive social outcomes for the Haitians, the performance of this revived community will increase. O'Toole (2011: 18) suggests that a programme of events and festivals are crucial to increasing national pride in small developing countries in a post-colonial state of recovery. He goes on to give examples of destination management organisation led strategies that combine events and tourism objectives and gives examples of how these have been successfully implemented in other countries. These provide both an overview and an insight into the complexities of such strategies and reinforce the notion that both tourism and events are interdependent. Thus the development of Voodoo events will enhance Haiti's tourism offering and provide opportunities for locals to embrace their cultural heritage and come to terms with their past, if this process is carefully managed.

Butler and Séraphin (2014) argue that social enterprises in the tourism sector can contribute to a peaceful relationship between local and visitors via an increase of trust. This is possible if corporate social responsibility practices are locally embedded, addressing not only environmental, philanthropic and economic aims but particularly citizen diplomacy and transparency aims. The tourism sector in Haiti is still in its infancy and therefore it is very difficult to assess its impact on the country. However, many academics have highlighted the fact that mass tourism has positive and negative impacts on a destination. With the development of the tourism sector in Haiti we can rightly assume that the industry is going to progressively have an impact on the different components of Haitian society, including religion.

For the moment there is no evidence to confirm that tourism will bring prosperity to Haiti or that Voodoo events can play a significant role in the country's tourism sector. While Voodoo is sometimes used as a commercial product in

Haiti, so far this has been occasional and thus the religion has managed to keep its essence and original function. However, our research indicates that Voodoo events are a viable means to supporting the tourism industry. How they are developed requires further, detailed investigation and involvement of the local community and religious leaders. The challenge here is to develop an enjoyable and authentic visitor experience of Voodoo rituals that does not detract from the role of the religion in the Haitian community.

References

Andrews, H. and Leopold, T. (2013) *Events and the Social Sciences*, Abingdon: Routledge.

Barnett, T. (2010) 'Haiti: Ripe for tourism?' *Tourism Concern*. Online: www.tourismconcern.org.uk (accessed 16 February 2014).

Bladen, C., Kennell, J., Abson, E. and Wilde, N. (2012) *Events Management: An introduction*, Abingdon: Routledge.

Bonnet, F. (2010) 'Haïti: L'ile de toutes les tragédies', *Marianne*, 65, 6–12.

Bowdin, G., Allen, J., O'Toole, W., Harris, R. and McDonnell, I. (2010) *Events Management* (3rd edn), Oxford: Elsevier.

Butler, C. and Séraphin, H. (2014) 'An exploratory study of the potential contribution to peace through sustainable enterprise in the tourism industry in Haiti and Kenya', *International Journal of Human Potential Development*, 3(1), 1–13.

Chronis, A. (2005) 'Coconstructing heritage at the Gettysburg storyscape', *Annals of Tourism Research*, 32(2), 386–406.

Cooper, C. and Hall, M. (2004) *Contemporary Tourism: An international approach*, London: Elsevier.

Damoison, D. and Dalembert, L.P. (2003) *Vodou: Un tambour pour les anges*, Paris: Editions Autrement.

De Ascaniis, S. and Grecco-Marasso, S. (2011) 'When tourists give their reasons on the web: The argumentative significance of tourism related UGC', *Information and Communication Technology in Tourism*, 125–137.

Deaux, K. and Philogene, G. (2001) *Representations of the Social*, Oxford: Blackwell.

Getz, D. (2012) *Event Studies* (2nd edn), Abingdon: Routledge.

Gilles, A. (2012) 'The social bond, conflict and violence in Haiti', *Peace Research Institute*. Online: www.prio.no (accessed 3 August 2013).

Higate, P. and Henry, M. (2009) *Insecure Spaces, Peacekeeping, Power and Performance in Haiti, Kosovo and Liberia*, London: Zed Books.

Hinch, T. and Butler, R. (1996) 'Indigenous tourism: A common ground for discussion', in R. Butler and T. Hinch (eds), *Tourism and Indigenous Peoples* (pp. 3–19), London: International Thomson.

Hirschman, E. and Holbrook, F. (1982) 'Aspects of consumption', *Journal of Consumer Research*, 9, 132–140.

Holden, A. (2013) *Tourism, Poverty and Development*, New York: Routledge.

Huxley, F. (1969) *The Invisibles: Voodoo Gods in Haiti*, New York: McGraw-Hill.

Lovelock, B. and Lovelock, K.M. (2013) *The Ethics of Tourism: Critical and Applied Perspectives*, New York: Routledge.

Meliou, E. and Maroudas, L. (2010) 'Understanding tourism development: A representational approach', *Tourismos*, 5(2), 115–127.

Metraux, A. (1958) *Le vodou haitien*, Paris: Gallimard.

Moscovici, S. (1961) *La psychanalyse: Son image et son public*, Paris: Presses Universitaires de France.

Nunn, N. (2008) 'The long term effects of Africa's slave trades', *The Quarterly Journal of Economics*, February, 139–176.

Nunn, N. and Wantcheckon, L. (2011) 'The slave trade and the origins of mistrust in Africa', *American Economic Review*, 101(7), 3221–3252.

Ogude, S.E. (1981) 'Slavery and the African imagination: A critical perspective', *World Literature Today*, 55(1), 21–25.

O'Toole, W. (2011) *Events Feasibility and Development*, Oxford: Elsevier.

Paul, B., Dameus, A. and Garrabe, M. (2010) Le processus de tertiarisation de l'economie Haitienne, *Etudes Caribeennes*. Online: http://etudescaribeennes.revues.org/4728 (accessed 24 July 2014).

Pearce, P.L., Moscardo, G. and Ross, G.F. (1991) 'Tourism impact and community perception: An equity social representational perspective', *Australian psychologist*, 26(3), 147–152.

Reader, J. (1998) *Africa: A biography of the continent*, London: Penguin.

Roc, N. (2008) 'Haiti-environment: From the "Pearl of the Antilles" to desolation', *Fride*. Online: www.fride.org (accessed 3 August 2013).

Saint-Louis, F. (2000) *Le vodou haitien: Reflet d'une societe bloquee*, Paris: L'Harmathan.

Séraphin, H. (2010) 'Quel avenir pour le tourisme en Haïti?' *Revue Espaces* (281), 4–6.

Séraphin, H. (2011) 'Hispaniola: The future destination of the Caribbean', *Journal of Tourism Consumption and Practice*, 3(2), 38–44.

Séraphin, H. (2013) 'The contribution of tour guides to destination understanding and image. The case of Haiti via an analysis of: "Bonjour blanc, a journey through Haiti"', *International Research Forum on Guided Tours, Breda University of Applied Sciences.*

Séraphin, H. and Butler, C. (2013) 'Impacts of the slave trade on the service industry in Kenya and Haiti: The case of the Tourism and Hospitality sector', *Journal of Hospitality and Tourism*, 11(1), 71–89.

Sheller, M. (2004) 'Natural hedonism: The invention of Caribbean islands as tropical playgrounds', in D.T. Duval (ed.), *Tourism in the Caribbean: Trends, developments, prospects*, London: Routledge.

Thomson, I. (2004) *Bonjour Blanc: A journey through Haiti*, London: Vintage.

16 Setting a research agenda for rituals and traditional events

Jennifer Laing and Warwick Frost

The genesis for this book was our realisation that most of the research to date on the role of rituals and traditional events in contemporary society has not been carried out from an events studies perspective. We decided that it was important that this book be multi-disciplinary in scope, showcasing the work of a wide variety of researchers from around the globe, and that it set future research directions, to advance the field. Nevertheless, we are conscious that this is only a first step and there are numerous areas that warrant further research. This final chapter draws together some of the key themes developed in this book, sets out a research agenda and considers the future outlook for rituals in an events context.

Revival and rebranding of traditional events

The revival and rebranding of traditional events to suit modern sensibilities or needs is often done with an eye to the tourism benefits of these spectacles. This phenomenon is exemplified by one of the most iconic events of the twenty-first century, the Running of the Bulls festival in Pamplona. When Ernest Hemingway wrote about it in his book *Fiesta* (also known as *The Sun Also Rises*) in 1927, the Festival of San Fermin (to use its proper name) was not a household name, and was largely patronised by locals.

Fiesta

In his novel *Fiesta* (1927), Ernest Hemingway tells the story of a group of Americans who venture to Pamplona in Spain for the Festival of San Fermin. The group are rich but aimless; members of the *Lost Generation* who have fought in the First World War and now cannot bear to return home. Instead they hang around the cafes of Paris, occasionally travelling to remote areas for new experiences. In Pamplona they are off the tourist track, and most of those participating in the festival are locals, either from the town or nearby villages.

Generally, Pamplona is quiet. However, 'at noon on Sunday, July 6th, the fiesta exploded. There is no other way to describe it' (Hemingway 1927: 122). The streets and squares fill with people. There are processions, bands and groups of street performers; the medieval carnivalesque still performed in the twentieth century:

It kept up day and night for seven days. The dancing kept up, the drinking kept up, the noise went on. The things that happened could only have happened during a fiesta. Everything became quite unreal finally and it seemed as though nothing could have any consequences. It seemed out of place to think of consequences during the fiesta.

(Hemingway 1927: 124)

The narrator Jake is there with his friends Bill and Brett – the girl he might have married if it were not for the war and the injury he suffered. In the street,

Some dancers formed a circle around Brett and started to dance. They wore big wreaths of white garlics around their necks. They took Bill and me by the arms and put us in the circle. Bill started to dance, too. They were all chanting. Brett wanted to dance but they did not want her to. They wanted her as an image to dance around.

(Hemingway 1927: 125)

In addition to the merriment, this is a religious festival. Following a procession, they try to enter the church, but Brett is refused entry because she is not wearing a hat. They are not too fussed and return to the drinking. The next day they are hungover, so only Jake sees the Running of the Bulls. Intriguingly, Hemingway only provided a few lines on this ritual; he was much more interested in the bullfights.

This famous account introduced the modern world to the traditions of the Festival of San Fermin. Over time, worldwide interest grew – fuelled by a film version in 1957 (*The Sun Also Rises*) and a wide variety of travel and news shows. The recent Woody Allen film *Midnight in Paris* (2011) has added to the Hemingway mystique (Laing and Frost 2012). As the modern world has embraced Pamplona, the elements of the carnivalesque have remained at the forefront (Ravenscroft and Matteucci 2003), particularly its signature ritual involving youths proving their bravery by running through the streets with the bulls. International media coverage largely focuses on this thrill-seeking element and the number of people who have been gored by the bulls. Yet there is evidence that this ritual may have a deeper significance, viewed as a rite of passage by participants (Wilson *et al.* 2008) or a form of initiation (see discussion below). Other research has explored the role of this festival and its rituals as a focus for sexual permissiveness (Ravenscroft and Matteucci 2003). There might be similar findings for other traditional events, perhaps a fruitful area for further research.

It is also important to note that the revival of traditional festivals might not necessarily be linked to a desire to boost tourism, or even any economic purpose. Nor might they be the outcome of a deliberate and strategic planning process. Chapter 10 discusses the example of the Beltane Fire Festival in Edinburgh, which resurrects the Celtic rite marking the passing of the seasons. The staging of this festival is described as an organic process, which was underpinned by a desire to bring a community together and contribute to identity. The meaning that this rite appears to have for the current generation suggests that it fulfils a deep psychological need. More studies of this genre would be useful to tease this out further. In particular, qualitative studies might assist in drawing out the subtle nuances of this behaviour.

Appropriation of rituals

The example of the San Fermin Festival could also be conceptualised as an example of the *appropriation* of a ritual by mainstream contemporary society. As discussed in Chapter 1, rather than inventing tradition, appropriation may involve remaking the traditional event or rituals within it to suit modern purposes or adapting it for different purposes. For example, Chapter 4 by Hua and Zhu examines traditional wedding rituals in China that are still being followed in contemporary times, but are now also used to attract tourists to the village of Gouliang. Voodoo events, discussed by Séraphin and Nolan in Chapter 15, are similarly finding a market as a tourist attraction in Haiti. Other purposes are more subtle, less about commercial imperatives and more about meeting deep-rooted social or cultural needs. Gould, in Chapter 12, considers the use of the rite of purification through punishment, a 'spectacle of discipline' creating a public scapegoat, within a new context – the prison rodeo.

Appropriation of rituals within mainstream society is not necessarily evidence of widespread acceptance of the culture within which these rituals originated. Haverluk (2003: 181) notes the broad appropriation of Hispanic fiestas, food, dress and music by Anglo-Americans, despite the fact that Hispanics 'still suffer from economic and political marginalization'. Wearing their clothes or playing their music has not dismantled the barriers to opportunity nor necessarily overcome prejudice. Similar observations have been made about Australian multicultural society, where acceptance and assimilation of different foods came a long way before tolerance of other cultural practices and acceptance of diversity more broadly.

Appropriation may be multi-layered. From the 1960s onwards, English Heritage was pressured by New-Agers to allow the staging of druidic events for the summer solstice at Stonehenge. In a number of cases this led to clashes between participants and the police and these events became something akin to protests. In 2000, English Heritage relented and allowed a summer solstice event. Over the next few years attendance grew, reaching 31,000 in 2003. However, by then there were further changes and tensions. For many who attended, the event was similar to a 'rave' and there were now criticisms by regular attendees that the event had been appropriated by people with less interest in the religious elements (Blain and Wallis 2004).

An intriguing example of commercial appropriation involves the Holi festival, one of the best-known Indian religious festivals. It involves using brightly tinted powder and coloured water to drench people in the streets, sometimes using water pistols, in a kind of mock fight, celebrating love and the brilliant colours of life. This anarchic rite has captured the imagination of marketing executives, who have used it most recently in an advertisement for the Expedia 'Bucket List'. In the Heineken beer 'Legendary Travelers' campaign, one television advertisement depicts a young man who appears to be in India. He chases a goat, encounters a brightly painted elephant, has coloured powder thrown over him and later relaxes over a beer with a friend while covered in paint. In Australia, an action was brought against Heineken in 2013 over the television advertisement, which was claimed to be 'offensive to the Hindu culture'. It was ruled by the Panel adjudicating the Alcohol Beverages Advertising Code that the behaviour in the advertisement was not offensive as it did not portray someone adversely affected by alcohol. Regardless of the result, the case shows how cultural sensitivities might be upset by advertising that alludes to or suggests religious rites, particularly where it involves products that might be antithetical to that faith, such as alcohol, gambling or skimpy or tight-fitting clothing.

The appropriation of the use of coloured paint is less controversial in the case of the Color Run (www.colorrun.com.au) 'a unique paint race that celebrates healthiness, happiness and individuality'. Entrants wear white clothing and run through four different 'Color Zones' (Pink, Orange, Blue and Yellow). Their website states that the 'color is 100% natural, food dyed, food grade cornstarch' and suggest 'wearing a bandanna, glasses or goggles' to avoid entrants getting the paint in their eyes or mouth. The end of the race involves a

> Finish Festival ... where we count down to our famous Color Throws. As you cross the finish line you will receive your colour packet. Color Throws happen approximately every 15 minutes. Our Cleaning Zone is located in the festival area and our Color Blowers will do their best to help clean you off.

The throwing of paint in this instance is presumably designed to be cathartic, and the focus on ideals such as happiness is in accordance with broad community values.

Given the prevalence of appropriation of rituals within a number of different contexts, there might be value in exploring whether this denudes the ritual of its meaning and how this process is received by different groups within the community.

Place identity through rituals and traditional events

Traditional events or the rituals performed at an event may reinforce identity with respect to the places where they are staged. For example, there might be a link between satisfaction with a traditional event and place identity, as Ramkissoon postulates in Chapter 3. Our discussion of the Helldorado festival in Tombstone in Chapter 14 depicts a place where cherished stories of common heritage can be shared and performed during the festival, contributing to identity and the bestowing of mythic status on the town. More work could be done to explore this phenomenon more deeply, including the potential link with place identity, sense of place and place attachment.

Commodification of traditional events

Some of the chapters in this book highlight concerns about the commodification of traditional events, often for reasons connected with tourism but also due to other business interests seeing a profit to be made from these events. There has been long-standing disquiet over the so-called commercialism of Christmas, discussed in Chapter 8, even if it might be argued that 'there never was a time when Christmas existed as an unsullied domestic idyll, immune to the taint of commercialism' (Nissenbaum 1996: 318). While traditionally a community event, Halloween is becoming increasingly commodified and organised, and has diffused beyond its European roots and identification with North America to become a global phenomenon. Others argue that this commodification is not necessarily a cause for concern, with Lee and Kim in Chapter 5, in their case study of the Kangnung Danoje Festival in South Korea, arguing that tourism is keeping some of these traditional rituals alive, and helping people to respect and understand their heritage and the heritage of others.

Setting a research agenda

We identify ten areas for future research on rituals and traditional events, which build upon the contributions in this book.

1 Intersection of traditional events with contemporary concerns

As Shinde notes in Chapter 2 on the Ganesh festival, this traditional event is now accommodating green concerns, such as minimising the pollution of water caused by immersing the idol in the river. This chapter makes a contribution to the growing literature on green events, as most of this (admittedly scarce) body of work has taken place in the context of modern events such as outdoor music festivals or business events (Laing and Frost 2010; Mair and Jago 2010; Mair and Laing 2012). It is interesting to see that this trend is also having an impact on events with a long history, or the rituals performed within events. Other trends that may affect rituals and traditional events involve the use of new technology such as smartphones and the impact of communication tools like social media. Are they changing the nature of these events, including making attendees and participants more self-conscious or less engaged in the moment? Or are they making people feel more connected through the interactivity of social media?

The clash between ritual and contemporary mores can be seen in sharp relief in the festivities surrounding Christmas, where some people feel that custom and ritual is being overthrown due to political correctness and the diversity of our populations. Do these rituals still have a place in a multicul-

Figure 16.1 McDonald's holiday pie (source: W. Frost).

tural society? In North America, McDonald's advertises the generic 'holiday pie', rather than referring to Christmas and potentially alienating some of its customer base (Figure 16.1). In 2013, no carols from a cathedral, local or otherwise, were broadcast on Australian television. Many schools and kindergartens have stopped staging the traditional nativity play, substituting a play or concert without Christian content, to acknowledge the existence of multiple faiths and atheism/agnostic beliefs. This is controversial, with some arguing that the nativity play has become its own tradition, regardless of one's religious persuasion or that this represents a 'dumbing down of Christmas' (Sky News 2004).

Other changes are largely accepted, yet still linked to the mutable nature of contemporary society. The booming sales of German *stollen*, a cake of dried fruit and marzipan, in the United Kingdom in 2013 now rival the traditional mince pie (Smallman 2013), while the Italian *panettone* is increasingly popular in Australia as a way to round off the meal, perhaps reflecting a more multicultural society, and a desire for something different, yet traditional to the Italian culture, arguably the most popular national brand in the world today (Gill 2010; Laing and Frost 2013). Further research is needed to explore some of these issues in more depth.

2 Rites of initiation into adulthood through participation in events

Many anthropological studies have examined rites of initiation into adulthood through participation in events, often in an indigenous context. An example is the land-diving rite on Pentecost Island, Vanuatu, where the men 'negotiate what is a potentially perilous rite of passage' (Cheer *et al.* 2013: 447) to gain status and power, jumping from a tower of approximately 60 metres and made of traditional materials, which becomes a symbol of masculinity (Cheer *et al.* 2013; de Burlo 1996). This tradition is now staged for tourists, which has raised concerns about whether this has created any lasting benefits for the grass-roots community. The importance of this initiation rite might perhaps be dissipating, which might affect the status of men in this society, as well as the way in which they regard themselves as reaching adulthood. Researchers might wish to focus on the role of events in these rites of initiation or rites of passage, not just with respect to traditional events, and consider how both attendance at and participation in events affects these rites. Examples of contemporary events that might play a part in rites associated with the shift from childhood to adulthood include outdoor music festivals and Spring Break for Americans (schoolie's week for Australians) (Hobson and Josiam 1993; McKercher and Bauer 2003; Schwartz *et al.* 1999).

3 Liminality and liminoid experiences

Tinsley and Matheson in Chapter 10 discuss how liminoid experiences resulting in personal (rather than public, as discussed above) rites of passage might be the result of involvement in an event. These experiences may seep into the everyday life of the participant, and be ultimately transformative. They can build identity, a sense of belonging to a community, or feelings of connection to a shared past or heritage. The distinction between liminal and liminoid experiences in an events context needs further examination, including exploring the role played by ritual and/or involvement in traditional events in these experiences.

4 Links with well-being and quality of life

The growing interest in the potential nexus between attendance at or involvement in events and well-being elicits a question about the effects of rituals and traditional events in this process. For example, festivals marking the passing of the seasons, including planting and harvest festivals and mid-winter festivals, might have a concomitant effect on well-being and quality of life by helping us to come to terms with the passing of time, experience gratitude for nature's bounty or experience a sense of looking forward to better times (Frost and Laing 2011). Another example can be found in Matteucci's (2014: 121) examination of flamenco festivals and parades in Seville, Spain, which suggests that they might be 'spiritually enriching and transformative' for participants. There is evidence of challenge, arousal, self-enrichment or self-actualisation and a sense of the ineffable in these experiences.

Seligman's (2011) theoretical model of well-being known as PERMA (positive emotions, engagement, relationships, meaning and achievement) might be a useful framework to explore this issue. Certainly many of the events showcased in this book involve all of these elements of well-being. Cogent examples include the Ganesh festival in India (Chapter 2), Catholic processions in Macau (Chapter 7), the Mardi Gras Indians' parade in New Orleans (Chapter 13), the masked rites within the Sant'Antonio festival in Sardinia (Chapter 9) and the Helldorado festival in Tombstone (Chapter 14). These events heighten or draw out emotions, promote engagement through active participation and/or the liminality of the event space, build relationships or connections or create social cohesion through activities such as volunteering or attendance, have a deep and often symbolic meaning for participants and attendees and may offer challenge or a sense of achievement in taking part or in the messages that the event is promoting. Further research might usefully explore some of these elements in the context of other rituals or traditional events.

5 Paradoxes inherent in rituals and traditional events

Chapter 8 provides some examples of the paradoxes inherent in the celebration of Christmas. There are many other festivals with pagan roots that have been appropriated for religious reasons, yet retain this duality and thus a tension between their secular and sacred elements. St Lucia's Day, celebrated on 13 December, can be traced back to festivities surrounding the winter solstice, as this used to be the shortest day of the year before the Gregorian calendar was introduced (Barber 2013). St Lucy was a Sicilian saint in the third or fourth century CE, who was revered as a protector of marriage. Her name is a reinterpretation of *Santa Lucia* or Holy Light (Barber 2013). On St Lucia's Day, young girls, most notably in Scandinavian countries but also in Eastern Europe, wearing a headdress or crown of candles or carrying a candle, go from house to house, a symbol of the bringing of light in the depths of winter. This was originally a fertility ritual (Barber 2013). Rather like the Halloween tradition, the girl would curse your house if she didn't receive a present. Pagan elements of this festival are centred on the idea that St Lucia, while a saint, is also a witch, and must therefore not be angered. Aside from infertility, she may bring bad luck or ill-health. This link to witchcraft led to the tradition of making *Lucia's stool*, starting on 13 December. If the wooden stool is taken to midnight mass at Christmas and the person who made it stands on it, they can tell who in the congregation is a witch. These paradoxes could be usefully explored with respect to other traditional events, including why this duality between secular and sacred elements is so ubiquitous.

6 Lost traditions

Some of the discussion above about St Lucia comes from oral tradition, with Jennifer's stepfather telling her about Hungarian country customs when he was growing up in the 1920s and 1930s. Much of this tradition may have been discontinued in the modern era and be lost if it is not documented before those who remember it pass away. Similarly, Warwick's father told him stories of Glassite rituals in Coventry between the wars, a religious movement that has now completely disappeared. Well dressing in Great Britain, where the well would be adorned with flowers as a form of blessing, is an example of a tradition that lapsed but has been revived (Bird 1983). Research on lost traditions might include rituals associated with food, dance, music and costume.

7 The invention of traditional events

Chhabra *et al.* (2003) examine the staged authenticity of the Flora MacDonald Scottish Highland Games in North Carolina, an example of an event based on ethnic heritage and depictions of culture which is a mixture of 'elements of truth and falsehoods' (Timothy and Coles 2004: 292). So-called traditional events are being invented for a number of reasons. They might be seen as appealing to tourists, or creating a sense of identity for a disparate and fractured community. Future research might consider invention of traditional events in specific contexts. For example, many royal events and the rituals within them have been invented in recent times, such as the Imperial Assemblage of 1877 in Delhi, which was designed to establish the legitimacy and authority of the British monarch as the ruler of India (Cohn 1983), the Queen's Christmas Speech, discussed in Chapter 8, and the Royal Command Performance, now known as the Royal Variety Performance, which first took place in 1912 and has been an annual event to raise money for charity since 1921.

8 The intersection between rituals and memory

There are rituals inherent in commemorative events, which may be used to reinforce or create collective memory, invoke feelings of nostalgia or act as a form of catharsis to express gratitude, relief or grief. Examples of a ritual structure have been discerned within commemorative re-enactments (Frost and Laing 2013a), such as the devalorisation rite that occurs at the end of the Battle of Hastings re-enactment, where a minute's silence is observed to bring the audience and participants back to the modern world. There are rites of inversion involving banter or tomfoolery, even within a recreation of a battlefield scenario, while rites of conspicuous display are evident in the careful attention to detail in the costumes (Figure 16.2), and the pleasure clearly gained from wearing something that attracts attention from the audience. ANZAC Day commemorations at Gallipoli have been criticised for drunken and disorderly behaviour, which is possibly another example of a rite of inversion (Frost and Laing 2013a). There is scope for exploring the role and importance of rituals within other types of commemorative events, such as anniversaries of independence such as the Fourth of July in North America and Bastille Day in France, or the overthrow of some form of oppression, such as the 2007 bicentenary of the Abolition of the Slave Trade Act in the British Empire.

Figure 16.2 Re-enactors firing a salute at the Tomb of the Unknown Revolutionary
Soldier, Alexandria, Virginia, USA (source: W. Frost).

9 Festivals of reversal

There are numerous examples of festivals that are based around *rites of reversal*, where roles are assumed that people would normally not have the ability to take on (whether this barrier is self-perceived or actual), or what happens is the mirror image of what occurs in everyday life (Falassi 1987). Rites of reversal associated with Halloween include dressing up as a ghost, ghoul, witch or wizard, or decorating the garden and facade of one's house (Figure 16.3) to make light of fears about the twilight world and black magic. Taking part in this event is comforting and helps us to make sense of the world in which we live and to confront the difficult aspects of life, including the inevitability of its ending. The Helldorado Festival, discussed in Chapter 14, involves reversing gender roles in some instances, empowering women in a festival based on a Western theme which is normally considered to be founded on a myth of masculinity. More research is needed to explore the importance of these reversals from a societal dimension. Do they provide a safety valve for tensions and anxieties? How do they evolve? And why is a festival the right forum for this phenomenon?

Figure 16.3 Halloween garden decorations in St Helena, California (source: W. Frost).

10 *Festivals and rites of consumption*

Studies of food festivals or feasting within events might shed light on rituals connected with consumption. Some of the rites may be more complex than just being an exercise in gluttony. Trick-or-treating during Halloween, where children visit people's homes to receive gifts of sweets is a rite of consumption, but also acts as a way to diffuse terrors about the dead and death itself (Santino 1994). Slow food festivals link consumption of food with political messages relating to how food is grown, prepared and consumed (Frost and Laing 2013b). Chapter 6 by White and Leung looks at the food rites associated with Chinese New Year and how they are used to emphasise family values and strong familial connections. Frew and Mair in Chapter 11 refer to the gathering of the community to celebrate Hogmanay and the rites of consumption that take place there, almost as a site of pilgrimage. Research might extend this work to cover, for example, consumption rites within farmers' markets, more prosaic food choices served at contemporary events and the importance of consumption rites in forming and shaping identity.

The outlook for rituals in an events context

As discussed in Chapter 1, we argue that the contributions in this book point the way towards rituals becoming even more important in anchoring events and imparting meaning for those who participate in them. This effect is not limited to traditional events. It would appear that events conceived in the contemporary era incorporate rituals such as celebrating the opening and closing of the event or encouraging consumption and display, even if this is largely unconscious and unplanned. While Brown and James (2004: 53) argues that 'event managers have sacrificed the ritual element' in favour of economic imperatives, we suggest the opposite, namely that ritual elements are largely organically present within events and contribute to their economic success. Event design should encompass these ritual elements and might benefit from a more strategic approach. The embedding of ritual within modern events is thus an important area for research, considering the way in which it enhances (or not) the experience and how it manifests itself in different contexts or cultures.

There is also evidence of growing interest in using traditional events to brand destinations and attract tourists, as well as how they might build or contribute to strong communities. Further research might deliver a deeper understanding both of their potential economic benefit, but also the ways in which these events might deliver social outcomes such as social capital, community building, place identity and social cohesion.

References

Barber, E.W. (2013) *Dancing Goddesses: Folklore, archaeology, and the origins of European dance*, London and New York: Norton.

Bird, S.E. (1983) 'Derbyshire well-dressing: An annual folk festival', *Journal of Cultural Geography*, 3(2), 61–72.

Blain, J. and Wallis, R. (2004) 'Sacred sites, contested rites/rights: Contemporary pagan engagements with the past', *Journal of Material Culture*, 9(3), 237–261.

Brown, S. and James, J. (2004) 'Event design and management: Ritual sacrifice?' in I. Yeoman, M. Robertson, J. Ali-Knight, S. Drummond and U. McMahon-Beattie (eds), *Festival and Events Management: An international arts and cultural perspective* (pp. 53–64), Oxford: Elsevier.

Cheer, J.M., Reeves, K.J. and Laing, J.H. (2013) 'Tourism and traditional culture: Land diving in Vanuatu', *Annals of Tourism Research*, 43(1), 435–455.

Chhabra, D., Healy, R. and Sills, E. (2003) 'Staged authenticity and heritage tourism', *Annals of Tourism Research*, 30(3), 702–719.

Cohn, B.S. (1983) 'Representing authority in Victorian India', in E. Hobsbawm and T. Ranger (eds), *The Invention of Tradition* (pp. 165–209), Cambridge: Cambridge University Press.

De Burlo, C. (1996) 'Cultural resistance and ethnic tourism on South Pentecost, Vanuatu', in R. Butler and T. Hinch (eds), *Tourism and Indigenous Peoples* (pp. 255–276), London: Thompson.

Falassi, A. (1987) 'Festival: Definition and morphology', in A. Falassi (ed.), *Time out of Time: Essays on the festival* (pp. 1–10), Albuquerque: University of New Mexico Press.

Frost, W. and Laing, J. (2011) *Strategic Management of Festivals and Events* (2nd edn), Melbourne: Cengage.

Frost, W. and Laing, J. (2013a) *Commemorative Events: Memory, identities, conflict,* London: Routledge.

Frost, W. and Laing, J. (2013b) 'Communicating persuasive messages through slow food festivals', *Journal of Vacation Marketing*, 19(1), 67–74.

Gill, A.A. (2010) 'Italy, Inc.', *Gourmet Traveller*, May, 115–117.

Haverluk, T.W. (2003) 'Mex-America: From margin to mainstream', in G.J. Hausladen (ed.), *Western Places, American Myths: How we think about the West* (pp. 166–183), Reno and Las Vegas: University of Nevada Press.

Hemingway, E. (1927) *Fiesta*, in *The Essential Hemingway*, London: Arrow, 2004 edn.

Hobson, J.S.P. and Josiam, B. (1993) 'Spring break student travel: An exploratory study', *Journal of Travel & Tourism Marketing*, 1(3), 87–98.

Laing, J. and Frost, W. (2010) '"How green was my festival": Exploring challenges and opportunities associated with staging green events', *International Journal of Hospitality Management*, 29(2), 261–267.

Laing, J. and Frost, W. (2012) *Books and Travel: Inspiration, quests and transformation,* Bristol: Channel View.

Laing, J. and Frost, W. (2013) 'Food, wine … heritage, identity? Two case studies of Italian diaspora festivals in regional Victoria', *Tourism Analysis*, 18(3), 323–334.

McKercher, B. and Bauer, T.G. (2003) 'Conceptual framework of the nexus between tourism, romance, and sex', in B. McKercher and T.G. Bauer (eds), *Sex and Tourism: Journeys of romance, love, and lust* (pp. 3–17), Binghamton, NY: The Haworth Hospitality Press.

Mair, J. and Jago, L. (2010) 'The development of a conceptual model of greening in the business events tourism sector', *Journal of Sustainable Tourism*, 18(1), 77–94.

Mair, J. and Laing, J. (2012) 'The greening of music festivals: Motivations, barriers and outcomes – Applying the Mair and Jago model', *Journal of Sustainable Tourism*, 20(5), 683–700.

Matteucci, X. (2014) 'Experiencing flamenco: An examination of a spiritual journey', in S. Filep and P. Pearce (eds), *Tourist Experience and Fulfilment: Insights from positive psychology* (pp. 110–126), London: Routledge.

Nissenbaum, S. (1996) *The Battle for Christmas*, New York: Knopf.

Ravenscroft, N. and Matteucci, X. (2003) 'The festival as carnivalesque: Social governance and control at Pamplona's San Fermin Fiesta', *Tourism, Culture and Communication*, 4(1), 1–15.

Santino, J. (1994) 'Introduction', in J. Santino (ed.), *Halloween and Other Festivals of Life and Death*, Knoxville: University of Tennessee Press.

Schwartz, R.H., Milteer, R., Sheridan, M.J. and Horner, C.P. (1999) 'Beach week: A high school graduation rite of passage for sun, sand, suds, and sex', *Archives of Pediatrics and Adolescent Medicine*, 153(2), 180–183.

Seligman, M.E.P. (2011) *Flourish*, Sydney: Random House.

Sky News (2004) 'Quarter of schools axe nativity plays', *Sky News*, 24 December: Online: http://news.sky.com/story/316925/quarter-of-schools-axe-nativity-plays (accessed 3 January 2014).

Smallman, E. (2013) 'The German cake that's stollen Christmas', *Daily Mail*, 19 December. Online: www.dailymail.co.uk/femail/article-2526026/The-German-cake-thats-stollen-Christmas-FEMAILs-master-baker-reveals-buy-yours.html (accessed 5 January 2014).

Timothy, D.J. and Coles, T. (2004) 'Tourism and diasporas: Current issues and future opportunities', in T. Coles and D.J. Timothy (eds), *Tourism, Diasporas and Space* (pp. 291–297), London: Routledge.

Wilson, J., Fisher, D. and Moore, K. (2008) ' "Van tour" and "doing a Contiki": Grand backpacker tours of Europe', in K. Hannam and I. Ateljevic (eds), *Backpacker Tourism: Concepts and profiles* (pp. 113–127), Clevedon: Channel View.

Index